| AMERICAN COURTS EXPLAINED

A Detailed Introduction to the Legal Process Using Real Cases

GREGORY MITCHELL
SCHOOL OF LAW
UNIVERSITY OF VIRGINIA

DAVID KLEIN
THE WOODROW WILSON DEPARTMENT OF POLITICS
UNIVERSITY OF VIRGINIA

WEST
ACADEMIC
PUBLISHING

The publisher is not engaged in rendering legal or other professional advice, and this publication is not a substitute for the advice of an attorney. If you require legal or other expert advice, you should seek the services of a competent attorney or other professional.

© 2016 LEG, Inc. d/b/a West Academic
444 Cedar Street, Suite 700
St. Paul, MN 55101
1-877-888-1330

Printed in the United States of America

ISBN: 978-1-63459-879-8

Preface

This book is a descendant of Professor Dan Meador's *American Courts*, a book that one of the current authors had the privilege of joining in its last edition. Dan's book introduces beginning law students to topics that they will cover in detail in law school and provides a good introduction to American courts for others interested in learning about our legal systems. *American Courts Explained* has the same mission but greatly expands on and adds to the topics covered in Dan's book and provides many concrete examples of how American courts work by following two real cases—one involving criminal laws and one involving civil laws—as the cases make their way through state and federal trial courts and appellate courts.

American Courts Explained provides broad but sufficiently detailed coverage of the American legal process that it can serve as the main text in an undergraduate course on American courts. Alternatively it can be used as a fact-filled supplemental text in a course that might otherwise leave students thirsty for more detail on the nuts and bolts of our legal systems. An accompanying website (www.amcourtsbook.com) provides access to the legal documents from the cases that we follow so that you can examine these documents in more detail. The documents and other information available on this website should be a rich resource for instructors who want to develop additional assignments for a class and for readers who want to learn more about the topics discussed in the book.

We are grateful to the Washington and Lee University School of Law for permitting us to reproduce portions of the papers that former Supreme Court Justice Lewis F. Powell, Jr. donated to the school and to archivist John Jacob for his help with those papers. We appreciate the assistance of Valerie Dormady, Kay Mitchell, Gabriel Fulmer (Virginia Law Class of 2016), Adam Johnson (Virginia Law Class of 2016), and James Paulose (Virginia Law Class of 2017) in the preparation of this book. We also appreciate the helpful reviews provided by Judge Andrew Wistrich and Professors Sheldon Goldman and Herbert Kritzer. Responsibility for any errors remains, of course, with the authors.

As with any first edition, there are surely places where we could have been clearer or where more detail would have been helpful. We welcome your input so that we can improve the next edition.

Gregory Mitchell &
David Klein
University of Virginia,
January, 2016

About the Authors

GREGORY MITCHELL is the Joseph Weintraub–Bank of America Distinguished Professor of Law and the Thomas F. Bergin Teaching Professor of Law at the University of Virginia. Professor Mitchell holds a J.D. and a Ph.D. in psychology from the University of California at Berkeley. He teaches courses in civil litigation and psychological aspects of legal practice and regulation, and his research focuses on judgment and decision-making with respect to legally significant behaviors, employment discrimination, expert evidence, the psychology of justice, and the application of social science to legal theory and policy. Professor Mitchell clerked for Judge Thomas A. Wiseman, Jr., in the Middle District of Tennessee, and then practiced civil litigation with the Nashville law firm of Doramus, Trauger & Ney for six years before returning to academia.

DAVID KLEIN is an Associate Professor in the Woodrow Wilson Department of Politics at the University of Virginia. Professor Klein holds a Ph.D. in political science from the Ohio State University. He has taught undergraduate courses on judicial process for twenty years. His research focuses on appellate court policy making, the psychology of judging, and judicial elections. Professor Klein is the inaugural editor of the *Journal of Law & Courts* and is the author of the book, *Making Law in the United States Courts of Appeals*.

Table of Contents

|AMERICAN COURTS EXPLAINED

A Detailed Introduction to the
Legal Process Using Real Cases

| CHAPTER 1

Introduction to Two Cases
and Important Information
About What Is to Come

I n 1998, Robert Keith Woodall, having pled guilty to kidnapping, raping, and murdering a sixteen-year-old girl, was sentenced to death in a Kentucky trial court on the recommendation of a jury. More than ten years later, a United States District Judge ruled that the procedures under which Mr. Woodall had been sentenced violated the U.S. Constitution and ordered the case back to the Kentucky courts for resentencing. The state of Kentucky contested this order all the way to the U.S. Supreme Court, where it won in April, 2014, leading to the reinstatement of the death sentence nearly sixteen years after it was first imposed. Mr. Woodall presently resides on Kentucky's Death Row.[1]

Woodall's case is highly unusual in some respects, especially in that it reached the Supreme Court: these days, out of the millions of cases that start out in the judicial system each year, fewer than one hundred end up there. But in many other respects the case is fairly typical. Many criminal convictions in state courts are reviewed by federal courts, and many of these cases take a decade or more to reach a final resolution. In this book, we will explain how a case such as Woodall's can make it all the way from a small Kentucky court to the highest court in the land, and we will explain why this process takes so long. We will also introduce you to the prosecutors, defense lawyers, jurors, and judges who had Woodall's life in their hands and explain the role these people played in deciding his fate.

---

1   A list of inmates on Kentucky's Death Row can be found at: http://corrections.ky.gov/communityinfo/Pages/DeathRowInmates.aspx

In a criminal case, like Woodall's, the government seeks punishment for some crime. Criminal cases constitute a large percentage of the work of American courts, but every year American courts also resolve many non-criminal disputes. These are called "civil" cases. The term "civil" refers to the nature of the laws at issue rather than to how the parties conduct themselves: in civil cases, one *party* claims that (a) the other party acted improperly (or failed to act properly) and (b) the law allows the first party to obtain relief from the second for its improper actions (or inaction). For instance, if you are injured in a car wreck because of someone else's negligent driving, you could sue that person for injury to yourself and to your car under civil laws that provide a remedy for injuries caused by another person's *negligence*. If you win your civil case, you will receive a *judgment* from a court ordering the other person to pay you a sum of money to compensate you for the personal injuries and property damage you suffered in the wreck.

Although a state or federal agency may be a party in a civil case, none of the laws at issue in civil cases will authorize the judge or jury to impose a punishment of incarceration or death. However, the law in a civil case may authorize a judge or jury to impose a large monetary penalty, called *punitive damages*, to punish a party and deter similar misconduct by that party or others who might be thinking of misbehaving. In addition to differences in the form of punishment that may be imposed, civil cases differ from criminal cases in many other respects. This book will take you through the full legal process for both criminal and civil cases, from how each type of case makes it to court in the first place to how each proceeds through the different levels of courts built into the American system until it reaches a final conclusion.

◼ WHAT IS A CASE?

The term "case" is shorthand for a dispute that has formally reached a court. A case involves two or more parties who disagree about something of legal significance. For instance, in Woodall's case, the Commonwealth of Kentucky contended that Woodall had violated Kentucky's criminal laws and that Woodall should be sentenced to death under these laws. Woodall did not dispute that he broke Kentucky's laws against kidnapping, rape, and murder, but he denied that he should be condemned to death under Kentucky law. We will follow Woodall's case as it makes its way through a succession of courts at different levels within Kentucky's court system and the U.S. government's court system.

Although you were probably already familiar with the term "case," American courts use lots of other jargon that will be unfamiliar to you. Rather than stop in the middle of the text to define all of this jargon, we provide a glossary at the end of the book that defines and translates much of this jargon for you. If a word is italicized, that means it can be found in the glossary.

The complexity of the American legal system can seem overwhelming to students thinking of pursuing law as a profession or to laypeople who get caught up in the system as *litigants* or as *jurors*. A central aim of this book is to cut through that complexity and help readers become much more familiar and comfortable with how the American legal system works. But we hope to do more than demystify the American judicial process—we hope to give you the knowledge and conceptual apparatus needed to judge how well the American system functions in resolving disputes. Each of the many formal rules and informal norms that make up the American legal system can have implications for who prevails in the case and for what the winner wins and what the loser loses. For citizens to evaluate their judicial system, they need a solid understanding of its intricacies.

But learning about a highly complex, jargon-filled system can be quite tedious (just ask anyone who has gone to law school). The challenge when explaining a complex system is to present the details in a way that is absorbing and makes the details memorable. Our strategy begins with recognition that what fascinates most people about American courts are the cases themselves and the unique way these cases are dealt with in the United States. All the rules and norms only matter to the extent they affect real cases, and these rules and norms are best understood in the context of real cases. Accordingly, every important concept and procedure covered in this book will be illustrated through two real cases, one criminal and one civil. For each of these cases we provide excerpts from real court documents and provide links to the full set of case documents so that you can explore the cases—and the operations of the legal system—in more detail.[2]

Commonwealth of Kentucky v. Woodall

To take you through the twists and turns of a criminal case, we will examine Robert Woodall's case, from his arrest and sentencing to his attempts, initially

---

promising but ultimately unsuccessful, to have his death sentence invalidated. This journey involves visits over many years to many different courts between the state trial court and the U.S. Supreme Court. We will not dwell on the details of Mr. Woodall's crime, but it is important to understand that, in American courts, even those who have committed horrendous crimes are (at least theoretically) entitled to the same treatment as innocent persons who have been falsely accused of a crime. And there is no doubt that the crime that Mr. Woodall ultimately confessed to was horrendous.

Early in the evening of January 25, 1997, sixteen-year-old Sarah Hansen drove the family minivan to a Minit Mart in Greenville, Kentucky to rent a movie. When Ms. Hansen did not return within a couple of hours, her parents alerted the police, who began a search. Later that night, after locating her vehicle and following a long trail of blood to the lake's edge, the police found Ms. Hansen's body floating in nearby Luzerne Lake. A coroner's examination concluded that Ms. Hansen's throat had been cut twice by a box cutter or similar sharp instrument, completely severing her windpipe, that she had been raped, and that she had been left in the lake while still alive.

At the time, Woodall was twenty-two years old and had been released from prison only ten months earlier, after serving three years for sexual abuse of a minor. Woodall had been seen at the Minit Mart on the night in question

Robert Keith Woodall, courtesy Kentucky Dept. of Corrections

and was known by police to be a former sex offender. Accordingly, the police questioned Woodall about his possible involvement in the Hansen crime. Woodall gave conflicting statements about his whereabouts. A police officer noticed that Woodall wore sneakers that might match shoeprints found at the crime scene and confiscated his shoes. The police also consulted fingerprint records from his prior conviction for comparison with fingerprints recovered from Ms. Hansen's vehicle. When Woodall's shoeprints and fingerprints were found to match the crime scene prints, he was arrested. A search of his home led to the seizure of a bag of wet, muddy, and bloody clothes from underneath his bed, and his DNA was found to match DNA recovered from Ms. Hansen's body. On March 18, 1997, a *grand jury*, after hearing the state's evidence against Woodall, indicted him for violations of Kentucky's laws proscribing murder, rape, and kidnapping. Following the indictment, the *prosecuting attorney* for Muhlenberg County (the county in which the crime occurred) filed papers with the Muhlenberg Circuit Court (the trial court in Kentucky that handles serious crimes) giving notice that he intended to seek the death penalty in the case.

At his appearance before a judge to enter a plea of guilty or not guilty (this proceeding is known formally as the *arraignment*), Woodall pled not guilty. After entering this plea, Woodall's court-appointed attorney asked that the site, or *venue*, of Woodall's trial be moved two counties to the west, from Muhlenberg County to Caldwell County, for fear that pretrial publicity and community members' familiarity with the victim and her family would make it impossible to assemble an impartial jury in Muhlenberg County.[3] The trial judge granted this change of venue *motion*, and trial was set to begin in the Caldwell County Circuit Court in April of 1998.[4] However, just days before the trial was to begin, Woodall changed his plea to guilty on all charges in the indictment.

AOC-320 Rev. 8-91	[SEAL]	Indictment No. 97-CR-00035
Commonwealth of Kentucky Court of Justice		County MULHENBERG
		Circuit Court Division
RCr 6.06, 6.08, 6.10	INDICTMENT	

(Filed Mar. 18, 1997)

COMMONWEALTH   KRS: 507.020
OF KENTUCKY,   509.040
                                                    510.040
v.

ROBERT KEITH WOODALL , DEFENDANT

The Grand Jury charges: That on or about the 25th day of January, 1997, in Muhlenberg County, Kentucky, the above-named defendant(s):

COUNT 1: committed the capital offense of murder by cutting Sarah Hansen with a sharp object and drowning her;

COUNT 2: committed the capital offense of kidnapping Sarah Hansen in which she was not released alive;

COUNT 3: committed first-degree rape by engaging in sexual intercourse with Sarah Hansen through the use of forcible compulsion in which she received serious physical injury;

Against the peace and dignity of the Commonwealth of Kentucky.

                            /s/   Paul G. Moore
                                              Foreman

Presented by the foreman of the grand jury to the court, in the presence of the grand jury, and received from the court by me and filed in open court this 18th day of March, 1997.

                            /s/   Janet [Illegible]   Clerk

BAIL $_____ ARRAIGNMENT:_____, 19__ at _____a.m./p.m.

Defendant's date of birth_____ Social Security #_____

The following appeared before the grand jury as witnesses:

Mike Drake
Dr. Mark LeVaughn
Terry Lohrey
Donna Harrison
Matthew Clements
Sylvester Johnson
Mark Johnson
Brian Turner
Catherine Tarrants
Amanda Daugherty
Barbara Woodall
Angie Phelps

Indictment of Robert Keith Woodall

---

3   Approximately 5,000 people lived in Muhlenberg County at the time of the crime, and many of those people probably were acquainted with the Hansen family or with friends of the Hansen family. By all accounts, Sarah Hansen was a well-liked and successful student who was a member of the school band and local swim team.

4   Outrage over the crime extended beyond Muhlenberg County. Within a year of the crime, the Kentucky legislature passed the Sarah Hansen Act, which requires that convicted sex offenders first complete the sex offender treatment program before they may receive good behavior credits that can be used to shorten their period of incarceration (codified at Ky. Rev. Stat. Ann. § 197.045). The Act was designed to motivate sex offenders to participate in the treatment program. Woodall had not completed the voluntary sex offender treatment program before his release from prison for his sexual abuse convictions.

In light of this change in plea, a trial on guilt became unnecessary, but a sentencing hearing was still needed to determine whether Woodall's crimes warranted the death penalty that the prosecuting attorney sought. At a four-day penalty trial, the Commonwealth presented testimony from eleven witnesses, all of whom were cross-examined by Woodall's attorneys, and Woodall presented testimony from fourteen witnesses. The Commonwealth put on evidence aimed at demonstrating the brutal nature of the crime and its impact on the victim's family. The main theme of Woodall's defense was that deficiencies in his upbringing and personality caused him to fail to appreciate the consequences of his actions. Woodall did not testify in his own defense, and his lawyers asked the trial judge to instruct the jury not to draw any negative conclusions from Woodall's choice not to testify. The judge refused to give this instruction to the jury, however. (Although Mr. Woodall would subsequently complain about a number of things that occurred at his penalty trial, the question whether the trial judge properly refused to give this jury instruction is what ultimately would bring the case to the U.S. Supreme Court.) The jury rejected Woodall's defense and recommended the death penalty for the murder charge and two life-without-parole sentences for the rape and kidnapping charges.[5] The trial judge agreed with the jury's sentencing recommendations and, on September 4, 1998, imposed two life sentences and condemned Woodall to death by lethal injection.[6] As we will see, however, the trial judge's death sentence was just the first chapter in a long history of Woodall's experiences with American courts. We will follow Woodall as he exhausts all legal avenues at several different courts in his attempt to avoid execution by the Commonwealth of Kentucky.

---

5   Alternatively, the jury could have recommended life without possibility of parole until twenty-five years had been served, life without the possibility of parole until twelve years had been served, or a fixed number of years of incarceration up to fifty years. (Sentences are imposed for all of the crimes because longer sentences may have to be served after shorter sentences are completed. Where the sentence for one crime is death, sentences for the other crimes are still imposed in case the conviction of the death penalty crime is overturned.)

6   Woodall became the second person sentenced to die by lethal injection in Kentucky, which previously had used the electric chair for executions.

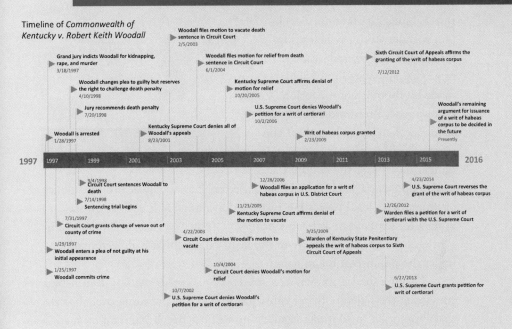

TIMELINE: COMMONWEALTH OF KENTUCKY v. WOODALL

Timeline of *Commonwealth of Kentucky v. Robert Keith Woodall*

Woodall files motion to vacate death sentence in Circuit Court
2/5/2003

Grand jury indicts Woodall for kidnapping, rape, and murder
3/18/1997

Woodall files motion for relief from death sentence in Circuit Court
6/1/2004

Sixth Circuit Court of Appeals affirms the granting of the writ of habeas corpus
7/12/2012

Woodall changes plea to guilty but reserves the right to challenge death penalty
4/10/1998

Kentucky Supreme Court affirms denial of motion for relief
10/20/2005

Jury recommends death penalty
7/20/1998

U.S. Supreme Court denies Woodall's petition for a writ of certiorari
10/2/2006

Woodall's remaining argument for issuance of a writ of habeas corpus to be decided in the future
Presently

Kentucky Supreme Court denies all of Woodall's appeals
8/23/2001

Woodall is arrested
1/28/1997

Writ of habeas corpus granted
2/23/2009

1997 | 1997 | 1999 | 2001 | 2003 | 2005 | 2007 | 2009 | 2011 | 2013 | 2015 | 2016

9/4/1998
Circuit Court sentences Woodall to death

7/14/1998
Sentencing trial begins

7/31/1997
Circuit Court grants change of venue out of county of crime

1/29/1997
Woodall enters a plea of not guilty at his initial appearance

1/25/1997
Woodall commits crime

12/28/2006
Woodall files an application for a writ of habeas corpus in U.S. District Court

11/23/2005
Kentucky Supreme Court affirms denial of the motion to vacate

4/22/2003
Circuit Court denies Woodall's motion to vacate

10/4/2004
Circuit Court denies Woodall's motion for relief

10/7/2002
U.S. Supreme Court denies Woodall's petition for a writ of certiorari

4/23/2014
U.S. Supreme Court reverses the grant of the writ of habeas corpus

12/26/2012
Warden files a petition for a writ of certiorari with the U.S. Supreme Court

3/25/2009
Warden of Kentucky State Penitentiary appeals the writ of habeas corpus to Sixth Circuit Court of Appeals

6/27/2013
U.S. Supreme Court grants petition for writ of certiorari

Promotion in Motion, Inc. v. Beech-Nut Nutrition Corporation

To take you through the twists and turns of a civil case, we will examine Promotion in Motion, Inc. v. Beech-Nut Nutrition Corporation. This civil law dispute began in 2008 when a product made for Beech-Nut by Promotion in Motion—a product known as Fruit Nibbles™— generated complaints from toddlers and their parents about the supposedly revolting appearance, smell, and flavor of the product, which one customer described as "shriveled, disgusting-looking snacks." These customer complaints, along with Beech-Nut's own quality control checks, prompted much discussion between Promotion in Motion and Beech-Nut about whether problems existed with the manufacturing and packaging of the product and, if so, how best to correct those problems.

When Promotion in Motion could not rectify the problems to Beech-Nut's satisfaction, Beech-Nut withdrew Fruit Nibbles from the market and refused to accept, or pay for, any more Fruit Nibbles made by Promotion in Motion.[7] In response, Promotion in Motion sued Beech-Nut for breach of contract, claiming that it had met its obligations under the contract and

A photo from Beech-Nut's investigation showing normal (left) versus degraded (right) Fruit Nibbles™

had produced acceptable Fruit Nibbles. Beech-Nut not only denied the validity of Promotion's legal claims but instituted a counter-suit of its own, seeking money to compensate it for the economic injury caused by Promotion in Motion's shoddy manufacture of the Fruit Nibbles that had been marketed under the Beech-Nut brand name.

Using a device known as a *summary judgment motion*, Beech-Nut convinced the federal district court judge who was presiding over the case that Promotion in Motion's legal claims against Beech-Nut had no merit.[8] Promotion did not pursue a similar motion with respect to Beech-Nut's counterclaims, and Beech-Nut's counterclaims against Promotion went before a jury in 2012. On September 12, 2012, the jury decided the case in Beech-Nut's favor, awarding Beech-Nut *damages* of $2.2 million (i.e., Promotion in Motion was ordered to pay this sum to Beech-Nut). Promotion appealed the jury's verdict to the court of appeals, but it lost again. Ultimately, this civil *lawsuit* that began with Promotion in Motion suing Beech-Nut for an alleged breach of contract ended four years later with Promotion in Motion having to pay millions of dollars to Beech-Nut for its own breach of contract. That sum came on top of the many thousands of dollars in legal fees that Promotion in Motion surely had to pay to its own lawyers.

This brief sketch of the dispute between Promotion in Motion and Beech-Nut omits many important details about how this case turned out as it did. We will examine this case in much more detail because it is a wonderful microcosm of the full civil litigation process. It is rare nowadays to find a civil

---

7   Initially, Beech-Nut used a different supplier to produce Fruit Nibbles, but eventually Beech-Nut discontinued the Fruit Nibbles™ product.

8   In federal courts, the trial court is called the district court. In the next chapter, we will provide an overview of the various kinds of courts found within the state and federal legal systems that comprise the American court system.

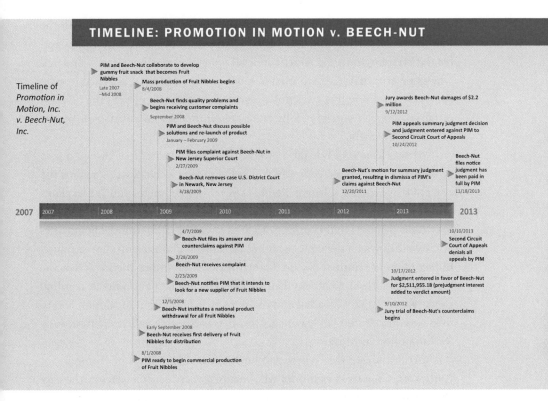

TIMELINE: PROMOTION IN MOTION v. BEECH-NUT

Timeline of Promotion in Motion, Inc. v. Beech-Nut, Inc.

PIM and Beech-Nut collaborate to develop gummy fruit snack that becomes Fruit Nibbles
Late 2007 –Mid 2008

Mass production of Fruit Nibbles begins
8/4/2008

Beech-Nut finds quality problems and begins receiving customer complaints
September 2008

PIM and Beech-Nut discuss possible solutions and re-launch of product
January – February 2009

PIM files complaint against Beech-Nut in New Jersey Superior Court
2/27/2009

Beech-Nut removes case U.S. District Court in Newark, New Jersey
3/18/2009

Jury awards Beech-Nut damages of $2.2 million
9/12/2012

PIM appeals summary judgment decision and judgment entered against PIM to Second Circuit Court of Appeals
10/24/2012

Beech-Nut's motion for summary judgment granted, resulting in dismissa of PIM's claims against Beech-Nut
12/20/2011

Beech-Nut files notice judgment has been paid in full by PIM
11/18/2013

2007   2007   2008   2009   2010   2011   2012   2013   2013

4/7/2009
Beech-Nut files its answer and counterclaims against PIM

2/28/2009
Beech-Nut receives complaint

2/23/2009
Beech-Nut notifies PIM that it intends to look for a new supplier of Fruit Nibbles

12/5/2008
Beech-Nut institutes a national product withdrawal for all Fruit Nibbles

Early September 2008
Beech-Nut receives first delivery of Fruit Nibbles for distribution

8/1/2008
PIM ready to begin commercial production of Fruit Nibbles

10/10/2013
Second Circuit Court of Appeals denials all appeals by PIM

10/17/2012
Judgment entered in favor of Beech-Nut for $2,511,955.18 (prejudgment interest added to verdict amount)

9/10/2012
Jury trial of Beech-Nut's counterclaims begins

case that goes all the way through jury trial and appeal and ends with the losing party satisfying the judgment from the trial court by making full payment to the prevailing party. Relatively few civil cases reach trial, with most cases being resolved through a voluntary *settlement* or being dismissed by the judge before trial, and of those few cases that do go to trial and result in a verdict for one of the parties, many settle voluntarily after the losing party has appealed the jury's verdict to a higher court but before the appellate court has ruled.

The Rest of the Book[9]

This chapter has introduced you to the cases that will serve as our tour guides through the federal and state court systems that collectively make up the American legal system. Our first extended stop on this tour will be an overview

9   Please do read this section of the chapter. It is not your usual boring preview that gives cryptic summaries of what is to come but actually contains some interesting information that will help you understand the lifecycle of a case.

of both the federal and state court systems, which will provide you with the foundation needed to understand the relationship between state courts and federal courts within the American legal system. If you have ever wondered why some criminal cases are tried in federal court and some are tried in state court, Chapter 2 will answer this question for you as it explains the division of labor between courts run by state governments and courts run by the federal government.

If you have ever bought a product over the internet that turned out to be defective and wondered where you could pursue a civil lawsuit against the seller of that product, Chapter 3 will answer this question for you as it explains the law that sets limits on when state and federal courts can issue *orders* and *judgments* that are binding on persons located outside the territorial boundaries of the state in which the injury occurred. Chapter 3 also explains the mechanics of beginning a criminal case and a civil case. It examines the steps that the Commonwealth of Kentucky had to follow to initiate and pursue criminal charges against Mr. Woodall and the steps that Promotion in Motion had to follow to initiate the civil lawsuit against Beech-Nut that ended so disastrously for Promotion in Motion.

After touring the "where and how" of the beginnings of criminal and civil cases, Chapter 4 examines what happens between the start of the case and the start of the trial in that case. This period in a case's life is often called the pretrial phase, and it may last between a few months and many, many years.[10] The pretrial procedures that apply in civil cases differ considerably from the pretrial procedures that apply in criminal cases, and the pretrial phase is typically much longer in civil cases than criminal cases.[11]

One very important difference between civil and criminal cases during the pretrial phase concerns the acquisition and exchange of case-relevant information. In civil cases, the parties can use several legally-authorized maneuvers to obtain information about the other party's case and to gather information helpful to their own case that they might not otherwise be able to obtain. To many people's surprise, the information-gathering process, which is known formally as the *discovery* process, is much less extensive in criminal cases. Indeed, a criminal defendant has relatively few legal devices at his disposal to obtain information that might be helpful to his defense. Chapter 4 explains

---

10   For instance, one of the authors of this book (Mitchell) practiced law full time before becoming a professor. One of the very first cases that he worked on when he joined a law firm had begun approximately a year before. When he left the firm six years later, it had not yet reached trial.

11   One reason for shorter pretrial periods in criminal cases is that the Sixth Amendment to the U.S. Constitution guarantees criminal defendants a right to a "speedy trial."

why this disparity in information-gathering exists: the short answer is that the police and prosecuting attorney are supposed to investigate crimes vigorously and turn over to the person accused of a crime evidence that could be helpful to his defense.

The approach to information-gathering in civil cases is very different: each party is expected to do its own investigation, with relatively little information having to be disclosed to the other party until that other party has asked for it.

In both civil and criminal cases, the information gathered about each side's case will be very valuable, for it will influence the willingness of criminal defendants to enter into plea agreements with the prosecuting attorney and will influence the willingness of civil parties to settle a case rather than take it to trial. But the gathering and exchange of case-relevant information are not the only important things that occur during the pretrial phase. During this period, the judge will rule on criminal defendant's motions to suppress (i.e., bar the use of) evidence that the government allegedly obtained improperly, the judge will rule on motions by civil parties to dismiss legal claims for factual or legal deficiencies, and in civil cases new parties may be added where the discovery process has revealed additional persons or companies who may have some responsibility or interest in the case.

After we visit this very important period in a case's life, we will attend trial. People who are familiar with the American court system primarily through their viewing of television and films may believe that jury trials are common, but in fact jury trials are quite rare in both criminal and civil cases, usually making up less than five percent of both types of cases annually. When we add trials in which a judge, rather than a jury, renders the verdict (trials before only a judge are commonly known among lawyers as *bench trials*), the percentage goes up a bit, but trials by judge or jury still only occur in a small percentage of all cases decided by state and federal courts. (In any given year, between five to ten percent of cases filed go to trial.) Nonetheless, trials are an essential part of the American legal system: the mere possibility of a trial by jury casts a shadow over the pretrial phase of a case that can greatly influence whether a criminal case ends in a plea agreement between the prosecuting attorney and defendant or whether a civil case ends through a settlement agreement. But not all criminal and civil cases are automatically eligible for trial by jury. Chapter 5 explains the limits of the constitutional right to a trial by jury. Chapter 5 also walks you through the trial process itself, from pretrial motions, opening statements by the lawyers, the presentation of evidence, closing arguments by the lawyers, the judge's instructions to a jury in a jury trial, and the verdict, as well as the post-trial motions that can be made by the parties to try to get out from under an unfavorable verdict.

Chapter 6 stops at a destination where no party or lawyer ever wants to go, the court of appeals, because a visit to the court of appeals means that a loss has occurred in the trial court. The power of courts of appeals to overturn verdicts and orders from trial courts is somewhat limited: courts of appeals are supposed to defer to the judgment of the jury or trial judge on matters of fact, such as who pulled the trigger that fired the fatal shot. However, courts of appeals do not have to defer to trial courts on matters of law, such as how best to interpret a statute that imposes penalties for murder. Chapter 6 will help you understand the role and power of courts of appeals relative to the trial court.

It will also introduce you to a controversial process that closely resembles an appeal and raises difficult questions about the relationship between state and federal courts. This is the *writ of habeas corpus*, which allows federal courts to determine whether state prisoners are being held lawfully. Woodall's case made it to the Supreme Court through his invocation of this habeas corpus procedure, and detainees from the Iraq war who have been held at Guantanamo have invoked the *writ of habeas corpus* to try to obtain release.

Chapter 7 will help you understand the status of the U.S. Supreme Court in relation to all of the other courts in the U.S., whether state or federal and whether a trial court or a court of appeal. The Supreme Court truly is supreme in that it has the power to overturn decisions by any other court in the U.S., but there are limits to the Supreme Court's power. We will discuss these limits, will explain why so few cases make it to the Supreme Court, and will study how opinions by the Supreme Court justices get written.

One of the most important functions served by the U.S. Supreme Court is being the final arbiter on legal decisions: the litigation process must end somewhere. But another very important function of the Supreme Court is to serve as a check on the other branches of the federal government, the legislative and executive branches. Chapter 7 gives more attention to these two functions served by the Supreme Court: the Court's role overseeing lower courts and as protector of the Constitution against encroachments by Congress or the Presidency. The Supreme Court's role as protector of the Constitution is achieved through a doctrine known as *judicial review*. This doctrine, because it gives American courts the power to overturn acts of Congress and the President, is important and controversial and consequently has provoked much scholarly debate. We do not take a position on the proper conception and application of judicial review, but you should leave the chapter with a good understanding of what is at issue in the debate over the doctrine of judicial review.

By the time you reach Chapter 8, you should have all of the information you need to understand how American courts handle most criminal and civil cases. Chapter 8 complicates things just a bit by discussing an important, but less common type of case—*class actions*—and examines some details that were omitted previously but are important to understanding how

```
2.2   Arbitration Agreement

(1) AT&T and you agree to arbitrate all disputes and claims between
us. This agreement to arbitrate is intended to be broadly
interpreted. It includes, but is not limited to:

    •  claims arising out of or relating to any aspect of the
    relationship between us, whether based in contract, tort,
    statute, fraud, misrepresentation or any other legal theory;
    •     claims that arose before this or any prior Agreement
    (including, but not limited to, claims relating to
    advertising);
    •     claims that are currently the subject of purported class
    action litigation in which you are not a member of a certified
    class; and
    •    claims that may arise after the termination of this
    Agreement.

References to "AT&T," "you," and "us" include our respective
subsidiaries, affiliates, agents, employees, predecessors in
interest, successors, and assigns, as well as all authorized or
unauthorized users or beneficiaries of services or Devices under this
or prior Agreements between us. Notwithstanding the foregoing, either
party may bring an individual action in small claims court. This
arbitration agreement does not preclude you from bringing issues to
the attention of federal, state, or local agencies, including, for
example, the Federal Communications Commission. Such agencies can, if
the law allows, seek relief against us on your behalf. You agree
that, by entering into this Agreement, you and AT&T are each waiving
the right to a trial by jury or to participate in a class action.
This Agreement evidences a transaction in interstate commerce, and
thus the Federal Arbitration Act governs the interpretation and
enforcement of this provision. This arbitration provision shall
survive termination of this Agreement.
```

Excerpt from AT&T's Wireless Customer Agreement
(for the latest version, go to http://www.att.com/legal/terms.wireless
CustomerAgreement.html#howDoIResolveDisputesWithAtt)

American courts operate. A class action lawsuit is a type of civil case in which one or more persons sue on behalf of a group of persons who all have allegedly been injured by the same defendant in the same way. Many of you have probably been members of one or more class action lawsuits without even knowing it, because in a class action someone can sue on behalf of a large group of people without first getting the consent of all those people. For instance, if you have a contract for wireless internet service, you have probably been a member of a class action lawsuit accusing the provider of your internet service of some kind of deceptive or inappropriate billing practice, such as allowing young children to make in-game purchases without parental approval. Because the persons affected by a class action lawsuit usually will not have authorized the case or had any personal involvement in the lawsuit, American courts impose special requirements on class actions that are aimed at protecting the interests of those absent persons.

Chapter 8 will also contrast the legal process with alternative forms of dispute resolution, especially the use of *arbitration*. Many civil law disputes are decided today by an arbitrator rather than a judge or jury because many contracts require this form of dispute resolution rather through a lawsuit filed in court. For instance, the current default contract for wireless customers of AT&T includes a clause establishing that arbitration will be the exclusive means of resolving disputes between the customer and AT&T. (An excerpt from this contract is provided for you so you can read the detailed language). One of the benefits of choosing arbitration over a lawsuit is that you can have some say about who will be your arbitrator, whereas your filing in court will most likely be randomly assigned to a judge.

Chapter 8 also contains some sobering and perhaps disturbing information. A final, unappealable judgment in a criminal case ends the case and sends the defendant home or to his punishment. A final, unappealable judgment in a civil case in favor of the defendant also brings the litigation process to an end. However, a final, unappealable judgment in favor a civil plaintiff is equivalent to a promissory note: the plaintiff still needs to convert the favorable judgment into money or action. It is this feature of the American civil court system that perhaps more than any other encourages the parties to enter into a settlement agreement: a settlement agreement is not effective until one of the parties has been paid. A civil court's judgment is a very valuable piece of paper, but it is not money. In order to convert the judgment to money, a prevailing party must take steps to enforce or collect on that judgment, and this collection process may spawn a whole new round of litigation.

You should leave this book with a detailed, realistic understanding of how American courts work. There will still be much more to learn about American courts and American law—and many of you will probably do just that by going to law school—but you will have the basic information you need to critically evaluate the structure and functioning of the American legal system (and to debunk courtroom dramas that you see at the movies). ■

CHAPTER 2

An Overview of American Courts

A lthough people often speak of "the American judicial system," there really is no such thing. Instead, there are multiple court systems, all with their own sources of law. Each of the fifty states has its own judicial system, as do the District of Columbia and Puerto Rico. Also located in the states and territories, but operating independently, are the courts of the federal judicial system. That makes for plenty of variety and plenty of confusion. Courts in one system often have to apply and interpret the law of another system, and frequently a single case can properly be decided by courts in more than one system. (The figure on the next page provides a graphic overview of the federal and state courts and their relationship within the American system of governance.)

This state of affairs is not an accident. It originated with the Constitution itself and the Framers' decision to create a system of federalism, in which some powers were delegated exclusively to the national government, many others remained exclusively with the states, and still others were to be shared between the national and state governments. Although the power of the national government has grown enormously over time and the relationship between national and state governments has changed, the fundamental federalist structure persists, not least in the country's court systems.

State courts overshadow federal courts both in the number of cases they handle and in the number of litigants, lawyers, and judges. According to statistics from the National Center for State Courts and the U.S. government, in 2013 more than 39 million cases (civil and criminal cases combined) were filed in the trial courts of the fifty states, compared with approximately 375,000 in the principal federal trial courts (U.S. District Courts) and one million in the federal bankruptcy courts. There are over 30,000 judges in the state trial courts, while there are fewer than 1850 federal district, bankruptcy, and magistrate judges.

The Court Systems of the United States[1]

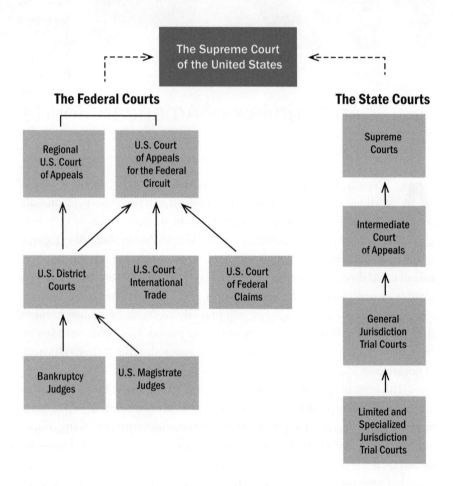

Volume of business and number of judicial personnel do not tell the whole story. Much of the business of the federal courts affects government operations throughout the country and touches many people's lives. Still, state courts matter more in the daily life of the average citizen.

The federal and state court systems vary considerably in the details of their organization and business, but their basic structures are all similar. Each system is shaped like a pyramid, with trial courts at the base, where cases begin; these courts are also often called "courts of first instance." At the top of the pyramid is the court of last resort, often called the supreme court[2]; this court has power to review and overturn decisions of courts lower in the pyramid. In most states and in the federal system there is a middle tier of courts that have power to review and overturn decisions by the courts of first instance and whose decisions can be reviewed and overturned by the court of last resort.

In most states there are two levels of trial courts. The major trial courts are called courts of "general jurisdiction" because they have authority to hear and decide numerous types of cases, civil and criminal. The particular name given to these courts varies from one state to another. They are called "circuit courts" in some states, "superior courts" in others, and "district courts" in still others.

Below the trial courts of general jurisdiction are courts that can only hear a limited range of cases, often only one specific type of case. For example, in some states there are traffic courts that handle only fairly minor motor vehicle offenses. Many states have "small claims" trial courts that hear civil cases in which the damages do not exceed $5,000 or some other relatively small amount.

Some of these specialty trial courts hear major cases. A probate court, for example, can administer estates worth millions of dollars. Family or domestic relations courts found in some states have authority to grant divorces, determine custody of children, and fix alimony and child support. Some states have a hodgepodge of specialty courts, usually resulting from the legislature's unsystematic creation of special courts from time to time (e.g., as shown in Appendix D, New York has a wide variety of specialty courts that operate as the point of first access into the New York legal system). Whatever their structure, these specialized courts handle a far greater volume of cases than general jurisdiction trial courts—approximately twice as many cases in most states.

---

2   For instance, Kentucky and New Jersey call their top court the Supreme Court, but other states use another name for their top courts and may even call one of the lower courts the Supreme Court, as New York does. (See Appendices D—F for full diagrams of the Kentucky, New Jersey, and New York courts.)

The U.S. Constitution leaves most decisions about the organization of the federal courts to Congress, saying simply in Article III that "[t]he judicial Power of the United States, shall be vested in one supreme Court, and in such inferior Courts as the Congress may from time to time ordain and establish" (The U.S. Constitution, including Article III, is set out in its entirety in Appendix A). After the Constitution was ratified, the first Congress passed the Judiciary Act of 1789, setting up the federal judicial system with federal trial courts in every state. In 1891 Congress established a set of intermediate courts with purely appellate jurisdiction called U.S. Courts of Appeals. The structure put in place in 1891 is essentially what exists today.

Congress has divided the United States and its territories into ninety-four federal judicial districts (a map of these districts is found on the next page). There is at least one district in each state, as well as in the District of Columbia and Puerto Rico. The largest and most heavily populated states have multiple districts; Florida, for instance, has a northern, middle, and southern district.[3] Each district contains a United States District Court. These ninety-four courts are the major trial courts of the federal judiciary. Each has at least two judges; the largest have more than twenty. Because each district covers either an entire state or a large part of a state, the court typically holds sessions in several cities in the district. For example, the United States District Court for the Eastern District of Virginia sits in Richmond, Norfolk, and Alexandria.

Each district falls within a circuit overseen by a Court of Appeals. For example, the Eastern District of Virginia is part of the Fourth Circuit. The Northern District of California is in the Ninth Circuit. There are twelve of these circuits. The District of Columbia Circuit, which hears many cases challenging the actions of federal agencies, covers only D.C., as its name suggests. The other eleven circuits are numbered, and each covers at least three states. The Fourth Circuit's territory is Maryland, Virginia, West Virginia, and North Carolina. The Ninth Circuit is by far the largest in terms of both area and population, covering California, Nevada, Arizona, Oregon, Washington, Idaho, Montana, Alaska, Hawaii, Guam, and the Northern Mariana Islands. A district court decision can only be appealed to the Court of Appeals for the circuit in which the district court is located. For instance, decisions from the

---

3   With minor exceptions, no judicial district crosses state lines: all of Yellowstone National Park is assigned to the District of Wyoming, even though parts of the park are in Montana and Idaho, and some territories possessed by the U.S. in the Pacific Ocean have been assigned to the District of Hawaii. In addition, two specialized trial courts hear certain types of cases no matter where they arise in the U.S.: the Court of International Trade (physically located in New York) hears cases involving international trade and customs issues; the Court of Federal Claims (physically located in Washington, D.C.) hears most claims against the federal government seeking monetary damages that might have to be paid from the U.S. Treasury.

Eastern District of Virginia go to the United States Court of Appeals for the Fourth Circuit, and no other Court of Appeals has the authority to review decisions from that district court.

Map of Federal Circuits and Districts[4]

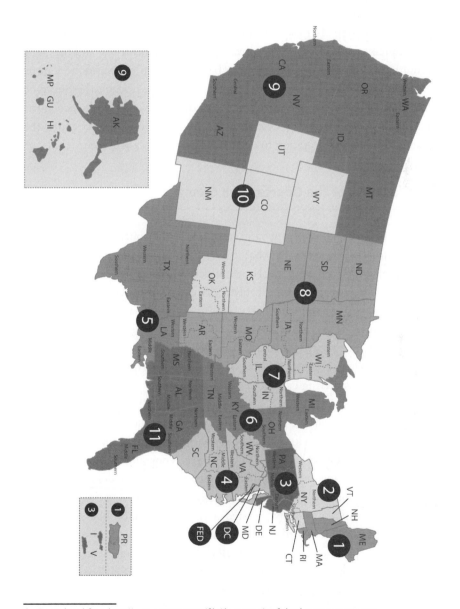

The only federal appellate court not organized on a territorial basis is the United States Court of Appeals for the Federal Circuit. This court hears appeals from all district courts in cases arising under federal patent law and cases in which monetary damages are sought from the federal government. This court also hears appeals from several administrative agencies and from decisions of two special trial courts: the Court of Federal Claims and the Court of International Trade.

The next step after the Court of Appeals for a dissatisfied litigant is the U.S. Supreme Court. A case that involves issues of federal law and has gone through a state court system can also be appealed to the Supreme Court. However, as we will explain in Chapter 7, most cases reach the Supreme Court only if that court agrees to hear them. In other words, while the Courts of Appeals have to hear any case appealed from a federal district court, the Supreme Court has discretion to decide which appeals it will hear.

The Business of the Courts: Civil Cases

With an understanding of the basic structure of the courts in place, we can now begin to examine exactly what it is that American courts do. Both state and federal courts hear cases involving both criminal and civil law. On the civil side, the quintessential state case involves a situation where one party has caused some sort of injury to the other party. This doesn't necessarily mean a physical injury; often, as in the case of Promotion in Motion v. Beech-Nut introduced in Chapter 1, the injury is financial in nature. But parties certainly can seek a remedy for physical injury and in some cases for injury to their reputations or for pain and suffering caused by an opposing party's behavior. Whatever the nature of the injury, the remedy in a civil case usually takes the form of an order by the court that one party pay the other a specified amount of money. An order to pay money is known as an award of damages. In some cases, where the behavior in question has not yet occurred or is ongoing, courts will order a party to do something, refrain from doing something, or stop doing something. For example, a court might order a company to stop releasing pollutants into a stream, to clean a previously polluted stream, or not to build another plant on its property. Such an order is called an *injunction*, because it enjoins, or commands, a party to act or not act. Both federal and state courts have the power to issue injunctions, but it is much more common for them to provide a monetary remedy, or damages, for injuries.

ENGLISH COURTS OF LAW AND EQUITY

When the American colonies were founded, the English courts were divided between "Courts of Law" and "Courts of Equity." Courts of Law were presided over by judges with juries deciding the cases based on the common law of England (because Courts of Law decided cases arising from the common law, these courts are also called common law courts). Juries could order one party to pay the other party damages, or a sum of money to compensate for injuries, but they did not have power to order the parties to do something or stop doing something. Courts of Equity were presided over by an official called a Chancellor (which explains why these courts are also called the Court of Chancery), and many Chancellors were members of the clergy. The Chancellor decided cases based on what the Chancellor determined to be fair and equitable. The Chancellor did have the power to order the parties to do something or cease doing something, such as ordering one party to deliver property in its possession to the other party, and this kind of relief came to be known as equitable remedies. The colonial and early U.S. courts largely followed English procedural traditions and had common law courts in which cases were decided by a jury and equity courts in which the judge resolved the case. Eventually, all of the states and the federal government permitted their trial courts to award damages and/or equitable relief.

Civil law cases often involve *contract* claims or *tort* claims. In a contract case, one party alleges that the opposing party failed to live up to its written or oral promises. The Fruit Nibbles case is an example of a business-to-business contract dispute, but contract disputes also arise frequently between individuals or between individuals and businesses. For instance, if you buy a used car from another person and the car turns out to be a lemon, you might sue the seller for breach of the contract because you thought you were buying a working automobile rather than a clunker. Or if your insurance company denies a claim following a traffic accident caused by your malfunctioning car, you might sue your insurance company for breaching the insurance contract you signed with the company.

Tort cases, which form an especially large part of state court business, are like contract cases in that one party accuses the other of breaching some duty that it owed to the first party. But in tort cases the duty does not arise from a promise; in fact, the parties in a tort case may not have even known or communicated with each other before the injury occurred. Rather, torts involve duties inherent in situations or relationships. For instance, we have a duty not to intentionally harm others without good reason. People who violate this duty can be sued for an intentional tort, such as battery. The law of every state also requires that we act reasonably, or without negligence, when performing everyday activities such as driving a car or performing work on the job. We also have a duty to keep places where others might walk, such as the front steps of our house or the floor in a grocery store, in safe condition. Some professionals, such as financial advisors and lawyers, owe special duties of loyalty and care to their clients. When someone violates a duty owed to another person and that breach of duty causes the other person harm, we say that the first person committed a tort, and the person who has been harmed can file a civil case seeking relief under tort law.[5] Traffic accidents are an especially common source of tort suits.

In addition to laws that can be used to redress torts and breaches of contracts, every state has civil laws that regulate family matters, public safety, work, and commerce within the state, among other things. People who stand to benefit from these laws can sometimes rely on them to make legal claims against others: for instance, one spouse can sue another for divorce, an employee can sue an employer for failure to pay overtime, and a customer of an electric company can sue to challenge a rate hike. Some civil regulatory laws are enforced by state agencies, such as a department of insurance or public utilities commission, and these agencies may sue to get a court order forcing a regulated entity to abide by the law.

▪ WHAT DO WE CALL THE BASIS FOR A CIVIL LAWSUIT?

(a) Claim

(b) Cause of Action

(c) Private Right of Action

(d) Any of the Above

The correct answer is "(d) Any of the Above." Although the terms claim, cause of action, and right of action have different origins and historically have had different connotations, today these terms can be used interchangeably to refer to civil laws that regulate interpersonal relationships and business

---

5 The behavior that constitutes some torts may also constitute a crime. If your professor intentionally hits your hand with a ruler for giving a bad answer in class, you may sue that professor for committing the tort of battery and the prosecutor in your county may also begin a criminal case against your professor for committing the crime of battery. A murder case will sometimes be followed by a civil case in which the defendant is accused of committing the tort of battery that led to the victim's wrongful death. Because the burden of proof is higher in a criminal case than in a civil case (the prosecutor must prove beyond reasonable doubt that the defendant committed the crime, whereas the plaintiff only has to prove that it is more likely than not true that the defendant committed the tort), the civil case may succeed even when the criminal case failed. This is what happened in the criminal and civil cases involving O.J. Simpson and the death of his former wife, Nicole Brown Simpson: Ms. Simpson's estate obtained a $33.5 million verdict against Mr. Simpson in the civil case even though Mr. Simpson was acquitted in the criminal case.

transactions. If someone has harmed you in violation of civil law, then you have a claim or cause of action against that person through this civil law. If you can prove all of the necessary elements of your claim, then you will be entitled to relief from the other person. In English Courts of Law, only a single claim could be pursued in a case. In modern American courts (at both the federal and state level), multiple claims can be joined together in a single case, and these claims can arise from different sources of law (e.g., claims arising from contract law can be joined with claims arising from tort law).

The most fundamental source of civil law is a constitution. In addition to delineating governmental powers—and limitations on those powers—constitutions set out the rights of individuals. Every state government is bound by both the U.S. Constitution and its own state constitution. People who feel their federal or state constitutional rights have been violated can sue for relief. For instance, if you thought you were turned down for a hunting license because of your race or sex, you could sue the offending official under a federal or state equal protection clause.

Laws passed by legislatures, called statutes, are less fundamental in the sense that they are subordinate to constitutions: a statute that violates a constitution lacks the force of law. (When a court declares a statute unconstitutional, it has exercised the power of judicial review. We will have more to say about judicial review in Chapter 7.) However, the civil laws that affect people's lives from day to day come far more often from statutes than from constitutions. This makes the state legislature the most important source of civil laws. Many other civil laws come from regulations promulgated by state agencies; these regulations have the force of law if they are enacted according to the procedure required by the state legislature. Finally, a small but important number of civil laws are made by state courts through their decisions in cases and the opinions explaining those decisions. For instance, in most states the tort of negligence was created by decisions of the state's supreme court rather than the legislature or executive. Finally, some laws are even passed directly by the people of a state through ballot initiatives or referenda.

Civil laws based on constitutions, statutes, regulations, and referenda are often referred to as the "positive law," because the legislature, executive or the people have formally "posited" or explicitly pronounced what the law is. In contrast, when a state court creates a civil law, such as the tort of negligence, the law is referred to as the "common law," because the law is the product of commentary of the courts that is supposed to reflect the expectations of citizens within the state and promote the state's public policies. Whether a claim is created by positive law or by the common law process, the end result is a law that specifies the elements of a claim that must be proved in order for the claimant to win damages or an injunction. For instance, if a defendant is alleged to have committed the common law tort of battery, the plaintiff must prove that it is more likely than not true that (1) the defendant knowingly or intentionally (2) made contact with the plaintiff (3) without the plaintiff's consent, (4) the defendant was not otherwise privileged to make such contact, and (5) this contact caused some harm to the plaintiff. By looking to the cases or statutes that create claims, the claimant will be able to determine what facts must be proved to prevail on a claim.

Whereas many of the state civil laws that give rise to lawsuits are formed through the common law, federal civil laws are exclusively the product of the U.S. Constitution, congressional legislation and regulations promulgated by the executive branch. Federal judges have the power to interpret and apply federal statutes and federal regulations. This includes the power to decide that a statute implicitly authorizes private individuals, not just government actors, to file a suit to enforce the statute. However, federal judges do not have the power to create common law causes of action—that is, they cannot make up new grounds for lawsuits, unlike their state judge counterparts. This difference in judicial power derives from differences between federal and state constitutions and statutes. The U.S. Constitution reserves the lawmaking power to Congress, and Congress has been unwilling to delegate lawmaking authority to federal courts. In contrast, some state constitutions or state legislatures grant state courts the power to create common law causes of action, though if the courts go too far, the legislatures may pass laws that revoke or alter the law as announced by the courts.

The Business of the Courts: Criminal Cases

With few exceptions, all criminal laws are now positive law.[6] Although initially the states continued to recognize common law crimes when the United States was formed, eventually all of the states and the federal government passed statutes codifying, and sometimes changing and often adding to, what were previously common law crimes. For instance, for many years the American

---

6   A few states, including Florida and Michigan, still enforce some common law crimes (i.e., crimes that are the product of judicial decisions instead of statutes). Most states and the federal government no longer recognize common law crimes.

states followed English common law with respect to murder, but eventually every state passed a statute defining the crime. The primary idea underlying this shift to positive law, as the U.S. Supreme Court has put it, is that "because of the seriousness of criminal penalties, and because criminal punishment usually represents the moral condemnation of the community, legislatures and not courts should define criminal activity. This policy embodies 'the instinctive distastes against men languishing in prison unless the lawmaker has clearly said they should.'"[7] The role of the courts is to interpret rather than create the criminal laws.

■ MAKING SENSE OF LEGAL CITATIONS

Here is a quick guide to deciphering the legal citations you will find throughout this book. Let's take the example of *U.S. v. Bass*, 404 U.S. 336, 348 (1971) (quoting H. Friendly, *Mr. Justice Frankfurter and the Reading of Statutes*, in BENCHMARKS 196, 209 (1967)), which is the legal citation found in note 5 for this chapter. In this citation, "*U.S. v. Bass*" refers to the two parties in the case (the U.S. government brought criminal charges against Bass). "404 U.S." directs us to volume 404 of the Supreme Court Reports, a government publication that compiles the opinions of the U.S. Supreme Court. The numbers 336 and 348 that immediately follow refer respectively to the page in this volume where the opinion for this case begins and to the specific page on which the quotation appears. The year in parentheses is the year the opinion was written. The final parenthetical provides information on a source quoted by the Supreme Court in its opinion. If you are interested in learning more about one of the opinions that we cite, you can search the Internet using the opinion citation we provide and you will probably find the opinions publicly available at no charge.

Statutes and administrative rules also have their own special citation format. All federal statutes are collected in a set of books called the U.S. Code that are organized by title and section numbers. For instance, the federal statute making internet gambling illegal is found in Section 5362 of Title 31 of the U.S. Code; the formal legal citation for this law is 31 U.S.C. § 5362. Federal administrative rules and regulations are collected in the Code of Federal Regulations, organized by title, section name, and year. For instance, the most recent regulation enacted by the Department of Treasury aimed at preventing banks or credit card companies from funding internet gambling is found in Section 132 of Title 31 of the Code of Federal Regulations; the formal legal citation for this regulation is 31 C.F.R. § 132 (2015).

---

7   *U.S. v. Bass*, 404 U.S. 336, 348 (1971) (quoting H. Friendly, *Mr. Justice Frankfurter and the Reading of Statutes*, in BENCHMARKS 196, 209 (1967)).

The Relation of Federal and State Laws in Our Federalist System

The existence of fifty different states, each with its own lawmaking powers and court system, situated within a federal sovereignty with its own lawmaking power and court system, creates the potential for conflicts among the states' laws and between state and federal law. When a state law and a valid federal law conflict, the Supremacy Clause of the U.S. Constitution tells us that the federal law trumps the state law:

> This Constitution, and the Laws of the United States which shall be made in pursuance thereof; and all treaties made, or which shall be made, under the authority of the United States, shall be the supreme law of the land; and the judges in every state shall be bound thereby, anything in the constitution or laws of any state to the contrary notwithstanding.

Thus, if a state tries to impose voter registration requirements that conflict with federal voter registration requirements (as the U.S. Supreme Court ruled Arizona did in a law that required additional proof of American citizenship[8]), then the state law cannot be enforced.

The Supremacy Clause also requires state courts to ensure that parties in legal cases receive the minimum level of protections guaranteed by the federal Constitution, such as the right to a trial by jury in certain kinds of cases. (We discuss the right to trial by jury in more detail in Chapter 4.) States are free to grant additional protections to criminal defendants and civil parties, and a number of states have expanded protections for criminal defendants through their state constitutions, but states cannot give less protection than that guaranteed by the federal Constitution.

The Supremacy Clause only applies to conflicts between federal and state law. Another provision of the Constitution addresses conflicts that arise between state laws. Under the Full Faith and Credit Clause each state is supposed to honor the laws and legal decisions of the other states:

> Full faith and credit shall be given in each state to the public acts, records, and judicial proceedings of every other state.

---

8   For the full opinion by the Supreme Court, see *Arizona v. Inter Tribal Council of Arizona, Inc.*, 133 S.Ct. 2247 (2013). ("S.Ct." refers to the *Supreme Court Reporter* published by West; the official U.S. reports version of the case often takes a year to be published, while the S.Ct. version will appear much earlier.)

Therefore, when one state court has followed proper procedure and reached a decision in a case, the courts and public officials in the other forty-nine states are supposed to recognize and enforce that state court's decision, even if they disagree with the outcome in the case. A similar rule applies to federal courts and officials through a congressional statute that orders the federal government to give full faith and credit to lawfully-rendered state court decisions.[9]

The Full Faith and Credit Clause and the Full Faith and Credit statute are very important not only because they promote harmony among the states and federal government but also because they bring finality to legal disputes. Without the requirement that state and federal courts give full faith and credit to each other's verdicts, a civil plaintiff in New Jersey who was unhappy with the outcome in the New Jersey court could try for a better result in another court, and could continue trying until he found a court that agreed with his views on how the case should be decided. Because of the full faith and credit doctrine, that plaintiff gets one and only one bite at the litigation apple.

Selecting Judges

Yet another way that state courts differ from each other and from federal courts is in the methods they use to choose judges for office. As the framers of the U.S. Constitution understood well, the rules by which officials gain and retain office can profoundly affect what influence other people have on their thinking and actions. The framers thought members of the House of Representatives should be highly aware of and responsive to the views of their constituents, so they made them electable directly by the people and only gave them two-year terms. Senators, in contrast, were elected by state legislatures and given six-year terms; this was to encourage them to act more independently of public opinion. Views about who should influence judges and to whom they should be accountable—and the way those views have changed over time—are reflected in the diverse methods of judicial selection employed in the U.S. at various times in various places.

One selection system rejected by all U.S. jurisdictions is popular else-where, especially in continental Europe. In this system young people begin their professional careers as judges after specialized training, and, in many

---

9   *See* 28 U.S.C. § 1738. (This citation directs you to Section 1738 in Title 28 of the U.S. Code, which is the official government publication of laws passed by the U.S. Congress. For more information, visit http://www.gpo.gov/fdsys/browse/collectionUScode.action?collectionCode=USCODE.)

cases, successful passage of an entry exam. Having begun their judicial careers at the lowest level of courts, they are then promoted through the several higher levels of the judiciary by judges above them in the hierarchy. Think of a typical bureaucracy, such as an army. In the U.S., for some reason, it has always been the practice to have people become judges only after a substantial time spent practicing or teaching law or holding legislative or executive office. For that reason, regardless of the specific method, it is quite uncommon to see American judges in their twenties or early thirties. Furthermore, the career paths of American judges once they join the bench are far less predictable.

The Constitution mentions only one method for choosing federal judges: the president nominates and the Senate decides whether to approve. All judges on federal district courts, circuit courts of appeals, and the Supreme Court are chosen this way.[10] Especially with lower court nominations, the president's involvement is usually minimal. Advisers in the White House and Justice Department generate a list of candidates in consultation with senators and interest groups. Interested candidates fill out an extensive questionnaire and are vetted by the FBI, with the hope of eliminating candidates with serious ethical or legal issues. Depending on the administration, candidates may also be vetted by the American Bar Association. Normally the president will enter the discussion only once the list has been narrowed to a few approved candidates.

Once the nominee is chosen and the name is sent to the Senate, the nomination is referred to the Senate Judiciary Committee. The committee is responsible for holding hearings at which the nominee and the nominee's supporters and opponents speak and are questioned by senators. Hearings for lower courts, especially district courts, tend to be brief, with little drama; often a few nominations are combined into a single hearing. Contemporary Supreme Court nomination hearings tend to be multi-day affairs, with senators opposed to the nominee probing for weaknesses that might derail the nomination. After the hearings, the committee votes on the nomination and sends it to the floor with its recommendation for or against the nominee.

At least this is what the nominee and president would like to see happen. There is no absolute requirement that the Judiciary Committee hold hearings and report the nomination to the floor. If the chair or other important members of the committee oppose a nomination, they may simply refuse to move ahead with it. Even if a nomination does make it out of committee, that does not mean

---

10   The judges on these courts are called "Article III judges" because their appointments are authorized by Article III of the Constitution. Other federal judges, such as bankruptcy judges and magistrates, are authorized by federal statutes passed by Congress under Congress's powers under Article I of the Constitution. Thus, judges authorized by statute are called "Article I judges."

there will be a vote on the floor. The majority leader may refuse to schedule a vote, or a minority might filibuster the nomination, taking advantage of the Senate's general rule allowing unlimited debate to keep the nomination from coming to a vote. (The Democrats disallowed filibusters of lower court nominations in late 2013, but that change can be reversed by the majority party in the Senate at any time.) In recent decades it has become increasingly common for lower court nominations to die in the Senate without a vote; after months go by without a vote or sign of one to come, nominees ask the president to withdraw their nomination and allow them to get on with other things.

The role played by individual senators depends a great deal on the level of court. Individual senators matter most for district court nominations because of the practice of senatorial courtesy. Traditionally the practice is understood to mean that a senator from the same political party as the president can veto the president's nomination of a district court judge in that senator's state. If the senator informs the Senate leadership that the nominee is unacceptable, hearings will not be held and a vote will not be taken. Sometimes the norm is interpreted more broadly to give a veto to senators from the majority party even if the president is from the other party. In any case, the power of home-state senators means that presidents are well advised to consult with them before making their nominations.

Those nominees fortunate enough to make it through the process and be confirmed by the Senate are given their seats for a term of "good behavior," meaning that they cannot be removed from office except through impeachment for "high crimes and misdemeanors." For all practical purposes, this means a life term; these judges can decide cases as they see fit without having to worry about losing their jobs.

Congress occasionally creates specialized courts or judgeships. The methods of choosing judges for these vary. The most numerous of the specialized judges today are bankruptcy judges, who are chosen by Court of Appeals judges and serve for renewable fourteen-year terms.[11]

State court selection in the early years of the republic tended to look a good deal like federal court selection. Judges were appointed either by governors, with appointment subject to approval by the state legislature or a special commission, or directly by the legislature. Most appointments were for life. This began to change in the first half of the 19th century as part of a greater

---

11 http://www.fjc.gov/history/home.nsf/page/judges_bank.html. We cannot do justice to the importance and variety of specialized courts. For further reading on them, we recommend Lawrence Baum's *Specializing the Courts* (University of Chicago Press, 2011).

emphasis on democracy and public participation in American politics more generally. When Indiana joined the union in 1816, its constitution provided that most trial judges would be elected by the people for seven-year terms.[12] Mississippi changed its method in 1832 from legislative appointment to popular election for all judges. In the late 1840s, the pace picked up considerably, with new states choosing elections and existing states switching from appointment to election. By the time of the Civil War, judges were being elected in more than a dozen states.

The next major wave of reforms came with the Progressive movement in the late 19th and early 20th centuries. A key goal of the movement was to overthrow political party machines, which were accused of manipulating voters and, through their control of access to public office, filling offices with party hacks and exerting undue influence over their actions. Judicial offices were among those that party machines controlled. In an effort to reduce machine influence, a number of states, led by Washington and California, moved to a system of non-partisan election of judges. In non-partisan elections, candidates do not need their party's approval to get on the ballot, and party labels do not appear next to candidates' names on ballots. In some states there are also restrictions on activities parties can engage in to support candidates they favor. Non-partisan elections have remained a popular choice since they first appeared, and states have switched over to them with some frequency. Most recently, West Virginia decided that its judicial elections would be non-partisan as of 2016.[13]

Non-partisan elections do not always remove parties from the selection process; political parties can still manage to have considerable behind-the-scenes, or even public, influence over outcomes. Recognition of this fact, together with a feeling that the public isn't well equipped to choose judges wisely, is behind the rise of the final major method. Usually called the merit system, or because Missouri was the first to adopt it in 1940, the Missouri system, it combines appointment and election. There is some variation across states, but the basics of the merit system are as follows. When a judicial vacancy opens, a specially constituted commission vets interested candidates and forwards a short list of the candidates it deems best to the governor. The governor must choose a candidate from the approved list. That person assumes the judgeship but must face voters after a short probationary period (often a year)

---

12   All state-specific information in this overview comes from the National Center for State Courts, http://www.judicialselection.us.

13   Chris Dickerson, *Legal Newsline*, available at: http://legalnewsline.com/news/255608-judicial-elections-in-west-virginia-will-now-be-nonpartisan.

in what is called a retention election. In a retention election, voters' only options are yes or no. If there are enough yes votes (50% plus one in most states, but this varies), the judge stays on the bench for the full term; otherwise the judge loses the seat and the process begins again. At the end of the several-year term, the judge must face another retention election to stay in office.

Most states have changed their methods of selection at least once, some employ different methods for different courts, and there are many variations on the basic methods. This variety makes it difficult to say much about judicial selection in general. We can, however, point to one striking fact that causes the U.S. to stand out in a world where few judges are elected. A majority of American judges have to face voters at some point, whether at their initial selection or at retention time, if they want to sit on a court. This is not true of federal judges, as you know, but it is true of judges presiding over Kentucky's courts and was true at the time of Woodall's sentencing and appeal. (Kentucky began electing judges in 1850 and moved to non-partisan elections in 1975). As you read on, you may want to ask yourself whether you think these different methods of selecting the judges who sat on Woodall's case at one time or another played any role in the events described in the coming chapters. To what extent might concerns about a future election affect a state judge's decision in a high profile case? To what extent should we worry that federal judges, who are appointed for life and largely politically unaccountable, may feel free to insert their own politics into a case? And do these concerns make a good argument for having trial by jury rather than by judge? ■

| CHAPTER 3

Where and How a Case Begins

N ow that you have a basic understanding of our federal and state court systems and how they interrelate, we are ready to consider how a case makes it into one of these court systems in the first place. Given that the events giving rise to a lawsuit may occur in many different locations and may have consequences in multiple states, how do we know in which state a case should be adjudicated? How do we determine whether the case should start in a federal or state court? And what has to be done to start the case? We will first address the question of where, then we will turn to the question of how.

Where a Criminal Case Begins: Geographic Restrictions

When Robert Woodall, a resident of Kentucky, murdered Sarah Hansen, another resident of Kentucky, in a Kentucky county, it was no surprise that the prosecuting attorney for that county sought criminal penalties against Woodall in a court in that county. But what if Woodall had abducted Ms. Hansen in Muhlenberg County, Kentucky and had then taken her to another county or across state lines before murdering her? Would a prosecutor in the other county or state where the murder occurred have had the power to prosecute Woodall in a court outside Muhlenberg County, Kentucky?

Section 2 of Article III of the U.S. Constitution requires that crimes be tried in the state in which the crime was committed, and the Sixth Amendment to the Constitution contains similar language. Accordingly, the basic rule for the location of criminal cases is that they should be tried in the county (in the case of state courts) or the judicial district (in the case of federal courts) where the crime allegedly occurred.[1] The formal legal term for the specific locale in which a criminal case is tried is venue. Because Woodall did in fact commit his crime in Muhlenberg County, Kentucky, that county would normally have been the proper venue for his case. Recall from Chapter 1, however, that Woodall requested a change of venue to Crawford County because of concerns about pretrial publicity in Muhlenberg County. Absent this request from Woodall, the Crawford County Circuit Court would not have had authority to hear the case.

This rule makes sense because the evidence necessary to a case will likely be found in the locale where the crime was committed and because the jury can be drawn from the community that was harmed by the crime. But what if Woodall had transported Ms. Hansen across state lines? What venue would be appropriate in that situation? When the federal Constitution was passed in 1789, travel was of course much slower than it is today, and the Constitution did not contemplate the possibility that a crime would begin in one state and be completed in another. Congress filled this gap for federal prosecutions by passing a statute authorizing trial in any district where the crime began, was continued, or was completed.[2] The states, by statute or common law, likewise permit a criminal case to be filed in any of the counties where part of the crime occurred.

Similarly, if the defendant's actions constituted a number of connected crimes, all of those connected crimes could be prosecuted in any place where one of the crimes occurred. For instance, if Woodall had abducted Hansen in Muhlenberg County and then transported her to a neighboring county where he killed her, criminal charges could have been pursed in either county. The same is true if Woodall had committed connected crimes in two states: a prosecutor in either state could have pursued criminal charges for acts that violated each state's criminal laws.

So a crime or set of connected crimes committed in two different states can be prosecuted in *either* state. But can they be prosecuted in *both* states—that is, could prosecutors in two states pursue criminal charges for the same crimes? You may have heard of the Double Jeopardy Clause of the U.S. Constitution

---

1   Article III of the Constitution directed Congress to establish the place where crimes that do not occur within any state, such as crimes at sea, should be tried. Congress passed a statute providing that such offenses should be tried in the district where the offender is arrested or first brought; if the accused is not arrested, then the indictment can be filed in the district of last known residence of the accused or in the District of Columbia if the last residence is not known. 18 U.S.C. § 3238.

2   18 U.S.C. § 3237.

and assume that the answer is "no."[3] But in fact, the Double Jeopardy Clause would not bar prosecutions in both states, for the U.S. Supreme Court has interpreted the Double Jeopardy Clause to apply only to repeated prosecutions by the same government. Under this "dual sovereignty" principle, prosecutors in different states could pursue criminal penalties for the same crimes, so long as those crimes were committed, at least partially, in each state. In reality, such dual prosecutions rarely happen because of limited resources, with most prosecutors deferring to the prosecuting attorney in the locale where the defendant was first arrested.

Where a Criminal Case Begins: Subject Matter Restrictions

American courts follow the principle that federal courts are the proper forum for enforcing federal criminal laws and each state's courts are the proper forum for enforcing each state's criminal laws.[4] The rationale behind this principle is that a court that imposes punishment is an instrument of the government and only the government that passed the criminal laws in question should have the power to impose punishment for, or the discretion not to impose punishment for, violations of those laws. Because Woodall was accused of violating only Kentucky's laws and not any other state's laws nor any federal criminal laws, he could only properly be prosecuted in a Kentucky state court.[5]

Had Woodall been caught selling a large amount of marijuana, then either a Kentucky state court or a federal court would have been a proper forum for Woodall's prosecution, because in that case he would have violated both Kentucky and federal laws against the possession and distribution of marijuana.[6] When federal criminal laws overlap with state criminal laws (as they do when it comes to the use and distribution of illegal drugs), then a crime may be prosecuted in either a state court or a federal court. Or it may

---

3   The Double Jeopardy Clause is found in the Fifth Amendment to the Constitution, which contains a prohibition on a person being "twice put in jeopardy of life or limb" for the same offense.

4   There are some rare exceptions to this principle that we need not discuss here. But if the topic interests you, please read Michael G. Collins & Jonathan Remy Nash, *Prosecuting Federal Crimes in State Courts*, 97 Va. L. Rev. 243 (2011).

5   If Woodall had kidnapped Ms. Hansen and taken her across state lines, then he would have violated a federal criminal law that was passed shortly after the kidnapping of Charles Lindbergh's son in 1932. In the same year, Congress passed a law making it a crime to transport someone across state lines for illegal purposes (although the bill that led to this law predated the kidnapping). *See* Barry Cushman, *Headline Kidnappings and the Origins of the Lindbergh Law*, 55 St. Louis U.L.J. 1293 (2011).

6   By some measures, marijuana is Kentucky's most lucrative crop. Both Kentucky law and federal law currently make it illegal to grow and sell marijuana. *See, e.g.*, Ky. Rev. Stat. § 218A.140.

be prosecuted in both; again the dual sovereignty principle applies and the Double Jeopardy Clause is no bar to prosecution by two sovereign governments (here federal and state).

A rough division of labor exists between federal and state courts with respect to prosecutions: where the crime implicates strong federal interests, state prosecutors will typically defer to federal prosecutors, but most "ordinary" crimes are not seen as sufficiently important to federal interests and thus are left to states for prosecution. Judgments about whether particular crimes justify federal prosecution vary over time and across presidential administrations. For instance, the first President Bush made drug trafficking a major priority for federal prosecutors and aggressively prosecuted crimes that could have been left to the state courts. Since the 2001 terrorist attacks on the World Trade Center and the Pentagon, criminal cases that affect national security have become a focus of federal investigation and prosecution.

Occasionally, federal prosecutors will try a case that has already been tried in state court, but it is the policy of the U.S. Department of Justice to engage in such dual prosecutions only where the crime implicates strong federal interests that were not vindicated in the state court.

DEPARTMENT OF JUSTICE POLICY ON FEDERAL-STATE PROSECUTIONS

The U.S. Department of Justice, in its policy manual giving guidance to federal prosecutors, sets out three reasons for pursuing a federal prosecution for criminal acts that were previously the subject of a state prosecution: (1) the case implicates a substantial federal interest, (2) that federal interest was left unvindicated by the state prosecution, and (3) there is sufficient admissible evidence to believe that the defendant committed a federal crime. You may read the Department of Justice's policy manual for criminal cases at *http://www.justice.gov/usao/eousa/ foia_reading_room/usam/title9/title9.htm.*

Even more rarely do state prosecutors pursue criminal cases that are or have been the subject of a federal prosecution in federal court. Where the federal prosecution was successful, a successful state prosecution would usually add little in terms of penalty, because federal penalties are usually harsher than state penalties. Where the federal prosecution was unsuccessful, state prosecutors are reluctant to take on a case that the federal government, with its greater resources, could not win.

Where a Civil Case Begins: Geographic Restrictions

The rules that govern where a criminal case should be filed are fairly simple and straightforward; the rules that govern the filing of civil cases are much more complicated. As we did with criminal cases, we will first examine geographic restrictions on filing civil law cases (i.e., which state within the U.S. is the right location for the civil lawsuit) and then will look at type-of-law restrictions for civil cases (i.e., whether the case should be filed in a state or federal court). We will illustrate how the rules work by following the *Promotion in Motion v. Beech-Nut* case from the initial filing in a state court to its relocation to a federal district court.

■ **CORPORATION, INC.**

You have probably seen the abbreviation "Inc." at the end of many company names. The "Inc." designation tells you that the company is organized as a corporation. A corporation is a type of entity recognized by law, with power to enter into contracts, hire employees, and even donate to political campaigns. Corporations are governed by a board of directors and are owned by shareholders, people or entities who have paid money to obtain shares—that is, official legal documents indicating that they own a small part of the corporation. Corporations can raise money by selling more shares or can obtain labor by issuing shares as compensation for the labor. Although shareholders and officers may, under some circumstances, become liable for corporate debts, organizing businesses as corporations provides a form of limited liability for investors because usually only corporate assets will be available to pay corporate debts owed to others.

In the United States, corporations are created pursuant to state law rather than federal law. Every state has a law under which corporations can be formed. Many companies choose to incorporate under Delaware law, even when they are located outside Delaware, because Delaware's corporate law, for historical reasons, has become the most developed corporate law within the U.S. Companies that incorporate under Delaware law can consult this well-developed law for guidance on the many legal matters that can arise during the life of a corporation.

To understand how this happened, it is important to know more about the parties to that case and how those parties interacted before the lawsuit began. Promotion in Motion (which we will sometimes refer to as PIM for short) is a corporation that was formed under Delaware law and, at the time of its lawsuit against Beech-Nut, had its headquarters in Bergen County, New Jersey. PIM's main business is the manufacture of confections and specialty foods.[7] Beech-Nut is a corporation formed under Nevada law, with its headquarters in Albany County, New York. Beech-Nut's main business is the sale of food for children, toddlers, and infants.[8]

In 2007 and 2008, PIM and Beech-Nut collaborated to develop an all-natural fruit product that would eventually, and briefly, be marketed as "Fruit Nibbles," a name which Beech-Nut reserved for its exclusive use with the U.S. Patent and Trademarks Office.[9] Developing this product involved communications between employees in PIM's New Jersey facilities and employees in Beech-Nut's New York offices. The physical production of Fruit Nibbles took place at PIM's facilities in New Jersey, with packaged products shipped to Beech-Nut for further distribution. Beech-Nut and PIM collaborated on the basic product and the nature of the ingredients, but PIM determined the ingredients, their formula, and the process for combining the ingredients to produce Fruit Nibbles.[10]

While developing the product, PIM and Beech-Nut almost reached a "co-packing agreement" under which PIM would make and package Fruit Nibbles to be sold under the Beech-Nut label for two years or some other amount of time, but the companies could never agree on all of the terms of this contract and never executed it. Rather than enter into a master agreement, the companies proceeded on an individual purchase order basis, under which a purchase order would be submitted by Beech-Nut to Promotion in Motion for batches of Fruit Nibbles and PIM would issue an invoice to Beech-Nut for payment when the Fruit Nibbles were provided. Each accepted purchase order was a separate contract. (This arrangement is similar to what happens every time you go to the store to buy something that you need at the time. When you buy a subscription to a magazine or other product, then you are entering into

---

7   For more details on the company, go to http://www.promotioninmotion.com/.

8   For more details on the company, go to http://www.beechnut.com/. You may have heard of Beech-Nut Fruit Stripe® gum, but Beech-Nut no longer manufactures or markets that gum, which is now sold by the Ferrara Candy Company.

9   You can search the Trademark Office's database for free at http://tmsearch.uspto.gov/bin/gate.exe?f=-search&state=4806:ql5hrl.1.1. If you search the database for "Fruit Nibbles," you will find that Beech-Nut originally owned the phrase but that the phrase is currently owned by Promotion in Motion.

10   Promotion in Motion disclosed the ingredients used to make the product (for labeling purposes) but did not share with Beech-Nut the specific formula and processes used to create Fruit Nibbles. Promotion in Motion applied for a patent from the U.S. Patent and Trademark Office to give it the exclusive right to use the formula and processes to produce the product, but no patent has yet been issued.

a long-term contract that would have been more like the co-packing master agreement the companies could never agree on).[11]

On August 1, 2008, Promotion in Motion told Beech-Nut that it was ready to begin commercial production of Fruit Nibbles. Production started on August 4, and the first batches of Fruit Nibbles were shipped to Beech-Nut in that same month for distribution to retailers.[12] Within just a few weeks, however, Beech-Nut found quality problems in its random inspections of the product, and Beech-Nut received hundreds of complaints from consumers and retailers in September, October, and November of 2008. Wal-Mart, for instance, pulled all Fruit Nibbles from its shelves because the product appeared moldy. Consumers used some very unflattering language to describe the Fruit Nibbles, such as "moldy and wilted," "nasty," "horrid smell," "choking hazard," and "looks like dead toes." Beech-Nut alerted Promotion in Motion to these problems, PIM's own investigations verified that problems existed with at least some batches of the product, and the two companies discussed possible causes and solutions. In the meantime, a number of invoices from PIM were not paid by Beech-Nut. In early December 2008, when Beech-Nut was not satisfied that the problems could be corrected, Beech-Nut withdrew Fruit Nibbles from the market and accepted returns of previously-purchased products. PIM disputed the scope of the problem and said that unreasonable demands by Beech-Nut with respect to timing and volume had led to quality control problems. Accordingly, PIM refused to accept returns of the product from Beech-Nut, refused to cancel outstanding invoices, and refused to refund money that had already been paid for past orders of Fruit Nibbles.

Despite these problems, in January 2009 Promotion in Motion and Beech-Nut continued to discuss possible solutions and a re-launch of the product. But these discussions were not fruitful, and, in February 2009, Beech-Nut notified Promotion in Motion that it intended to look for a new supplier of Fruit Nibbles. In response to this news, PIM contended that it had spent considerable funds in reliance on future orders from Beech-Nut in its unsuccessful attempt to maintain the relationship. Beech-Nut, for its part, contended that the debacle had cost it more than $3.4 million (including approximately $1 million paid for products it could not sell and $1.6 million in lost profits).

---

11   Ultimately, Beech-Nut issued four purchase orders that were accepted by Promotion in Motion in 2008, and Beech-Nut received and paid for approximately 230,000 cases of Fruit Nibbles.

12   Promotion in Motion contracted with a related company, PIM Brands, LLC, to produce the Fruit Nibbles, and PIM Brands would ultimately also sue Beech-Nut. For purposes of keeping things simple, we are going to ignore the role of PIM Brands in the lawsuit. Nothing important is lost by ignoring PIM Brands.

When it was clear that efforts to resolve the dispute informally would not be successful, Promotion in Motion's lawyers prepared a *complaint* alleging that Beech-Nut had broken promises to buy more batches of Fruit Nibbles from PIM, causing substantial economic harm to PIM. The first page of the complaint is reproduced below, and the whole complaint can be reviewed on the book's website.

McCARTER & ENGLISH, LLP
Four Gateway Center
100 Mulberry Street
Newark, New Jersey 07102
(973) 622-4444
Attorneys for Plaintiffs
 Promotion In Motion, Inc. and PIM Brands, LLC

PROMOTION IN MOTION, INC. and PIM BRANDS, LLC,	:	SUPERIOR COURT OF NEW JERSEY LAW DIVISION - BERGEN COUNTY DOCKET NO.
Plaintiffs,	:	Civil Action
v.	:	**COMPLAINT** **(JURY DEMAND)**
BEECH-NUT NUTRITION CORPORATION, a HERO GROUP COMPANY,	:	
Defendant	:	

Plaintiffs Promotion In Motion, Inc. and PIM Brands, LLC, by way of Complaint against Defendant Beech-Nut Nutrition Corporation, a Hero Group company, in order to recover the damages sustained as a result of the Defendant's breach of the parties' agreement, state as follows:

PARTIES, JURISDICTION, AND VENUE

1.   Plaintiff Promotion In Motion, Inc. ("Promotion In Motion") is a Delaware corporation whose principal place of business is located within Bergen County, New Jersey, at 3 Reuten Drive, Closter, New Jersey. It is a marketer of popular brand name confections, fruit snacks, fruit rolls, and snack and specialty foods.

Page 1 of the Complaint Filed by Promotion in Motion Against Beech-Nut

As you can see from the first page of the complaint, Promotion in Motion's lawyers (from the law firm of McCarter & English) decided to sue Beech-Nut in the Superior Court of New Jersey located in Bergen County (you will find the name of the court on the middle right of the page, partially covered by the stamp of the clerk of the court). Superior Courts are the main trial court for civil cases within the New Jersey court system. Given what we know about the transactions between Promotion in Motion and Beech-Nut, the choice of a trial court in New Jersey makes sense. PIM is headquartered in New Jersey, the product in question was manufactured in New Jersey, and PIM allegedly suffered harm inside the state of New Jersey. On the other hand, you probably would not have been especially surprised if PIM's lawyers had chosen a court in New York instead, since Beech-Nut is located there and a good portion of the interactions occurred in New York. Could PIM's lawyers have chosen to sue in New York rather than New Jersey? What about Hawaii? Apparently none of the events leading up to the lawsuit occurred in Hawaii, but it might be a fun place to have a lawsuit (if that is not an oxymoron). Can the plaintiff in a civil case pick a location that has no connection to the lawsuit? For reasons we will explain, Promotion in Motion could have properly begun its lawsuit in either New Jersey or New York, but not in Hawaii.

When deciding where to file this complaint against Beech-Nut, the lawyers for Promotion in Motion had to consider two major geographic restrictions. First, the court in which PIM filed the complaint had to have authority to issue a summons against Beech-Nut. A summons is an official court document that orders the defendant to respond to the complaint within a specified amount of time (usually between twenty-one and sixty days, though this depends on the court). If the defendant fails to respond to the complaint in the required time period, then the plaintiff can win its case by default. Every state has laws authorizing its courts to issue summonses to defendants. These laws are called "long-arm" laws because they authorize courts to extend the long arm of the law to compel defendants to respond to a complaint. Long-arm laws authorize courts to issue summonses, not only to defendants found anywhere inside the state, but also to defendants who are located outside the state but have some connection to the state, so long as this connection somehow relates to the events at issue in the lawsuit.

These long-arm laws apply to any court located within the state, whether it is part of the state court system or the federal court system. It may seem odd that the federal courts would follow state laws about issuing summonses, but there is a very long federal history behind this restriction. When Congress first created federal district courts in the Judiciary Act of 1789[13], it decided

---

13   Article II of the Constitution grants to the President the power to appoint federal judges, and Article III of the Constitution sets out the broad contours of the federal court system but leaves the specific organization of the courts to Congress. Passage of the Judiciary Act of 1789 was thus necessary to create the federal court system. In addition to restricting the geographic reach of the federal district courts, the 1789

that the federal courts should only hear cases involving defendants who were located within the district or who had a substantial connection to the district. Eventually, federal law was amended to make the summons power of the federal district court equivalent to that of the state courts located in the same state. What this means is that even though a federal district court located in New Jersey is part of a nationwide, federal court system, it does not have personal jurisdiction over everyone found anywhere inside the nation.[14] It only has as much geographic reach as a New Jersey state court has. Congress imposed this restriction on federal district courts to ensure that juries would be drawn from a geographic region having some connection to the dispute and to prevent federal courts from extending their power too far.

The second geographic restriction on filing a civil case comes from the Due Process Clause of the U.S. Constitution, which requires that no person be "deprived of life, liberty, or property, without due process of law."[15] The U.S. Supreme Court has interpreted the Clause to limit the reach of courts to persons who either are physically within the state in which the court is located or who have purposefully established contact with that state in such a way that they should have known that they might be sued in that state.

For instance, if you drive through Massachusetts on your way to Maine and have a car wreck that injures a resident of Massachusetts, the person you injured can sue you in Massachusetts without violating the Due Process Clause because you went into Massachusetts and caused some harm there. So, even if you are living in Maine when the lawsuit is filed in a Massachusetts court, that court in Massachusetts can issue an order for you to pay money to compensate the injured person and in doing so will not be depriving you of property without due process of law. The key idea is that if you commit a tort in a state or if you conduct business in a state and the business goes bad, then it is fair to force you to defend a civil lawsuit in that state[16].

Act authorized district judges to appoint a clerk in each district to assist in the administration of the courts and authorized the President to appoint a district attorney (who would have power to prosecute federal crimes) and marshal for each district (marshals provide courthouse security and witness protection, arrest fugitives, and have power to serve a summons on a defendant).

14   There are a few exceptional kinds of cases where Congress has passed statutes extending the geographic reach of federal courts. For example, the U.S. Court of Federal Claims located in Washington, D.C. has nationwide jurisdiction over most non-tort civil claims being pursued against the federal government, even if those claims arose outside of Washington, D.C.

15   This phrase is found in both the 5th and 14th Amendments to the Constitution. The language from the 5th Amendment binds the federal courts, and the language from the 14th Amendment extends this restriction to state courts.

16   Because states are bound to follow federal law, no state's long-arm laws can extend the geographic reach of courts beyond that allowed under the federal Constitution's Due Process Clause. Some states with

When a court has power over a defendant under the state long-arm law and the federal Due Process Clause, we say that the court has "personal jurisdiction" over the defendant. Without personal jurisdiction over a defendant, a court cannot command the defendant to pay damages to the plaintiff; in fact, it cannot legally order the defendant to do—or not do—anything. A defendant who believes that a court lacks personal jurisdiction must file an objection with the court at the first opportunity. If the defendant fails to object in his response to the complaint, then the defendant waives this objection and the court obtains personal jurisdiction over the defendant. This is so even if personal jurisdiction would not otherwise have been proper. American courts expect civil defendants to protect themselves from being sued in an improper state; a court will not investigate whether it has personal jurisdiction over the defendant unless the defendant asks it to do so.

New Jersey's long-arm law permits its courts to exercise personal jurisdiction over defendants to the greatest extent allowed under federal law. In the case of Promotion in Motion versus Beech-Nut, the New Jersey court had personal jurisdiction over Beech-Nut because, although Beech-Nut's operations are located outside the state of New Jersey, the company did substantial business with PIM inside the state of New Jersey and that business was the subject of PIM's lawsuit against Beech-Nut. Recognizing this, Beech-Nut did not object to the court's personal jurisdiction in its response to the complaint and thereby waived any objection it could have raised to personal jurisdiction.

What if the lawsuit had been filed in Hawaii? We hope it is obvious to you now that courts in Hawaii would not have personal jurisdiction over the Beech-Nut case. Because none of the events central to the case occurred in Hawaii, the Due Process Clause would not authorize filing the case in Hawaii. There is one final wrinkle to personal jurisdiction that we have to tell you about, though.

Let's imagine that Promotion in Motion and Beech-Nut had signed a contract containing a "forum selection clause" that said that the parties agreed to resolve their business disputes in a court located in Honolulu, Hawaii. In that case, the court in Honolulu would have had personal jurisdiction over Beech-Nut, because when two parties enter into a valid contract that contains

---

particularly busy courts, such as New York, have decided to restrict the geographic reach of their courts to less than what is allowed under the Constitution in order to reduce the number of cases filed within the state. Therefore, whenever a lawyer files a civil case, the lawyer needs to make sure (1) that the forum state's long-arm law will authorize issuance of a summons to the defendant, wherever the defendant is located, and (2) that the Due Process Clause will not be violated by filing the case in the chosen state. In most cases, answering the second question will answer the first question, but in a few states the long-arm law will be more restrictive than the Due Process Clause.

a forum selection clause, American courts will honor that agreement. Indeed, if the parties had such an agreement and one of the parties tried to sue somewhere other than Honolulu, then the non-Hawaiian court should respond to an objection from the other party by dismissing the lawsuit. The rationale behind this rule is that the geographic restrictions on where a civil case can be filed are meant to protect the parties from being sued in locations that are unfair and could not have been predicted. When the parties include a forum selection clause in their contract, they have anticipated and voluntarily submitted to personal jurisdiction in the chosen location. Of course, Promotion in Motion and Beech-Nut did not sign a contract choosing Honolulu or some other location for their lawsuit, so they were left with New Jersey or New York as the proper places for their lawsuit.

The jurisdiction-by-agreement principle, by the way, explains why you never have to be concerned about whether a court has personal jurisdiction over a plaintiff. By choosing the court in which to begin a lawsuit, the plaintiff is submitting to the personal jurisdiction of the court and thereby giving the court the power to issue orders that are binding on the plaintiff.

■ VENUE

In addition to finding a state that has personal jurisdiction over the defendant the plaintiff plans to sue, the plaintiff must also find a court within that state that has what is called "venue." When there are multiple locations in a state where a case could be filed, as often happens in larger states, venue rules tell the plaintiff which court to choose within the state. Each state court system and the federal court system has its own venue rules. In general, venue rules tell the plaintiff to file in a county or district where a substantial part of the events giving rise to the lawsuit occurred or where the defendant is regularly found (e.g., the county where he lives). Sometimes there will be more than one place in a state where venue would be proper, in which case the plaintiff can choose whichever one the plaintiff prefers. After the case begins, the defendant can then ask the judge to transfer the case to a different venue that is more convenient, but judges can only transfer cases to other courts within the same court system. For instance, a Texas state court judge who sits in Houston could transfer the case to a Texas state court located in Dallas, but not to a Louisiana state court located in New Orleans.

Where a Civil Case Begins: Subject Matter Restrictions

We are only halfway through our discussion of where a civil case begins. We have looked at how plaintiffs choose one of the fifty states in which to start a civil case, but we have not yet looked at how the plaintiff decides whether to sue in a state court or a federal court. If civil cases were like criminal cases with respect to the division of labor, this discussion would be very brief, because the rule in criminal cases is simple: violations of federal criminal laws are tried in federal court and violations of state criminal laws are tried in state court. The rules for civil cases are, unfortunately, more complex. Understanding these complex rules is essential to being a good lawyer, because choosing a court may have important implications for how a case is decided. For instance, state courts typically draw their jury pools from smaller geographic regions than federal courts, and federal courts tend to be located in more urban areas, so the composition of the jury pool may differ considerably between state and federal courts. Also, the state and federal courts will often differ in the rules of procedure that govern how a case is managed before trial and may differ with respect to the rules of evidence at trial. These differences in procedure and evidence may greatly affect the time and expense of litigation as well as the outcome of the case. Therefore, these technical and boring rules on where civil claims may be litigated can have great significance for many cases.

Let us first consider what kinds of claims can be filed in state courts. Generally, state courts have not only the power, but in fact the obligation to hear claims based on either state or federal law when presented with them: a state court cannot decline to decide a claim simply because the claim is based on federal law. The one exception to this rule is where Congress has decided that a federal claim should be tried exclusively in a federal court, as it has, for example, with claims that a defendant has violated a trademark or patent issued by the U.S. Patent and Trademarks Office.

Furthermore, the courts of one state can decide claims arising under the law of another state. When a court has authority to hear the state or federal law claims presented to the court, we say that the court has "subject matter jurisdiction" over those claims. Each of the four purchase orders from Beech-Nut that Promotion in Motion accepted contained a clause stating that the transactions were governed by New York law. Therefore, all of PIM's claims against Beech-Nut were based on New York law, and even though the trial court in which PIM filed suit was located in New Jersey, the New Jersey court had subject matter jurisdiction over all of those claims.

Many people are surprised to learn that the subject matter jurisdiction of federal courts is considerably more limited than that of state courts. The kinds of claims that can be pursued in federal court are defined by the Constitution and congressional statutes. The most important of these statutes create what are called "federal question" and "diversity of citizenship" subject matter jurisdiction.[17]

Under the statute creating federal-question jurisdiction, federal district courts have authority to hear any claim filed by the plaintiff that is based on federal law. The statute creating diversity-of-citizenship jurisdiction gives federal district courts authority to hear claims based on state law so long as the parties are from different states. More precisely, to trigger the diversity-of-citizenship statute, a state law claim must satisfy two requirements: (1) the claim must be between citizens of different states[18] or between a U.S. citizen and a citizen from another nation and (2) the claim must seek relief in excess of $75,000. For purposes of the statute, corporations are citizens; many diversity cases involve a corporation as a litigant on one or both sides, as in the case of PIM versus Beech-Nut.[19]

Just because a claim may be filed in a federal court does not mean that a plaintiff has to file it there. In many civil cases, the plaintiff can choose to sue either in state court or federal court. However, if the plaintiff chooses federal court, she needs to be sure that it has authority to hear all of the claims taken to the court. If a federal court lacks subject matter jurisdiction over a claim, then the court is supposed to dismiss that claim from the lawsuit and retain only those claims over which it has subject matter jurisdiction. And the court is supposed to undertake its own investigation into subject matter jurisdiction, regardless of whether one of the parties asks for such an investigation. A federal court's duty to ensure it has subject matter jurisdiction over each claim comes from Article III of the Constitution: if the court lacks authority to hear a particular type of claim, any order issued by that court with respect to that claim is lawless and invalid.

There are two other basic federal statutes on subject matter jurisdiction with which you should be familiar. Imagine that you reside permanently in

---

17 *See* 28 U.S.C. §§ 1331-1332.

18 To be a "citizen" of a state, one needs to be a U.S. citizen who resides in one of the states and intends to remain in that state indefinitely. U.S. citizens living permanently abroad are not "citizens" for purposes of the diversity-of-citizen statute. An alien living in the U.S. temporarily is treated as a citizen of a foreign nation. An alien living in the U.S. on a permanent residency visa is considered a citizen of the state in which she permanently resides. If the case involves multiple plaintiffs and multiple defendants, none of the plaintiffs can share citizenship with any of the defendants.

19 A corporation is considered a citizen of every state in which it is incorporated and the state where it has its principal place of business.

Virginia and work for a Virginia company and your manager fires you because of your sex. Sex-based discrimination violates both federal law and Virginia law, so you would have claims against your employer under both federal and state law. It would be much more convenient for you to pursue both claims in a single lawsuit. You could pursue both in a Virginia state court because federal discrimination claims can be heard in state courts (and of course a Virginia court can decide claims based on Virginia law). But you could also pursue both of your claims in federal court even though you and your employer are citizens of the same state and, therefore, your state law claim does not satisfy the diversity statute. You can do this thanks to the "supplemental jurisdiction" statute [20] which gives a federal court the authority to hear claims that would otherwise be outside its jurisdiction if those claims are related to claims that are within its jurisdiction. Since these claims arise from the same events and present common factual questions, the same evidence will be used to decide both claims. It would be tremendously wasteful to force the parties to litigate one of the claims in federal court and the other one in state court.

You might think that the plaintiff appears to have an unfair advantage. A plaintiff with able attorneys will surely choose the court where they think they are likely to do better—perhaps a state court where the local judge and jury would be expected to be sympathetic. The federal "removal statute"[21] evens things out some by allowing a defendant to undo the plaintiff's choice of court and "remove" the case from state court to federal court. This option is available when the claims in the case could have been filed in federal court in the first place. That is, a defendant who prefers to have a federal judge decide federal law claims can remove those claims from state to federal court under its federal question jurisdiction. A defendant who is a citizen of a state other than the forum state can move the case to a federal court if the defendant is concerned that the state court may favor the local plaintiff (as long as the amount in controversy exceeds $75,000).

Note that removal only works in one direction: from state court to federal court. Even though state court judges might have more expertise on state law matters than federal court judges, there is no comparable statute that permits state-law claims to be removed from federal court to state court.

---

20   *See* 28 U.S.C. § 1367.

21   Business entities can be parties under the diversity-of-jurisdiction state. Under the statute, a corporation is deemed a citizen of the state in which it was incorporated and the state where it has its headquarters. If a corporation's headquarter state is different from its state of incorporation, the corporation will be citizens of both states for purposes of the diversity statute.

There are a number of reasons why a defendant might prefer a federal court. Among the most important is the fear that a local court will be biased in favor of the plaintiff and against an out-of-state defendant. This concern about local prejudice comes from the fact that most state trial judges are elected officials, whereas federal trial judges, although located in the same state, are appointed for life and thus are not politically accountable to the local populace.

Beech-Nut took advantage of the federal removal statute to take the case from the Bergen County Superior Court to the federal district court located in Newark, New Jersey. Beech-Nut had the right to do this because PIM was seeking more than $75,000 in damages against Beech-Nut and Beech-Nut and PIM were citizens of different states.[22] To remove the case from state to

UNITED STATES DISTRICT COURT
DISTRICT OF NEW JERSEY

---x

PROMOTION IN MOTION, INC.   :   HON.   , U.S.D.J.
and PIM BRANDS, LLC,   :
                               :   CIVIL ACTION NO.
                  Plaintiffs,   :

         vs.   :
                               :   (Removal from Superior Court of New
BEECH-NUT NUTRITION CORPORATION, :   Jersey, County of Bergen,
a HERO GROUP COMPANY,   :   Docket No. BER-L-1890-09)
                               :
                  Defendant.   :
---x

NOTICE OF REMOVAL

PLEASE TAKE NOTICE that, pursuant to 28 U.S.C. §§ 1441 and 1446, the Defendant,

Beech-Nut Nutrition Corporation ("Beech-Nut" or the "Defendant"), hereby removes this action

to the United States District Court for the District of New Jersey, Newark Division, upon the

following grounds:

1.   On or about February 27, 2009, Plaintiffs Promotion in Motion, Inc. ("Promotion

in Motion") and PIM Brands, LLC ("PIM" (collectively, the "Plaintiffs")), commenced an action

Page 1 of Notice of Removal Filed by Beech-Nut

---

22   Beech-Nut is a citizen of Nevada (its state of incorporation) and New York (where its headquarters are located), while Promotion in Motion is a citizen of Delaware (its state of incorporation) and New Jersey (where its headquarters are located).

federal court, all that Beech-Nut had to do was file a "Notice of Removal" with the state and federal courts and serve a copy on Promotion in Motion. From that date forward the case was converted from a state court case to a federal court case.[23]

Statutes of Limitations

Once problems began to develop between Promotion in Motion and Beech-Nut, it was only a short time before PIM filed suit. Many other disputes take much longer to arise, and sometimes people do not even know they have been wronged until long after the wrong occurred. You may buy a house that has a hidden defect in the roof that you will not discover for years, even though the seller knew about that defect at the time of the sale. Will your claim for breach of contract or fraud exist in perpetuity (legalese for "forever")? What if that defect does not cause any real harm until twenty years later, when an unusually large snow storm combined with the defect causes the roof to collapse? Can you sue the seller twenty years after the purchase?

Every civil claim, whether based on state law or federal law, has some limit on how long someone can wait to pursue it, and that time limit is usually found in what is called a "statute of limitations." (Most crimes have statutes of limitations associated with them as well.) A statute of limitations usually allows one or more years to file a civil claim from the date on which you knew or should have known (a) that you were wronged and (b) who or what wronged you (the specific wording and requirements will of course vary by statute). Note the "should have known" language, which is there to prevent people from remaining blissfully ignorant of claims they may have. If a plaintiff misses the deadline for pursuing the claim, then the defendant can move for summary judgment on the basis of the affirmative defense that the statute of limitations has been exceeded.

Sometimes statutes of limitations lead to dismissals of seemingly strong claims, but these time limits are seen as a necessary evil for a variety of reasons: at some point, even people or companies who may have done something wrong should be free of the threat of litigation; putting time limits

---

23   The defendant also files with the federal district court copies of the legal documents that had been filed in the state court, so that the federal court will have a record of what transpired in the case before the removal. A defendant has to remove the case to federal court within 30 days of being served with the summons from the state court, so usually very little has happened in the state court by the time the case is removed to federal court. If the plaintiff believes that subject matter jurisdiction did not exist in federal court or that the defendant waited too long to remove the case, the plaintiff can challenge the removal. Promotion in Motion did not challenge Beech-Nut's removal and therefore the case remained in federal court for the remainder of its life.

on claims allows businesses to manage their litigation risks and insurance costs, which should keep the costs of goods and services down; and statutes of limitations encourage plaintiffs to be diligent about their rights and to pursue them while evidence needed to resolve the dispute is still available. Plaintiffs, and especially their attorneys, need to be aware of these time limits on their claims. A common source of legal malpractice claims is a lawyer's failure to file a claim on behalf of his or her client in a timely fashion.

The Mechanics of Beginning a Case

Despite the somewhat complicated rules that govern where cases can be filed, in most cases experienced attorneys can answer personal jurisdiction questions (i.e., in which state could the case be filed?) and subject matter jurisdiction questions (i.e., can the claims be filed in federal or state court?) quite quickly to determine a proper forum. Once the decision on where to pursue a case has been made, a number of steps must be taken to formally initiate a civil or criminal lawsuit against a defendant who is accused of violating either civil or criminal laws.

1. Beginning a Civil Case

A civil lawsuit officially begins when the plaintiff, or the attorney for the plaintiff, files a complaint with the clerk of the court and pays the court's filing fee.[24] The complaint is a very important document in the history of a civil case: it sets out the plaintiff's claims against the defendant and specifies what the plaintiff wants from the defendant. The complaint is a type of *pleading*: in civil cases, pleadings contain a party's claims for relief from another party or a party's defenses to another party's claims for relief. Pleadings set the boundaries of the legal dispute because they establish what legal issues must be decided by the judge or jury to resolve the case. If a complaint omits a claim that could have been asserted but was not, then the judge or jury will never have authority to decide that claim.[25]

---

24   The fee is typically quite small. For instance, presently the fee is $50 in U.S. District Courts (*http://www.uscourts.gov/FormsAndFees/Fees/DistrictCourtMiscellaneousFeeSchedule.aspx*). Every American court allows the plaintiff to apply for waiver of the filing fee on grounds of financial hardship.

25   Court rules will often allow a plaintiff to amend a complaint to add a previously omitted claim, but if the plaintiff wants relief on a particular claim, that claim at some point needs to be formally added to the case to permit the judge or jury to decide issues presented by the claim.

Access to Legal Representation

Although parties in both civil and criminal cases may represent themselves (unless the presiding judge finds them incompetent to do so), typically it is wiser to have the services of a lawyer. Laypeople can easily get lost in the intricacies of legal procedure and, lacking experience in the courtroom, can struggle to form and implement an effective strategy. Being emotionally invested, litigants—even if they are themselves attorneys—may find it hard to think dispassionately about how to approach their cases.

Recognizing the especially serious disadvantages that may face criminal defendants who lack an attorney, the framers of the U.S. Constitution enshrined the right to counsel in the Sixth Amendment. The Supreme Court has interpreted the amendment to require that the prosecuting government provide an attorney to any defendant who cannot afford to hire one and who faces incarceration if convicted. The defendant can choose to represent himself, but the trial judge will conduct a hearing to ensure that the defendant is competent to represent himself and will usually strongly encourage him to accept an attorney. Robert Woodall was represented by a court-appointed attorney at every stage of the legal proceedings recounted in this book.

There are two main types of court-appointed counsel in criminal cases. Public defenders, usually located in cities, are full-time employees of a government-funded office dedicated solely to representing criminal defendants. Assigned counsel, usually found in less populated areas, are attorneys in private practice who agree to represent defendants in individual cases and to be paid by the government for their services. Paying for lawyers for criminal defendants is not one of the more popular uses of taxpayer money, and states tend to skimp on funding, with the result that public defenders usually carry very heavy caseloads and private assigned counsel are reimbursed at rates considerably lower than lawyers typically charge private clients. Not surprisingly, many observers raise questions about the quality of legal representation provided to indigent defendants, both in itself and as compared with the quality of representation provided to defendants who can afford to hire their own attorneys.

Similar questions arise on the civil side. There is no constitutional right to an attorney in a civil case. A litigant who cannot afford to pay a private attorney an hourly fee that is rarely below $100/hour and often much higher has two other primary options. One is to check with the local legal aid society—perhaps nearby if one lives in a city, often many miles away for rural residents. Legal aid offices operate on a mix of public and private funds. They provide important services but, like public defenders offices, are almost always underfunded and overworked. Often their services are limited to certain types of legal problems and to people with the lowest incomes.

The other option is to seek an attorney who will accept what is called a contingency fee rather than an hourly rate. An attorney being paid by contingency fee does not receive money upfront and gets paid nothing if her client loses. If her client wins, she gets a percentage—often thirty-three percent—of the money awarded and gets reimbursed for case expenses that she paid on behalf of the client; in some states, if the case is lost the client is still responsible for payment of expenses other than attorney fees.

The contingency-fee arrangement, with its promise of a large payday, can secure whole-hearted representation from very able lawyers. However, it has important limitations. One you have probably spotted already: the contingency fee makes more sense for plaintiffs (or sometimes defendants with cross-claims). An ordinary defendant, with no prospect of winning any damages, typically has nothing to promise an attorney in return for a victory and will only be able to hire one by paying upfront. More subtly, attorneys do not want to waste their time litigating cases that don't yield an adequate payoff. Imagine a lawsuit for $3000. The attorney calculates that it would take her at least fifteen hours of work to reach a settlement for $1800. With a fee of $600, that would work out to $40 an hour, too little to warrant her effort if she has a healthy practice. Going to trial would take much more time and be even less worthwhile financially. So the contingency fee can be an excellent source of access for even the most indigent litigants, but only in a fairly narrow range of circumstances.

Pleadings should be distinguished from motions, which are documents filed with the court that ask the judge to take some action in a case. For instance, if a defendant fails to respond to a complaint in the time required in the summons, then the plaintiff can file a motion for default judgment asking the court to enter a final judgment in the case in favor of the plaintiff. If this motion is granted by the court, then the plaintiff wins the case by default and the defendant can be made to pay money to the plaintiff or do whatever else is required by the court. The remedy that the court can order will depend on the relief requested in the complaint: if the plaintiff asked for monetary damages of $25,000 in the complaint, then that is the most the court can award the plaintiff in a default judgment. Together, pleadings and motions are the basic legal documents in American civil law cases.[26] Pleadings structure the case, and motions make things happen inside this structure.

To prepare a complaint, the plaintiff's attorney has to learn about the dispute that led her client to seek legal help. After meeting with her client, she will begin a basic investigation to determine whether the defendant may have violated any civil laws. If she thinks the defendant did, then she can prepare a complaint for filing with a court. The complaint is supposed to tell a story about what happened between the plaintiff and defendant, how the plaintiff was injured, and why the defendant should be held legally responsible for the harm the plaintiff suffered. The complaint presents, of course, only one side of the story. As we will see later, the defendant will have the chance to tell its side of the story when it responds to the complaint. For now, let us focus on just the complaint and the plaintiff's perspective on the dispute.

The complaint filed by Promotion in Motion against Beech-Nut is a good example of what complaints filed in American courts typically look like.[27] After the headings identifying the court and parties, the body of the complaint is made up of numbered paragraphs. They are numbered for ease of reference in later documents (e.g., the defendant will admit or deny each numbered paragraph in the complaint when it files an answer to the complaint), and, like a paragraph in a story, each numbered paragraph in the complaint is supposed to present one basic point or idea.

The narrative presented in Promotion in Motion's complaint follows the standard narrative structure found in complaints: the body of the complaint begins by introducing and identifying the parties, or the protagonists in the story, and explains why the chosen court has jurisdiction over the case (¶¶ 1-4); then the complaint summarizes the parties' dealings ((¶¶ 5-32) and connects those background facts to the civil laws that Beech-Nut supposedly violated (¶¶ 33-60); finally, the complaint sets out the relief requested and demands that the case be tried by a jury (p. 13).

Each component of the complaint is necessary and important; for instance, in federal courts and some state courts unless a jury is demanded by one of the parties, the case will be tried by a judge. But the heart of the complaint is the connection of the factual allegations to the civil laws that supposedly were

---

26   A document presenting legal arguments to support a motion is called a brief or a memorandum in support of the motion. A document presenting facts in support of a motion is called an exhibit. Exhibits may also be attached to the complaint or other pleadings to provide the court with factual information relevant to the claims or defenses stated in the pleading.

27   Remember that you can access the full complaint at the book's website.

violated. Every complaint is supposed to assert facts that, if true, establish all the elements required for that claim to be successful. For instance, in a simple breach of contract case, the plaintiff must allege that the plaintiff entered into a contract with the defendant, that the defendant breached one or more terms of the contract, and that the plaintiff was damaged by the breach. The Promotion in Motion versus Beech-Nut case was slightly more complicated because PIM claimed that Beech-Nut agreed orally, or implicitly through its actions, to continue purchasing Fruit Nibbles from PIM and that Beech-Nut violated this oral or implied contract when it stopped issuing purchase orders for Fruit Nibbles. PIM claimed that it suffered damage because Beech-Nut breached the contract.

Once the complaint was filed with the court on February 9, 2009, PIM's civil case against Beech-Nut officially began. However, the case could not proceed yet. The defendant cannot know what it is accused of doing until it receives the complaint. Accordingly, due process requires that the plaintiff provide the defendant with a copy of the complaint along with an order from the court (in the form of a summons) to submit a response to the complaint within a specified time period. It is the responsibility of the plaintiff to make sure that the defendant is served with the summons and complaint, although the plaintiff can retain the services of the U.S. Marshal's office (for cases filed in federal court), a local sheriff's office (for cases filed in state court), or a private process server to deliver the summons and complaint. It is not clear from the record in the PIM case which method PIM used to serve the summons and complaint, but we do know from the record that Beech-Nut received the complaint on February 28, 2009, the day after it was filed in the Superior Court of Bergen County, New Jersey. With the complaint in hand, the next move in the case belonged to Beech-Nut, and we will see how Beech-Nut responded in the next chapter.[28]

2. Beginning a Criminal Case

The prosecuting attorney is the criminal-law equivalent to a plaintiff in a civil case. Citizens can initiate criminal investigations by filing complaints with the police, but citizens cannot act as prosecutors for serious crimes.[29] It is the

---

28   Actually, you already know that Beech-Nut's very first move was to "remove" the case from New Jersey's Superior Court to a federal court, because we discussed that move above in the section on choosing between state and federal courts. In the next chapter we will see what happened after removal to the federal court.

29   In the early years of the United States, citizens who had been victims or the victim's relatives did act as prosecutors in criminal cases, as was the practice in England at that time, and in some states citizen-victims can still act as the prosecutors for petty criminal offenses. But nowadays the prosecuting

responsibility of the prosecuting attorney to walk a potential case through a number of preliminary steps before formal charges are filed against the criminal defendant. The prosecutor at the federal level is the U.S. attorney for the judicial district where the crime occurred or, in some cases of national interest, an attorney from the Department of Justice in Washington, D.C. The prosecutor at the state level is usually an elected county official but occasionally—for certain kinds of crimes or where there is some reason to disqualify the local prosecuting attorney from trying the case—is an attorney from the state attorney general's office. (The state attorney general is the government official who has responsibility for legal affairs in the state; the attorney general in most states is selected through a state-wide election.)

MISDEMEANOR AND FELONY CRIMES

Criminal laws distinguish between misdemeanors and felonies. Misdemeanors are minor crimes that are subject to a maximum penalty of one year of incarceration in a local jail. (Shoplifting an item having only a few dollars in value is an example of a misdemeanor). Felonies are more serious crimes carrying a penalty of more than one year of incarceration in a state or federal prison. All of the crimes with which Robert Woodall was charged were felonies.

Ordinary traffic violations, like speeding, are normally considered civil infractions, not criminal offenses, and are handled fairly informally. The same is true of violations of local ordinances on matters like littering and noise. This is because violations of this sort result only in fines or the loss of privileges, such as the privilege to drive. When a person is accused of a crime that may result in prison time, greater protections are given to the defendant. These greater protections result in a more formal and involved case-initiation process than we saw with civil cases.

Robert Woodall was of course charged with very serious crimes: kidnapping, rape, and murder under circumstances that justify the death penalty. So he was entitled to the full panoply of protections available to a criminal defendant. The steps taken to begin the criminal case against him illustrate the steps that must be taken in any state or federal court to prosecute a defendant for a serious crime.

---

attorney has the sole authority to prosecute serious crimes, usually through passage of a statute conferring this authority.

The process leading up to formal criminal charges usually begins with notice to the police that a potential crime is in progress or has been committed. In the Woodall case, a call from Sarah Hansen's parents to the local police on the evening of January 25, 1997 that Ms. Hansen had gone missing instigated a police search for her. When Ms. Hansen's body was found, the police search turned into an investigation into who killed her. This investigation led quickly to Robert Woodall, who was arrested and booked on suspicion of kidnapping and murder on the evening of January 28, 1997.

As in any case involving a serious crime, Woodall was kept in jail until he made an initial appearance the next day before a state court judge who notified Woodall of the crimes that he was accused of committing and noted the presence of Woodall's court-appointed attorney. Had Woodall appeared without an attorney, the judge would have reminded him of his constitutional right to an attorney and to have an attorney appointed if he could not afford one. At this initial appearance, defendants accused of a felony sometimes enter a plea of guilty or not guilty but may delay that plea until a later proceeding.[30] Woodall entered a plea of not guilty at his initial appearance. The judge denied Woodall's request to be released from jail and scheduled a preliminary hearing for February 5, 1997.[31]

Given the nature of the crimes Woodall was accused of, it was not surprising that the judge refused to release him from jail. However, it was a departure from the norm; most criminal defendants are given the option of staying out of jail while awaiting trial, subject to certain conditions. The most common condition is the payment of bail. Bail is an amount of money deposited with the court by the defendant as an assurance that the defendant will show up for future proceedings; if the defendant fails to show, the money is forfeited and the absent defendant becomes a fugitive who can be arrested and jailed. The U.S. Constitution requires that bail not be "excessive." However, this does not mean that all defendants can get out of jail while awaiting trial. In the common situation where bail is set but the defendant cannot afford it, the defendant can go to a bond company, which charges a set fee, often 10% of the full bail amount, in return for posting the defendant's bail and taking the

30   Defendants accused of misdemeanors typically plead guilty at the initial appearance and are given a sentence at the initial appearance. A person charged with a misdemeanor may demand a trial, however, should they lose at the trial they will have to pay administrative fees that may be larger than the fine that may be imposed after trial.

31   Many jurisdictions allow a plea of "nolo contendere" (or no contest), where the defendant does not admit guilt but declines to fight the charge, but this plea is usually reserved for misdemeanors or felonies less serious than those of which Woodall was accused.

risk of losing the money if he flees. Even 10% of a moderate bail amount will be too much for some defendants. Furthermore, if the judge feels that releasing the defendant would be dangerous to others or that the defendant is likely to run away and evade capture, bail can be set prohibitively high or even denied entirely. At the other extreme, where the alleged crime was minor and there is no real danger that the defendant will flee, the judge may choose not to require any bail, releasing the defendant on nothing more than his word that he will appear at the next proceeding.

At the preliminary hearing, the judge reviews the evidence against a defendant to ensure that there is probable cause for the case to proceed. The preliminary hearing usually occurs fairly soon after the defendant has been apprehended, while evidence is still being developed by the police and prosecuting attorney. Because it comes at such an early stage in the case, the probable cause review is not very searching: the judge only has to have a reasonable belief that the defendant more likely than not committed the crime. Passing this threshold requires considerably less evidence than satisfying the guilt beyond a reasonable doubt threshold, which is the test that will be applied at trial. Still, the judge must have more than just a suspicion. If the judge finds no probable cause, then she orders the defendant released from custody. The release may be temporary, however. If the police and prosecuting attorney assemble more evidence against the defendant, the defendant can be re-arrested and the process started again.[32]

At Woodall's preliminary hearing, a police officer who searched Woodall's house testified that a bag of "bloody, wet, and muddy clothes" was found under Woodall's bed and that the blood type on the clothes matched Sarah Hansen's blood type. After hearing this evidence, the judge concluded that there was sufficient evidence for the case to proceed.

If the prosecuting attorney intends to take a felony case to trial, then formal criminal charges must be filed against the defendant. In many cases, no formal charges are ever filed by the prosecuting attorney following the arrest and initial appearance. This can be for a variety of reasons, such as lack of sufficient evidence or an agreement that the charges will be dropped if the defendant successfully completes a treatment program. If the prosecutor proceeds, then she must prepare a charging document that is analogous to a complaint in a civil case. When this document is signed only by the prosecutor, it is called an

---

32   The Double Jeopardy Clause does not prevent multiple preliminary hearings because the Clause only prohibits multiple proceedings that may result in a criminal penalty. Because no criminal penalty can be imposed at the preliminary hearing, it does not fall under the Double Jeopardy Clause.

information. When it is signed, under oath, by a victim or an arresting officer, then the document is called a criminal complaint.

In some states, the filing of an information after a probable cause determination by a judge at the preliminary hearing is sufficient to schedule a case for trial. In other states, and in the federal court system, the formal charges must be presented to a grand jury for a probable cause determination. A grand jury is composed of citizens assembled from the local community who have the power to compel witnesses to give testimony before them (via issuance of subpoenas) and who then determine whether there is probable cause to proceed with the criminal charges.[33] A grand jury is usually larger than a trial jury (federal grand juries have between sixteen and twenty-three members). And, unlike a trial jury, which is formed to hear a single case and is then dissolved, a grand jury is formed for a set length of time, usually measured in weeks or months, and meets periodically during that time to consider any case the prosecution is thinking of bringing.

Grand jury proceedings look very different from a trial. For one thing, they are secret until an indictment is issued, and much of the proceedings may remain secret even after the indictment has issued. More importantly, they are intentionally one-sided, dominated by the prosecutor, who presents evidence to and questions witnesses in front of the grand jury. The grand jurors can also ask questions. But neither the defendant nor the defendant's attorney has a right to participate in or even view grand jury proceedings. There is not even a requirement that a judge be present, and rules of evidence (which we talk about in Chapter 5) are much less strict at the grand jury hearing than at a trial. If this surprises you, recall that the grand jury does not have the power to convict a defendant; it can only decide that he should stand trial. Still, the result is that grand juries rarely refuse to indict when the prosecutor asks for an indictment. (The old saw is that a decent prosecutor can get a grand jury to indict a ham sandwich.) So the difference between indictment and information does not turn out to be all that important in practice.

If the grand jury concludes there is probable cause, then it issues an indictment of the defendant for all the crimes for which probable cause exists. If the defendant has already been indicted at the time he is arrested, then no preliminary hearing before a judge is required because the grand jury has made a determination that there is probable cause to believe the

---

33   Targets of the grand jury investigation can be called to testify, but these targets may invoke the privilege against self-incrimination and refuse to testify. A stenographic record of witness testimony before the grand jury is made, and the criminal defendant is entitled to a record of any testimony he gave along with testimony given by persons who will be witnesses against him at trial.

defendant committed a crime. In such cases, the next step after the arrest is a proceeding called the arraignment. At the arraignment, the judge informs the defendant of the crimes charged against him, informs him of his right to an attorney, takes a plea of guilty or not guilty from the defendant, and makes a decision on release and bail for the defendant. (You may notice that much of what the judge does here is similar to what happens if an initial appearance is held. If a plea is entered at the initial appearance, an arraignment will be unnecessary.)

The indictment issued against Woodall, on March 18, 1997, is shown on page 5 in Chapter 1. After the indictment was issued, the prosecuting attorney filed papers with the court and served notice on Woodall's attorney that the death penalty would be sought in his case. With these actions, the criminal case against Woodall was ready to be set for trial. Circuit Court Judge Dan Cornette of the Muhlenberg County Circuit Court initially set the case for trial on October 28, 1997, but the trial would be delayed until February, 1998. In the next chapter, we will examine what happens in a typical criminal case between the filing of formal charges and the trial, and we will look specifically at what happened in Woodall's case as the prosecution and defense prepared for trial.

More on Grand Juries

The Fifth Amendment to the U.S. Constitution requires indictment by a grand jury before someone can be tried for a "capital, or otherwise infamous crime." The Supreme Court has ruled that the Fifth Amendment's guarantee of a grand jury indictment does not extend to prosecutions in state court (*Hurtado v. California*, 110 U.S. 516 (1884)). Thus, whether and when a state uses a grand jury are determined solely by each state's own constitution and statutes.

There are two traditional functions of a grand jury: indicting and investigating. The federal government and states allow grand juries to perform these functions in a variety of ways.

Federal Grand Juries

Implementing the Fifth Amendment's grand jury guarantee, the Federal Rules of Criminal Procedure state that a felony that is punishable by death or by imprisonment for more than one year must be prosecuted by a grand jury indictment. Federal grand juries also have the responsibility of investigating criminal activity. Federal grand juries do not, however, investigate public or civil affairs, as that responsibility has largely been taken over by federal administrative agencies.

State Grand Juries

Because the federal Constitution does not require that states use grand juries, the states are free to determine when and how grand juries will be used. All states use grand juries to some extent, but the states differ greatly in these uses. All of the states except Connecticut use grand juries to indict at least some crimes. Seventeen states and the District of Columbia require an indictment for all felonies. Five states require an indictment for certain serious or "infamous" crimes (similar to the federal standard). Twenty-five states make indictments optional, allowing the prosecutors to use either an indictment or information to charge an individual with an offense.

Only Connecticut has abolished use of grand jury indictments completely. Since May 26, 1983, all crimes charged by the state have been prosecuted by complaint. In Connecticut today, grand juries are used only for investigative purposes. Pennsylvania is similar to Connecticut in that grand juries are primarily used only for investigatory purposes. However, in 2012 a law was passed authorizing indictments by grand juries in cases where witness intimidation has occurred, is occurring, or is likely to occur (this law was passed following the abuse scandal involving the Penn State football team and concerns that local prosecutors did not vigorously pursue crimes).

In addition to investigating crimes and issuing criminal indictments, some grand juries have the power to investigate civil matters. For instance, grand juries in some states have the duty to inspect jails and public facilities (Louisiana, Maryland, New Mexico), and in other states to investigate public officers (Oklahoma, South Carolina, Minnesota).

For detailed information on grand juries in each state, see Thomson Reuters, *Convening of Grand Juries, 50 State Statutory Surveys: Criminal Laws: Criminal Procedure*, 0030 Surveys 19 (2013). ■

| CHAPTER 4

The Post-Filing, Pretrial Phase

P romotion in Motion filed its complaint against Beech-Nut on February 9, 2009. More than three and a half years passed before a jury handed down its verdict in favor of Beech-Nut on September 12, 2012. Robert Woodall committed his crimes on January 25, 1997 and was apprehended three days later, yet his trial, for sentencing purposes only, was not held until February, 1998. Why did it take so long for trials to be held in these cases, and what happened in the interim?

Believe it or not, the time between the beginning of a civil case and its trial is often much longer than three and a half years. Criminal cases, on the other hand, even complex ones, are often completed in less time than it took to reach a sentence in Mr. Woodall's case. One big reason for this difference in duration is found in the Sixth Amendment to the U.S. Constitution, which requires that criminal defendants "enjoy the right to a speedy and public trial" ("enjoy" here is just an antiquated way of saying "have" instead of a bad joke by the Founders). The Speedy Trial Clause is vague about when a criminal trial must be held,[1] but state and federal statutes provide more specific guidance. In general, a criminal trial will be held within a year of issuance of the indictment or information unless the defendant seeks further delay. There is no equivalent guarantee of a speedy civil trial under federal or state law, though civil courts do regularly inspect their *dockets* for stalled cases and impose scheduling orders to move long-pending cases toward completion.

Another part of the explanation is that criminal cases typically involve fewer pretrial hearings on motions submitted by the parties and involve less

---

[1] The Supreme Court imposed a four-factor test for violation of this clause that looks at (1) the length of the delay, (2) the reason for the delay, (3) when the defendant asserted his right under this clause, and (4) the harm caused by the delay. See *Barker v. Wingo*, 407 U.S. 514 (1972). A violation of the speedy trial clause results in dismissal of the indictment or information with prejudice (i.e., the case cannot be refiled).

time spent in what is called discovery, the process of gathering information and evidence relevant to the case. Although the time spent between filing and trial will differ between civil and criminal cases, the post-filing, pretrial phase is very important in the life of both kinds of cases. What the parties learn through discovery and how the court rules on pretrial motions will strongly influence whether the case proceeds to trial: if the evidence strongly favors one side or the judge rules favorably on an important motion made by one of the parties, the case is more likely to be resolved by agreement rather than trial (through a "settlement" in a civil case or a "plea agreement" in a criminal case); if both parties emerge from pretrial discovery and motion hearings feeling that they can do no worse than the settlement or plea bargain option offered by the other side, then they are likely to put their fates in the hands of a judge or jury at trial.

In civil cases, even if one party refuses to settle, there is a good chance that the case will never get to trial. For judges have the power to terminate cases through decisions on pretrial motions, and they often use that power. There are multiple "dispositive motions" that may be filed during the pretrial phase and, if granted, will end the case before trial. Pretrial motions and the discovery of information go hand in hand, because the information and evidence obtained through discovery will often be used to support a motion asking the judge to dispose of all or part of a case. Indeed, one of the key pretrial motions—a motion for *summary judgment*—allows the parties to present extensive evidence to the court in support of their positions. If the evidence and law favor the moving party (i.e., the party who made the motion) strongly enough, the judge can end the case in favor of that party.

Paradoxically, the availability of pretrial motions that can end a case before trial will sometimes prolong the case. For instance, many civil defendants would rather pay their attorneys to try to win a case through a summary judgment motion than give the same amount of money to a plaintiff as a part of a settlement agreement.

Although a variety of pretrial motions can be filed in criminal cases, there is no criminal-case analog to the motion for summary judgment. In a criminal case, a prosecutor can only "win" a case at trial or through a guilty plea. The defendant may win a motion to dismiss an indictment where a prosecutor has applied a criminal law too aggressively—perhaps the prosecutor is testing the boundaries of what is and is not allowed under a medical marijuana law. Or the defendant may win a motion to suppress important evidence (perhaps because it was seized improperly by the police), with the result that the prosecutor chooses to withdraw the case. But, as defense attorneys know, such victories are rare. That means that during the pretrial phase of a criminal case, the main concern of the defendant and his attorney is whether to enter into a plea agreement or take the case to trial. Information gathered through discovery is very important to this decision, because the information gives the defendant more or less leverage to negotiate a favorable plea agreement and will be needed at trial if no plea agreement is reached.

In this chapter, we will explain the pretrial maneuvers taken by the parties to try to gain an advantage and the legal tools at their disposal to gather the information they need to bring out the strengths, and combat the weaknesses, of their cases. As we walk through the pretrial phase, you must keep in mind a very important fact about American courts: in American civil and criminal courts, the parties rather than the judges control how the cases proceed.

Our Adversarial System

American courts (like English courts) employ what is called an adversarial system of litigation. In an adversarial system, the burden is on the parties and their attorneys to identify the legal and factual issues in dispute and to present evidence to a judge or jury to resolve those issues. In this kind of system, the "adversaries" develop the case. Other countries, such as France and Germany, employ an *inquisitorial system*. In an inquisitorial system, after a case has been initiated, a judge (or sometimes a group of judges) determines the issues for resolution and is actively involved in developing the evidence. The parties and their counsel still play a role in inquisitorial systems, but they do not control the case to nearly the same extent as they would in an adversarial system.

As we explore the system we have, it is worth considering the alternative. If you were not familiar with either kind of system, which would make more sense to you? If you were designing a legal system from scratch, would you choose the adversarial approach? Try to picture the first prehistoric use of a judge to make a decision: say two members of a tribe engaged in a dispute over the ownership of a goat agreed to put the issue before a respected elder and abide by his decision. How do we imagine the case proceeding? Maybe the elder sat silently while the disputants, one by one, told their stories. But this seems unlikely. It is much easier to picture him interjecting with questions and calling on other members of the tribe to tell him what they knew about the issue. That approach would seem to fit an intuition that, in order to reach a responsible decision, the judge should do his best to make sure he had all possible relevant information.

However, relying on the judge to root out all the information comes with a major downside. Uncovering and making sense of all the evidence may require a great deal of effort. Even the most conscientious judge will feel less compulsion to ensure that every scrap of evidence favoring a litigant comes to light than that litigant will. The disparity is likely even greater when the judge has a crowded docket. The key assumption of the adversarial system is that parties, with the greatest stakes in the outcome, can best be trusted to make sure that all relevant information is brought out.

We will have more to say about how the adversarial system operates when we get to the trial in the next chapter. The important thing to understand for now is that the responsibility for researching the law, asserting violations of the law, asserting defenses to accusations of breaking the law, and gathering and presenting evidence for use in deciding whether the law has been violated falls squarely on the parties in American courts. If there is legal or factual information out in the world that would help one of the parties but that party fails to bring it to light, the judge or jury will never hear of it.[2]

The Pretrial Period in a Civil Case

1. Responding to the Complaint

Shortly after Beech-Nut received the complaint filed against it by Promotion in Motion, it took advantage of the federal statutes that permit a civil defendant to remove a case from a state court to a federal court so long as the case could have been filed originally in the federal court. (See Chapter 3 for a full discussion of federal court subject matter jurisdiction.) Removal of the case from state to federal court did nothing to engage the issues raised by Promotion's complaint. Removal is a procedural maneuver that places the civil defendant in what is hoped to be a more favorable forum than the state court, but the mere act of removal has no direct impact on the outcome of the case.

Once the case was removed, Beech-Nut still had an obligation to respond to the complaint. If Beech-Nut had not filed a response in a timely fashion, Promotion in Motion could have sought to win the case immediately, through

---

2   Judges can interject at times, or act sua sponte (Latin for "of its own accord"), to raise legal and factual issues, and judges may be more inclined to do this when one of the parties does not have an attorney, but American judges generally have no obligation to protect the parties from making mistakes or missing something important. Furthermore, some types of American legal proceedings resemble more inquisitorial than adversarial proceedings. For instance, in small claims courts, the judge often acts as active fact finder, and courts run by administrative agencies will often employ more active fact finding and case control than we see in the regular courts.

a motion for default judgment. But Beech-Nut did file a timely response. Beech-Nut had two options when responding to the complaint: it could file a *motion to dismiss* the claims against it, or it could file an *answer* to the complaint, responding directly to the allegations and raising new issues for the court to consider. Beech-Nut chose the second option, but let us consider the first option before examining its chosen path.[3]

There are two kinds of motions that may be filed as the initial response to a complaint. One kind claims that the case is not properly before the court and seeks to force the plaintiff to start over in another court. For instance, if the defendant believes that the court lacks personal jurisdiction over it or lacks subject matter jurisdiction over the claims in the plaintiff's complaint, then the defendant can ask the court to dismiss the complaint on these grounds. The plaintiff will get a chance to respond in writing to the defendant's motion, but if the court agrees with the defendant's argument that the court is not a proper forum for the case, then the complaint will be dismissed *without prejudice*—that is, this court will refuse to hear the case while recognizing that the plaintiff might be entitled to have the case heard in a proper forum. The defendant might hope that the plaintiff will not bother with the cost and hassle of refiling in a different court or might just believe that another court would be preferable to the present court (e.g., it might be in a more convenient geographic location).

The second kind of motion that may be filed in response to a complaint asks the court to dismiss the complaint because the claims made in it are for some reason defective. If there is some easy-to-prove fact that completely undercuts the plaintiff's claims, then the defendant can file a motion for summary judgment along with an *affidavit* swearing to the necessary facts. Perhaps, for example, the plaintiff sued the defendant thinking he was the driver of the car that hit the plaintiff but the defendant submits an affidavit from his doctor swearing that the defendant was in a coma on the day of the accident. If the plaintiff cannot present contradictory evidence, then the court will conclude that no one could reasonably believe the defendant hit the plaintiff and will grant summary judgment to the defendant and dismiss the complaint *with prejudice*. When claims are dismissed with prejudice, they cannot be refiled against the same defendant in any court. However, they can be pursued against other responsible persons. So if the accident victim could figure out who the real driver was, he could bring a claim for negligence against that defendant.

---

3   This discussion of the pretrial phase in a civil case applies to cases pending in both state and federal courts.

It is rare for a summary judgment motion to be filed as the initial response to a complaint because typically it takes a good deal of time to develop the evidence needed to support such a motion. More commonly, defendants file a motion to dismiss on grounds that the complaint "fails to state a claim upon which relief can be granted." This motion contends either that the law does not recognize the civil claim being asserted or that the allegations in the complaint are too vague or implausible to support the claim. Say the plaintiff and the defendant illegally agreed to make and distribute illicit drugs but the defendant breached his part of the agreement. The law does not allow breach-of-contract claims based on illegal contracts, so the defendant could move to dismiss the plaintiff's complaint on grounds that it fails to state a claim upon which relief can be granted. Or perhaps the plaintiff and defendant entered into a legal arrangement to do something together, but the plaintiff's complaint is so vague that it is unclear what exactly the defendant did wrong; the defendant could move to dismiss the complaint because the allegations in the complaint are insufficient to support whatever claim the plaintiff is trying to bring. If the plaintiff cannot amend the complaint to make the claim clearer, then the court will dismiss the plaintiff's complaint with prejudice.

A party can make both kinds of motions--to dismiss because the case is not in the right court and to dismiss because a claim is defective. The judge will first consider whether her court is the proper forum; if it is not, then the case will be dismissed without prejudice and arguments about the claims will not be reached. If the judge concludes that her court is proper, then she will rule on any argument that the claims in the complaint are invalid.

Beech-Nut did not file either kind of motion in response to Promotion in Motion's Complaint. Instead, Beech-Nut filed an Answer to the Complaint in which it responded to each numbered paragraph in the complaint with an admission or a denial of the paragraph's allegations. (Page 1 of that Answer is reproduced below; the full document is available on the book's website.) The complaint and the answer together establish what is and is not in dispute between the parties. Although Beech-Nut admitted some of the facts alleged in Promotion in Motion's Complaint (e.g., that Beech-Nut had submitted some purchase orders for Fruit Nibbles made by PIM), it denied the key allegations that it breached an oral or implied contract with Promotion in Motion.[4] But Beech-Nut's answer to the complaint did more than that. Beech-Nut asserted *affirmative defenses* and went on the offensive by asserting *counterclaims*.

---

4   If you compare the complaint and answer, you will see that the numbered paragraphs in Beech-Nut's answer correspond to the numbered paragraphs in Promotion in Motion's complaint.

Affirmative defenses respond to claims, not by denying the underlying facts, but by providing an independent reason for rejecting the claims. A well-known affirmative defense in criminal cases is self-defense: the criminal defendant argues that even if he did shoot the victim, the fact that his own life was in danger at the victim's hands justifies his actions and exonerates him. Defendants have the burden of establishing the elements of an affirmative

---

BLOOM KARINJA & DILLON, P.C.
70 South Orange Avenue, Suite 240
Livingston, New Jersey 07039
973.758.0900

KING & SPALDING LLP
1185 Avenue of the Americas
New York, New York 10036
212.556.2100

Attorneys for Defendant and
Counter Claimant

UNITED STATES DISTRICT COURT
DISTRICT OF NEW JERSEY

PROMOTION IN MOTION, INC. and PIM BRANDS, LLC,	HON. WILLIAM J. MARTINI, U.S.D.J.
Plaintiffs,	Civil Action No. 2:09-cv-1228 (WJM)
vs.	**ANSWER AND COUNTERCLAIMS**
BEECH-NUT NUTRITION CORPORATION, a HERO GROUP COMPANY,	
Defendant.	

Defendant Beech-Nut Nutrition Corporation ("Beech-Nut"), by and through its undersigned attorneys King & Spalding LLP and Bloom, Karinja & Dillon, P.C., answers the Complaint of Plaintiffs Promotion In Motion, Inc. ("Promotion In Motion"), and PIM Brands, LLC ("PIM") (collectively the "Plaintiffs"), dated February 27, 2009, as follows:

    1.   Beech-Nut is without knowledge or information sufficient to form a belief as to the truth of the allegations of paragraph 1 of the Complaint.

    2.   Beech-Nut is without knowledge or information sufficient to form a belief as to the truth of the allegations of paragraph 2 of the Complaint.

defense. In the Fruit Nibbles case, Beech-Nut asserted an affirmative defense based on what is called the "Statute of Frauds," which requires that certain kinds of agreements be put into writing to be legally enforceable. Beech-Nut alleged that PIM's claims violated the Statute of Frauds and thus were barred.

Counterclaims are claims by a defendant back against the plaintiff, with the defendant now alleging that it was the plaintiff who violated some civil law. The counterclaim part of an answer looks a lot like a mini-complaint: in the counterclaim section of its answer, Beech-Nut first alleged background facts (see ¶¶ 1-19) that supposedly supported claims against Promotion in Motion (see ¶¶ 20-38) and then closed with a demand for a judgment for damages. (Because Promotion in Motion had already demanded a jury trial, Beech-Nut did not have to make such a demand.) In particular, Beech-Nut claimed that the Fruit Nibbles manufactured by PIM breached express and implied warranties and that PIM negligently manufactured the Fruit Nibbles. In short, Beech-Nut contended not only that it owed Promotion in Motion nothing, but that Promotion in Motion owed Beech-Nut refunds of the money already paid plus money for injury to Beech-Nut's reputation and for other costs caused by the withdrawal of Fruit Nibbles from the national market. With the filing of Beech-Nut's answer and counterclaims, the legal claims to be decided in the case were set, and it remained for each party to develop the facts and evidence needed to prove that its legal claims were superior: either Promotion in Motion lived up to its obligations under its contracts with Beech-Nut and was entitled to full payment, or it did not, in which case it might have to pay Beech-Nut for harms caused by failure of the Fruit Nibbles product. The answer to this question of responsibility for the Fruit Nibbles failure was worth more than $3 million to the parties.

2. Discovery

With the legal issues set, discovering the facts and assembling the evidence took center stage. In a lawsuit, it is not enough for a party to believe that something is true. A reasonable belief that the other party violated a civil law is enough to file a complaint, but to win in court a party needs to be prepared to prove the important facts in the case using sworn statements by witnesses and physical evidence such as documents, email, and photographs. In a civil case, a party making a claim has the burden to prove each of the elements of the claim by a preponderance of the evidence. The preponderance standard means that the claimant's version of the facts must be more likely than not true: in terms of probabilities, the claimant's version of the facts has to be at least slightly more probable than the opposing party's version of the facts to satisfy the preponderance standard. (The "beyond reasonable doubt" standard of persuasion applied in criminal cases is supposed to require a much higher degree of belief in the prosecution's case in order to convict a defendant of a crime. We discuss both of these standards in more detail in Chapter 5.)

Recall that in a breach of contract case, the claimant has to prove three basic elements. Because Promotion in Motion and Beech-Nut had competing breach-of-contract claims, each needed to prove, by a preponderance of the evidence, (1) that the parties had entered into a contract, (2) that the other party had breached one or more terms of that contract, and (3) that the breach had caused harm to the non-breaching party. Since the parties never entered into a master written contract to govern their dealings, the first thing each party needed to prove was exactly what contract or contracts they had entered into and what the contract terms were. Once they did that, then they could move on to proving that the other party had breached one or more of those contract terms and that the breach(es) had caused harm.

Some of the evidence needed by the parties was surely easy to obtain because employees at each company had information about the events that led to the case and each company had relevant emails and other records at their disposal. The attorneys for each company could interview their client's employees and review their client's records to get a good idea of what transpired. But what if one party needed information from the other party, or from someone who was not a party to the case? With a few exceptions, the other party does not have to volunteer information, and people who are not parties to the case don't have to answer questions just because an attorney asks them. Recognizing that gathering information is essential to resolving cases, each state and federal court system has established rules that can be used to compel other parties and non-parties to share information. These rules are quite similar across courts.

Let us consider first how to get information from non-parties who are unwilling to share information. Say that Beech-Nut wanted to ask consumers about their experiences with Fruit Nibbles to try to prove that they were poor quality fruit chews that Beech-Nut should not have to pay for. An attorney for Beech-Nut could call consumers who complained about Fruit Nibbles, but the consumers could hang up on the attorney. In that case, the attorney could ask the court to issue a special kind of order, called a *subpoena*, which directs someone to appear at a legal proceeding to answer questions under oath. (The order can also force the person to bring specified types of physical evidence, such as documents that may be relevant to the proceeding.)[5] Someone who is the subject of a subpoena but fails to appear at the proceeding at the appointed time can be arrested and compelled to appear at another time.

If things get that far, a subpoena might be used to order someone to appear at a trial or a hearing before a judge. But in the discovery process, the point of a subpoena is to compel the person to answer questions at a legal proceeding called a *deposition*. A deposition may be held in a courthouse, but usually it is at the office of the attorney for one of the parties. A notice of the deposition must be sent to all of the parties in the case (or their attorneys) so that each party has an opportunity to attend the deposition and ask questions. The subpoenaed witness, known as the deponent, can also have an attorney present who can object to questions that are believed to be inappropriate. The deponent must answer the questions anyway, but putting objections on the record preserves the right to protest later if answers to those objectionable questions are used at trial or another court proceeding.

The deponent must answer under oath before a stenographer who creates a record of the questions and answers for future use in the case. The deponent's testimony thus becomes evidence that may be used later at a pretrial hearing before a judge or at trial. The same goes for any physical evidence that the deponent is ordered to bring to the deposition; items of physical evidence will be made "exhibits" to the transcript of the deposition. Subpoenas and depositions are the main legal devices for compelling non-parties to share information that is needed for a civil case.

■ "RAMBO ATTORNEYS" IN "CIVIL" LITIGATION

You may have heard the phrase "Rambo Attorney." Depending on your age, you may not understand that phrase at all, but if you are old enough to remember Sylvester Stallone as the former Army Special Forces soldier John Rambo in the film *First Blood*, then you have probably figured out that the phrase connotes a lawyer who lays waste to the opposition, just as John Rambo did to the small-town police force that attempted to arrest him. Lawyers gain reputations as Rambo Attorneys largely through their tactics during discovery in civil cases, especially during depositions. (Remember that "civil" does not refer to how the parties or attorneys behave but rather to the nature of

---

5   When the court order only directs the person to appear at a legal proceeding to answer questions, the Latin term for the court order is subpoena ad testificandum. When the court order also directs the person to bring physical evidence with her to the proceeding, the Latin term is subpoena duces tecum. When lawyers use only the term "subpoena," they are usually referring to orders just to appear and give testimony; lawyers use the phrase subpoena duces tecum when the witness is also expected to produce physical evidence.

the laws at issue in the case.) You could spend hours watching clips from videotaped depositions on YouTube, many of which are posted because of verbal and sometimes physical fights that broke out between the deponent and attorney. (If you do this, turn down the volume on your computer, because much of what you will hear is NSFW.) Asking tough, possibly even bullying, questions at depositions is just one way that attorneys signal to the other side that the case will not be easy or pleasant. Attorneys are not supposed to use deposition and other discovery tools just to increase the expense, duration, and psychological pain of a lawsuit, so few attorneys would admit that discovery requests were submitted to harass the other side. But the reality is that discovery, whether intended to do so or not, often adds huge monetary, temporal, and psychic costs to a case. Rules of procedure in both state and federal courts give deponents who feel they are being bullied and parties who believe they are being harassed through discovery requests some protection, but the burden is on the person on the receiving end of the alleged abuse to seek relief from the court.

Few trial judges enjoy dealing with disputes about discovery, with the result that all of the people in front of the judge in a discovery dispute—even the person seeking relief from abusive tactics--may receive a lecture on cooperation and civilized behavior. Consequently, parties are often reluctant to take discovery disputes to a judge unless things have gotten seriously out of hand and the attorneys can no longer cooperate. This reluctance has the effect of causing many low-level, and some high-level, unpleasantries and annoyances to be tolerated during discovery.

Subpoenas are necessary to obtain information from unwilling people who are not parties to the case. But they are not necessary to compel a party to attend a deposition. If you want to depose the other party, all you need to do is serve a notice of deposition specifying when and where the deposition will be held.[6] Beech-Nut, for instance, sought to learn what the manager of the plant producing the Fruit Nibbles knew about problems in the production process. Because this manager, Mr. Frank McSorley, was still an employee of PIM at the time of the lawsuit, Beech-Nut only had to serve a notice of deposition on PIM, which was then obligated to make Mr. McSorley available for his deposition. At his deposition, Mr. McSorley defended the quality of the Fruit Nibbles product when they left his plant, but he did concede that if the Fruit Nibbles had become "mummified and hard" within one year of production,

---

6   When the party to be deposed is a corporation or other entity, the notice of deposition will specify a particular office or employee to be deposed or will specify topics of questioning and instruct the other party to bring someone knowledgeable about those topics to be deposed.

then the product would not be saleable. Beech-Nut also wanted to learn what PIM's quality control manager knew about problems with the production process, but this manager, Ms. Dianne Bianchini, had left PIM by the time Beech-Nut sought her deposition. Accordingly, PIM was under no obligation to produce her, and Beech-Nut instead had to subpoena Ms. Bianchini to compel her attendance at a deposition. Taking this additional step turned out to be a wise move, because Ms. Bianchini testified that she believed the formula used by PIM to produce the Fruit Nibbles was not stable, allowing the product to degrade quickly. In fact, Ms. Bianchini admitted at her deposition that, given what she knew about problems with the product formula, she would not have wanted to feed Fruit Nibbles to her children.

In addition to depositions, there are a number of other legal devices you can use to obtain information from the other party. First, you can submit written questions that must be answered in writing within a set time period (usually thirty days unless the parties agree to something else). These written questions are called "interrogatories" and are useful for obtaining more detail on the allegations in a complaint or an answer to a complaint. Second, you can submit requests for production of documents and other tangible things (including electronic files) and for access to real property. The other side has to make the requested things available for inspection in a timely fashion. Interrogatories and document requests are often used before depositions because they help determine who should be deposed and provide documents that can be used at the depositions. For instance, it was through interrogatories that Beech-Nut found out which employees of PIM had knowledge of the production process and through document requests that Beech-Nut obtained many internal PIM e-mails that were discussed at depositions (and ultimately trial, as we will see in the next chapter).

Third, you can submit written assertions that the other side must admit or deny (e.g., if you are the plaintiff in a car wreck case, you could ask the defendant to admit that the defendant's car struck yours—a fact—and also that the defendant operated his car negligently—a legal conclusion). If they fail to respond in a timely fashion, that counts as an admission. Fourth, in cases where the mental or physical condition of a party is in issue, a party can ask the court to compel the other side to submit to a mental or physical examination.

◼ DISCOVERING COKE'S SECRET FORMULA: PROTECTIVE ORDERS IN DISCOVERY

What if you made a soft drink that tasted a lot like Coca-Cola™ and you believed that the makers of Coke had stolen your recipe? You might sue the Coca-Cola Company on a claim of misappropriation, which is a type of tort. To prove that claim, you'd want to compare your recipe to the recipe used to make Coke, and so you would need to submit a request for production to the defendant asking that it produce the recipe it uses to make Coke. Coca-Cola might think that your lawsuit was a sham aimed at using discovery to gain access to Coke's secret formula. (Supposedly the only written record of this secret formula is kept in a bank vault in Atlanta, Georgia that can only be opened by resolution of the board of directors of the Coca-Cola Company). The company might fear that once you had the secret formula, you would sell it to a competitor or threaten to do so unless a large amount of money was paid to you—in other words, that your lawsuit and your request for production of the secret formula were one big attempt at blackmail or misappropriation. What could the maker of Coke do in this situation?

It would have two options. First, it could try to get your claim dismissed using one of the dispositive pretrial motions we have discussed. Second, assuming the motion was unsuccessful, it could ask the court to enter a "protective order" against the requested discovery. Both state and federal courts have the power to prevent discovery of highly sensitive or confidential information if the information is not really needed, if there is a less sensitive alternative, or if it appears the information is being sought for improper purposes. Alternatively, the court could impose restrictions on access to and use of the sensitive information—for instance, the court might allow only attorneys to see the information and require that any documents filed in court that referenced the information not be made available to the public. (The hypothetical facts on which this example is based are not so hypothetical. The Coca-Cola Company was faced with a discovery request for its formula in a case brought against it by some of the companies that bottle and distribute Coke. The federal district court concluded that the formula had to be shared but subject to stringent protections. See *Coca-Cola Bottling Company of Shreveport, Inc. v. Coca-Cola Company,* 107 F.R.D. 288 (D. Del. 1985).)

If a party who receives one of these discovery requests believes that the request is inappropriate, then the burden is on the receiving party to object. If the parties cannot reach an accommodation, then the judge will have to decide whether to compel the receiving party to provide the requested information.

The use of depositions, interrogatories, requests for production, and requests for admission is very common in civil cases. The discovery rules do not require any specific sequencing of discovery requests, but it is common to submit interrogatories and requests for production first. The information acquired can then be used to structure questions in the depositions. Requests for physical or mental exams are less common than these other discovery devices because often the parties agree to exchange expert reports that address the physical or mental state of the plaintiff who claims injury, plus the defendant can subpoena the doctor who treated the plaintiff for a deposition and can subpoena the plaintiff's medical records. Experts are commonly used in civil cases that present medical questions or questions on some other topic that requires specialized knowledge to address, such as complex accounting questions or scientific questions. Neither Promotion in Motion or Beech-Nut relied on any independent experts in their case.

The Value of Information

The single most important factor in whether a civil claim will settle rather than go to trial is the extent to which the parties agree about the expected value of the claim. The expected value of a claim is a complex function of how much the claimant would gain from a win versus a loss, the expenses each side would incur in reaching each outcome, and the probability that each outcome will occur. The most important single factor affecting the extent of agreement between the parties is the amount of information they possess. This is not to suggest that either attorneys or their clients should be thought of as dispassionate calculators. Sometimes clients insist on a trial as a matter of principle, or because they want to have an official and public verdict rendered, or simply because they are angry. And lawyers, like other human beings, are subject to all kinds of cognitive limitations that can keep them from correctly evaluating a case's prospects (for more discussion, see Andrew J. Wistrich & Jeffrey J. Rachlinski, *How Lawyers' Intuitions Prolong Litigation*, 86 S. Cal. L. Rev. 571 (2013)). Nevertheless, more information usually translates into more agreement and, in turn, a higher probability of settlement.

The calculations involved in assessing the expected value of a claim can be complex, and they are shrouded in uncertainty. Here is a simplified example just to illustrate the concept.

Jim is driving down a county road with his son soon after a snowstorm. He hits a slush-covered patch of ice, spins out of control, and hits a tree. Jim and his son both suffer serious, though not life-threat-ening, injuries. His car is totaled. Arguing that the county failed to plow the road properly, Jim sues the county for $200,000 to compensate him for his car, medical bills, and wages he lost while unable to work.

Suppose Jim's lawyer estimates that his chance of winning the entire $200,000 if the case goes to trial is 50%. It is also possible that the jury will find Jim partially or wholly at fault, because there is some indication that he was driving too fast. Accordingly, his lawyer thinks there is a 30% chance that Jim will win $100,000 and a 20% chance that he will win nothing. Jim's lawyer thus puts the expected value of the case at ($200,000 x 0.5) + ($100,000 x 0.3) + ($0 x 0.2) = $130,000. Note that she does not expect Jim to win exactly $130,000. She is saying that if many cases like Jim's were to be tried, the average award (sometimes $200,000, sometimes half of that, sometimes nothing) would end up around $130,000.

Now imagine that the county's lawyers agree about the probabilities of the various outcomes and so agree that the expected value of the case is $130,000. Trials cost a lot of money. If the county takes the case to trial, it can expect to lose $130,000 plus a good deal more in expenses—say $180,000 total. From the county's perspective, it would be much better just to pay Jim $130,000 without going through the trial. What if it were to offer Jim $130,000? His perspective is much the same. If he insists on a trial anyway, he will incur additional costs—for instance, paying expert witnesses to testify about his injuries and perhaps paying more in lawyers' fees. And he will have to spend much more of his own time on the case, perhaps losing more work wages in the process. He does better if he accepts the county's offer than if he pushes for a trial. In such a situation, we would expect the two parties to settle the case before trial. Even if the parties' estimates differ, we would normally expect them to reach a settlement through bargaining, as long as the difference is fairly small.

But imagine instead that the estimates differ a great deal—say the county puts the expected value of the case at only $40,000. It is unlikely that Jim will accept an offer of $40,000 when his estimate of the case's value is so much higher. The case will probably go to trial.

Now you can see the importance of discovery, and the information it reveals, for settlement. Even if each side knows everything that the other side knows, they might disagree about a case's expected value; perhaps they read the law differently or have different expectations about how a jury will react to the evidence. But they are much more likely to disagree, and the gap between their estimates is likely to be larger, the more private information—such as what a witness would say or what a document shows—each party has. Well-conducted discovery helps the parties see a case in a similar light and reach a settlement, avoiding the time and expense of trial.

Similar calculations apply in criminal cases, but with potential prison time for the defendant taking the place of the damages the defendant might have to pay the plaintiff. The risk of imprisonment may weigh much more heavily in the calculation than the risk of losing out on $200,000. Another important difference is that in criminal cases the prosecution's economic costs are largely fixed—whether the case is resolved by plea bargain or trial, the prosecutor will draw her salary and the state and county are going to bear the costs of the trial. On the other hand, the prosecution may have much higher opportunity costs than civil attorneys have: prosecutors' offices simply do not have enough manpower to take every criminal charge to indictment, much less trial, and a high profile loss at trial may be politically damaging to an elected prosecutor. Even though the calculations of criminal defendants and prosecutors may differ from those of civil parties, in both kinds of cases the parties have to estimate the likelihood of different outcomes. Information obtained during the pretrial phase of the criminal case will be crucial to whether a plea agreement is reached before trial and to what the terms of that plea agreement are.

The acquisition of information from the other side is a key function of discovery. But it is not the only thing litigants use discovery for, or the only way in which it fosters settlement. Discovery can also be used to coerce the other side into settlement—by causing delay and by increasing the expected cost of litigation. But whether through the acquisition of information or the imposition of costs, discovery is an important determinant of whether a case is resolved voluntarily before trial.

3. Summary Judgment

Promotion in Motion and Beech-Nut each took a number of depositions and exchanged interrogatories and requests for production. Particularly noteworthy was the deposition testimony of PIM's quality control manager that she would not feed the Fruit Nibbles to her own children and the deposition testimony of PIM's plant manager, that, although some of the product had problems, the extent of the problems was unknown and much of the product was good when Beech-Nut recalled the product from the market. After obtaining this and other helpful information through discovery, Beech-Nut became confident that it could prove that it had not violated any agreement but that PIM had.

Therefore, rather than wait until trial to attack PIM's claims and prove its own, Beech-Nut decided to file a motion for summary judgment, with the aim of winning the case immediately, with no need for a trial.

A party who moves for summary judgment is saying something like this: "Judge, a trial is for resolving disagreements about the facts. There is no point in having a trial here because the evidence and law are already clear. The other party simply cannot reasonably claim that the facts and law support its side of the case. A trial would be a waste of time and money. Therefore, you should rule in my favor right now."

Either party can move for summary judgment, and summary judgment can be used offensively or defensively—that is, it can be used to prevail on one's own claim for relief or it can be used to defeat the other side's claim against you. It is easier to win a defensive motion for summary judgment: because the claimant has the burden of proving each material fact in order to prevail on its claim, the party making the defensive motion only has to show that the claimant's case fails on at least one material fact. Winning an offensive motion for summary judgment is rare because the party making the motion has to prove to the judge's satisfaction that the evidence clearly supports all of the essential elements of its claim before the judge can grant judgment on that claim and order the other party to pay damages; to beat the motion, the responding party only has to show that there is some genuine dispute in the evidence on at least one of the essential elements. If that is the case, then the claim has to go trial for a full airing of the evidence. Because defensive motions for summary judgment are much easier to win, they are pursued far more often than offensive motions.

Beech-Nut tried to use a motion for summary judgment both offensively and defensively: it asked the judge to rule that Promotion in Motion's claims should be dismissed because no reasonable jury could believe that Beech-Nut violated the law and to rule that the evidence and law clearly supported Beech-Nut's claims against PIM. Beech-Nut presented the judge with a set of sworn statements from witnesses (these documents are called "declarations" or "affidavits"), excerpts from deposition transcripts, and various documents—e.g., the purchase orders, pictures of degraded Fruit Nibbles, records of customer complaints, and email exchanges. Beech-Nut argued that these collectively proved that the purchase orders were the only contracts entered into by the parties and that many of the batches of Fruit Nibbles manufactured by PIM were defective.

With any motion for summary judgment, the opposing party gets a chance to respond. PIM responded to Beech-Nut's motion by emphasizing that Beech-Nut could not prove how extensive the problems with the Fruit Nibbles were (though PIM conceded that some packages of Fruit Nibbles were defective and were rejected by consumers) and that without such proof Beech-Nut could not establish that Promotion had substantially breached any warranties. (Perfection is not possible and was not required by the contract. Basically, the question came down to whether Beech-Nut had a reasonable basis for concluding that the problems with the Fruit Nibbles were sufficiently widespread to revoke its acceptance of all Fruit Nibbles, or whether Beech-Nut should have gathered more evidence before revoking acceptance and withdrawing the product from the market.) Thus, PIM argued that Beech-Nut's attempt to get summary judgment on Beech-Nut's own claims had to be rejected. Approximately twenty-five pages of PIM's response are devoted to explaining why Beech-Nut should not be awarded summary judgment on its claims against PIM. The last page and a half of PIM's response reads as a half-hearted effort to keep its claims against Beech-Nut alive.

The judge's ruling on Beech-Nut's motion for summary judgment is clear and concise, coming in at only nine pages. (The opinion, which is fairly free of legal jargon, should be comprehensible to non-lawyers, and we encourage you to read the whole thing on the book's website.) The judge first dealt with Beech-Nut's contention that the only contracts entered into by the parties were the purchase order agreements submitted by Beech-Nut and accepted by Promotion in Motion. The judge agreed with Beech-Nut, concluding that any agreements beyond these purchase order agreements were never sufficiently finalized to be binding on either party. With this decision, the judge brought to an end Promotion's claims against Beech-Nut, because all of those claims depended on proving that the parties had contractual arrangements beyond the purchase orders. Everyone agreed that Beech-Nut had paid for all of the shipments of Fruit Nibbles received under the purchase orders and that Beech-Nut had not breached any other obligation under the purchase orders. Therefore, the judge granted Beech-Nut's defensive motion for summary judgment and dismissed PIM's claims against Beech-Nut.

Beech-Nut did not fare as well with the offensive part of its motion (i.e., the request for affirmative relief as opposed to the attempt to dismiss claims pursued by PIM). The judge agreed with Promotion in Motion that Beech-Nut had not adequately proven that the manufacturing or packaging defects in *some* Fruit Nibbles substantially impaired the value of *all* of the Fruit Nibbles provided by Promotion to Beech-Nut. Therefore, a trial would have to determine whether the scope of the problem was sufficient to justify revoking acceptance of all shipments of the Fruit Nibbles and to place responsibility on Promotion for the costs associated with Beech-Nut's recall of Fruit Nibbles.

So, in the end, Beech-Nut won a big and important victory in the case through its filing of a motion for summary judgment, but it was a partial victory. Beech-Nut would not have to face Promotion's claims at trial because those claims were now dismissed, but if Beech-Nut wanted to recover damages against Promotion in Motion, it would have to win on its own claims against Promotion at trial. We will take up what happened at trial in the next chapter.[7]

The Pretrial Period in a Criminal Case

The criminal case has no exact analog to the civil case's answer to a complaint. But the criminal defendant's entry of a plea of guilty or not guilty serves part of the function of an answer to a complaint: it broadly establishes what is in dispute in the case.[8] The reason why criminal defendants cannot be made to respond to every allegation in an indictment or information in the same way that civil defendants can is found in the federal Constitution. The Fifth Amendment's privilege against self-incrimination, which applies in both state and federal courts, guarantees both guilty and innocent persons the right to refuse to answer questions if the answers could be used against them in a criminal prosecution. The clause does not provide general protection against revealing things you would like to keep secret, even if revealing them could be very embarrassing or cost you a great deal of money in civil damages. So at a deposition in a civil case, the defendant can be forced to answer whether or not she breached a contract, even though this answer could cause her to be liable for damages.[9] If the case makes it to trial, she can be ordered to answer the question in court or face a penalty for refusing to answer. What a civil court cannot do is force you to answer a question if the answer might be used to prosecute you for a crime. Neither can the police if they are questioning you about a crime they think you committed, and neither, of course, can a criminal court. Forcing defendants to admit or deny the specific allegations

---

7   Although many cases settle after the judge rules on a motion for summary judgment, Beech-Nut did not settle its outstanding claims against Promotion in Motion but rather took those claims to trial.

8   Federal Rule of Criminal Procedure 11 specifically states that in criminal proceedings the pleadings (i.e., the legal filings that set the legal boundaries of the case) are the indictment, the information, and pleas of guilty, not guilty, and nolo contendere. Recall that the primary pleadings in a civil case are the Complaint and the Answer to the Complaint.

9   Technically, no one can force anyone else to answer a question, but if the civil defendant refuses to answer this question at the deposition, she can be sanctioned with a fine or some other penalty, up to granting the plaintiff a judgment against her due to her refusal to answer. No sanction can be imposed on someone who refuses to answer a question by invoking the Fifth Amendment privilege against self-incrimination.

against them would be equivalent to forcing them to answer incriminating questions, so the court cannot do it.

What criminal courts can do is compel a defendant to tell the judge whether or not he accepts guilt for any of the charged crimes. A "not guilty" plea denies the indictment's allegations at the most basic level without having to respond to the specific charges or allegations in the indictment. (If a criminal defendant refuses to enter a plea, then the judge will presume the defendant generally denies the allegations in the indictment and will treat that refusal to enter a plea as a plea of not guilty.[10])

You may recall that Woodall initially pled not guilty but later changed his plea to guilty. This is very common, as a number of important events can occur during the pretrial period to motivate a defendant to change his plea. In most cases (though not Woodall's), the most important of these events is the prosecution's decision to engage in plea bargaining with the defendant. A plea agreement offer aims to induce a guilty plea by reducing the severity of the sentence faced by the defendant. A prosecutor can do this by agreeing to drop certain charges, replace charges with less serious ones (e.g., charge a misdemeanor instead of a felony), or recommend a shorter sentence to the judge in return for a guilty plea. Sometimes the prosecutor plea bargains to avoid the risk of an acquittal at trial. But the more important motivation is to save time. Prosecutor's offices typically process far more cases than they can possibly take to trial. To keep up, they must plea bargain in most cases, even where the prosecutor is sure the defendant is guilty. The main exceptions are especially serious and visible crimes, like Woodall's, where prosecutors feel a special obligation to seek a stiff penalty and want to send a message to the community and deter other offenses.

The pretrial process plays a crucial role in structuring negotiations between the prosecution and defense. For instance, information obtained through discovery might lead the prosecution to feel less confident in its case, or the judge might make a favorable ruling on one of the defendant's pretrial motions. If so, the prosecution will have more reasons for wishing to avoid trial and may offer a more generous deal. If discovery and pre-trial motions go against the defendant, the defendant will be motivated to avoid trial. In fact, the prosecution case sometimes appears so overwhelming that the defendant

---

10   A criminal defendant may have an obligation to notify the prosecution if he plans to rely on certain affirmative defenses. For example, the federal rules of criminal procedure require the defendant to notify the prosecution if he plans to rely on an alibi defense or an insanity defense, so that the prosecution can investigate the bases for those defenses. Such notice requirements do not run afoul of the Fifth Amendment privilege against self-incrimination because the defendant is just being asked to alert the other side if it plans to put on certain defenses—he is not being compelled to answer questions from the government about potentially incriminating facts.

elects to plead guilty even without a reduced plea through plea bargaining, simply to spare the effort and public humiliation of a trial.

The table on pages 82-84 contrasts criminal discovery with civil discovery in federal courts. State courts follow similar rules, although there can be important variations (e.g., Texas rules for procedures in criminal cases are silent on the sharing of witness statements). There are two crucial things to understand about discovery in criminal cases. First, it is less involved and extensive than discovery in civil cases. Second, the prosecution has some disclosure duties to the criminal defendant that a plaintiff does not have with respect to a civil defendant. Both facts can be explained by the typically huge disparities in resources between the prosecution and criminal defendant, together with society's view that the state should bear the burden of showing that a defendant is guilty and deserves punishment.

Prosecutors have immense investigative power at their disposal. They use law enforcement agencies, such as the FBI, local police, and forensic crime labs, to collect and analyze evidence, and they have access to digital repositories containing fingerprint and DNA information as well as criminal history records from all of the states. In contrast, criminal defendants normally lack the resources to conduct a substantial pretrial investigation. Most defendants don't have enough money to hire their own attorneys, and publicly-paid defense attorneys have very limited funds to conduct discovery.[11] Appointed counsel for indigent defendants can request additional funding for important discovery, but such requests provide only limited ability to conduct pretrial discovery and are usually reserved for particularly important requests because of the limited funds available.

---

11   The Sixth Amendment to the U.S. Constitution states that "[i]n all criminal prosecutions, the accused shall enjoy the right . . . to have the Assistance of Counsel for his defence." In *Gideon v. Wainwright*, 372 U.S. 335 (1963), the Supreme Court ruled that criminal defendants facing the threat of incarceration are entitled to a publicly-paid defense attorney if they cannot afford their own attorneys, even if facing charges in state court. Subsequent cases made clear that a defendant who did not have counsel could not be sentenced to a term of imprisonment. To meet the needs for counsel in criminal cases, larger cities usually have government-financed "public defender" offices, and other municipalities will employ private attorneys on a contract basis.

COMPARISON OF DISCOVERY IN FEDERAL CIVIL AND CRIMINAL CASES

	Federal Rules of Civil Procedure	Federal Rules of Criminal Procedure
Basic Limitation on Scope of Discovery	Information sought must be relevant to a claim or defense, or relevant to the subject matter of the action, but the information sought need not be admissible at trial.	Documents and objects sought by the defendant must be evidence the prosecutor plans to use or must be needed to prepare a defense. If the defendant requests evidence, the government can request similar evidence from the defendant if (a) the item is within the defendant's possession, custody, or control and (b) the defendant intends to use the evidence in his defense.
Automatic Disclosures	Early in the case, parties must exchange information about witnesses and physical evidence that may be used to support a party's case, as well as insurance information and information to damages calculation. Parties must also automatically exchange witness information before trial.	No automatic disclosures except that the government must automatically disclose obviously exculpatory material evidence and must automatically disclose to Defendant and the court that a government witness presented false testimony.
Depositions (answers under oath to questions from a party or a party's attorney; stenographic record is made for later use)	Presumptive limit of ten depositions per side and presumptive limit of one deposition of seven hours or less per witness. Party depositions by notice; non-party depositions by subpoena. Very commonly used.	The court may grant a motion to depose a witness to preserve testimony for trial and "in the interests of justice." A material witness can request to be deposed by giving notice to both parties. Not commonly used.
Interrogatories (written questions submitted to another party to be answered in writing)	Presumptive limit of twenty-five interrogatories per party that can be submitted only to other parties. Very commonly used.	No interrogatories.

COMPARISON OF DISCOVERY IN FEDERAL CIVIL AND CRIMINAL CASES		
	Federal Rules of Civil Procedure	**Federal Rules of Criminal Procedure**
Requests for Production of Documents and Other Physical Evidence	No limit. Requested information can include electronically-stored information and access to real property for inspection. Very commonly used.	Defendant can request access to physical evidence (including any statements given by defendant) and can request a copy of defendant's prior criminal record. Federal rule permits either party to request prior relevant written statements of a witness, other than the defendant, who testified at trial; by federal statute, the defendant can request evidence of any prior statements of government witnesses that relate to the subject matter of the witness' testimony at trial. Very commonly used.
Request for Mental or Physical Examination of Person (for good cause, a party or a person under the control of a party may be ordered to submit to an exam)	Any party seeking an examination must first seek court approval and must be willing to share results of examination with person examined and other parties. Not commonly used (because parties typically use their own experts and/ or medical doctors who have already examined the person in question).	No comparable rule but a party may seek an order from court that a person be examined. Not commonly used.
Requests for Admission (assertions submitted to another party that must be admitted or denied)	No limit. Failure to respond in timely fashion causes assertion in requests to be deemed admitted. Commonly used.	No requests for admission.
Expert Witnesses	Plaintiff must disclose summary of expert witness testimony ninety days before trial. Defendant must disclose summary of rebuttal expert witness testimony thirty days before trial. Commonly used.	If requested by the opposing party, a party must disclose a summary of expert witness testimony the party intends to use. Commonly used.

COMPARISON OF DISCOVERY IN FEDERAL CIVIL AND CRIMINAL CASES		
	Federal Rules of Civil Procedure	**Federal Rules of Criminal Procedure**
Witness Identity	A list of all witnesses and exhibits that may be used at trial is to be exchanged 30 days before trial.	No comparable rule, but judges may order exchange of witness and exhibit lists.
Failure to Comply with Discovery Request	The court can order compliance and impose sanctions for subsequent failure to comply, up to and including awarding judgment against a party.	The court can grant a continuance of the trial date, prohibit introduction of the undisclosed evidence, or make "any other order that is just under the circumstances."

One justification for the prosecution's advantage in investigative power is the burden on the prosecution to prove its case. The prosecution must marshal sufficient evidence to survive a preliminary review of the evidence by a judge and ultimately must prove any criminal charge beyond a reasonable doubt if the case goes to trial; the defendant need only raise some reasonable doubt about the charges to avoid conviction. In carrying its burden, the prosecution may not compel the defendant to assist in his own prosecution. As mentioned above, a defendant has a right not to answer questions that might incriminate him. He can refuse to take the witness stand at trial, and even before trial he can refuse to answer police questions. (He cannot, however, refuse to participate in a line-up or give a blood sample, because those actions are not considered giving testimony against oneself.)

An important counterbalance to the disparity in investigative power between prosecutors and defendants is the requirement that prosecutors turn over to criminal defendants evidence that could help them win an acquittal or a lighter sentence. In 1963, the Supreme Court ruled that the "suppression by the prosecution of evidence favorable to an accused upon request violates due process where the evidence is material either to guilt or to punishment,"[12] In a subsequent case, the Court ruled that "obviously exculpatory" evidence should be disclosed by the prosecution even if the criminal defendant has

---

12   *Brady v. Maryland*, 373 U.S. 83, 87 (1963). Subsequent court opinions have defined "material" evidence to be evidence that is reasonably likely to impact the outcome in the case (or, stated alternatively, there is a reasonable probability the evidence would undermine confidence in a pro-prosecution outcome).

not requested it (as sometimes happens with inexperienced counsel).[13] The Supreme Court decisions set a lower limit on the protection that must be given to criminal defendants; state courts are free to provide more protection, and some states have done so by imposing a more stringent disclosure standard on state prosecutors.[14] In addition, if the prosecution learns that one of its witnesses may have perjured himself or otherwise presented false evidence, it is required to bring this possibility to the attention of the court and defendant.

It is difficult to know what information was learned during discovery in the *Kentucky v. Woodall* case because any exchange of information between the prosecution and Woodall's attorneys happened privately.[15] We do know from the public record in the case that pretrial motions were filed, and rulings on these motions likely played an important role in Woodall's decision to change his plea to guilty.

First, Woodall successfully moved to change venue from the Muhlenberg County Circuit Court to a court two counties away, the Caldwell County Circuit Court. The judge chose this county because it was outside the circulation territory of the local newspaper, which had heavily reported on Woodall's case). In light of the publicity associated with the crime (the judge called the publicity "massive . . . to the point of saturation") and the familiarity of many persons living in Muhlenberg County with the Hansen family, the judge concluded that it would be difficult to pick an impartial jury from this county.

This change of venue may have increased Woodall's confidence in taking his case to trial, but the judge's ruling on Woodall's motion to suppress evidence likely undercut that confidence. During a second search of Woodall's apartment, a police officer found a bag of bloody, wet and muddy clothes underneath Woodall's bed. Subsequent testing found that the blood on these clothes matched Sarah Hansen's blood type. Woodall moved to suppress this evidence on grounds that it had been planted in his apartment, but the judge ruled there was insufficient proof to reach that conclusion and refused

---

13   *United States v. Agurs*, 427 U.S. 97 (1976).

14   For instance, New York courts require that state prosecutors turn over any evidence for which there is a "reasonable possibility" that that the evidence is exculpatory. The New York courts have made this that this possibly exculpatory standard is broader and more protective of defendants than the Supreme Court's probably exculpatory standard.

15   We have an idea of what was learned in discovery in the *Promotion in Motion v. Beech-Nut* case because the parties laid out evidence obtained through discovery in connection with Beech-Nut's motion for summary judgment. However, summary judgment motions are not available in criminal cases. At Woodall's plea hearing, Woodall's attorney did state that the prosecution had shared statements of witness and forensic testing results, but no specific details about the information shared were disclosed.

to suppress the evidence.[16] In addition, shortly before trial was scheduled to begin, Woodall unsuccessfully moved the court to order (and pay for) a Positron Emission Topography ("PET") scan of his brain. His lawyers had hoped that they could use the scan to argue that Woodall hadn't truly understood what he was doing or that what he was doing was wrong and so he shouldn't be held fully accountable for his actions. These rulings were substantial setbacks for Woodall's case: the evidence seized from his apartment was obviously damning if the jury believed that it was in fact found in Woodall's apartment, and he would not have brain scan evidence to try to show that he suffered from a neurological disorder.

Were Woodall's Concerns About Pretrial Publicity Valid?

When criminal defendants fear that pretrial publicity about a crime will have biased community members against them and make selection of an impartial jury from that community impossible, they often request a change of venue. They may support the motion with the testimony of a social scientist who conducted a survey in the community gauging the level of public exposure to news about the case and assessing whether people in the community had formed opinions about the case. When these surveys are properly performed and reveal evidence of prejudice against the criminal defendant, they can provide strong support for a defendant's change of venue motion. Woodall's attorneys did not present such evidence, but they did not need it to convince the judge that there was a serious risk of prejudice in his case. His crime was notorious and extensively covered by the local media, and many in the community knew the victim and her family. There was thus a real risk that people selected for the jury from this community would have formed an opinion about whether Woodall committed the crime and an opinion about the proper punishment before the trial began. Under these circumstances, the trial judge felt obliged to move the case to give Woodall a better chance of being tried by an impartial jury.

Motions for change of venue will only be successful when there are special circumstances, such as those in the Woodall case, that pose a high risk that the defendant will not receive a fair trial. Trial judges are reluctant to

---

16   The Circuit Court judge denied this request because he concluded that the defense presented insufficient evidence to contest the conclusion of the prosecution's psychological expert that Woodall did not suffer from organic brain damage. At the hearing on the request for the PET scan, the defense presented the testimony of a psychological expert in support of the scan, but the court discounted this testimony because the expert spent limited time with Woodall, kept no notes of the interactions, and issued no written report.

move a trial from the community in which the crime occurred, because they believe that members of the affected community should participate in the process of determining guilt and assigning penalties for the crime. Judges can take some steps short of changing venue to protect against publicity that might undermine the integrity of the process. For instance, they occasionally ban the parties and their attorneys from discussing the case with media representatives and may require that some sensitive documents be filed under seal. However, because of the Constitution's guarantee of freedom of the press, the general rule is that the press must be allowed to review court records, attend court proceedings, and report on the trial.

Social scientists have conducted extensive research to determine whether defendants' concerns about the effects of pretrial publicity are valid. Many studies have found that pretrial publicity about criminal trials is much more likely to portray the defendants in a negative light than to portray them as wrongfully charged and that negative publicity does lead potential jurors to evaluate the defendant more harshly and lean more toward conviction. These negative effects are more likely to occur where the charged crime is murder, rape, or a drug offense. On the other hand, this research has found that few crimes receive enough pretrial publicity for these negative effects to be likely to occur. Given that Woodall's case did evoke much negative publicity about the crime and his past, the empirical research supports the trial judge's decision to move the location of Woodall's trial. For more information on empirical research on pretrial publicity, *see* Chapter 4 in Dennis J. Devine, *Jury Decision Making: The State of the Science* (New York University Press, 2012).

Three days after the court denied Woodall's motion for a PET scan, Woodall changed his plea to guilty. Guilty pleas must be given under oath, in person, before the judge. Before accepting a guilty plea, the judge must advise the defendant of basic constitutional rights that will be relinquished by pleading guilty, including the right to a jury trial and the right to confront and cross-examine the prosecution's witnesses. In addition, the judge must determine that the plea is being knowingly and voluntarily offered, meaning that the defendant understands the consequences of pleading guilty and has chosen to do so willingly, without coercion. The judge must also determine that there is a factual basis for the plea. In order to determine the factual basis, the defendant must testify, under oath, to the crimes he committed.[17]

The plea colloquy is recorded, and a transcript of Woodall's exchange with the judge is available on the book's website[18]. At the plea proceeding, the judge first notified Woodall of the charges he was facing (murder, kidnapping, and rape) and put into the record that the judge had received a motion signed by Woodall asking that he be allowed to change his plea from not guilty to guilty. Woodall confirmed that he had signed the motion, and the judge made clear that the plea being offered was a "conditional plea": Woodall was agreeing to plead guilty to the charged crimes, but he was not giving up his right to appeal a number of the trial judge's pretrial rulings, including the judge's refusal to delay trial to allow Woodall time to obtain a neurological evaluation. Then Woodall was sworn in and answered questions from the judge about his satisfaction with his counsel, his voluntary consent to the plea, and his understanding that he was waiving constitutional rights. In addition, Woodall swore that, on January 25, 1997, he committed murder by cutting Sarah Hansen with a sharp object and drowning her while engaged in the offense of rape, and he swore that he kidnapped Sarah Hansen and did not release her alive. Finally, he swore that he understood the consequences of his plea, namely, that he could be sentenced to between twenty years to life for the kidnapping and rape offenses and either to life without the benefit of parole for twenty-five years or to death for the murder offense. Satisfied that Woodall did commit the crimes to which he was pleading guilty and that he was voluntarily consenting to the plea, the trial judge accepted Woodall's plea of guilty.

With entry of this conditional guilty plea, Woodall's attorneys telegraphed that they intended to file an appeal of his case after he was sentenced, and all that remained to be done in the case at the trial court level was for a sentence to be set for each crime. Initially, Woodall consented to have the judge set his sentence without the recommendation of a jury, but he withdrew that consent and a sentencing trial before a jury was set. In the next chapter, we will examine what happens in criminal and civil trials, with particular attention to what happened in Woodall's sentencing trial and in the trial of Beech-Nut's claims against Promotion in Motion.

---

17   This requirement does not violate the Fifth Amendment privilege against self-incrimination because, by pleading guilty, the defendant has already incriminated himself.

18   www.amcourtsbook.com

Guilty Pleas and Plea Agreements

In the vast majority of criminal cases in the U.S., including Robert Woodall's, the verdict is determined not by a trial, but by a plea of guilty. Why do so many defendants plead guilty? Two facts go far toward answering this question. First, many charged defendants did in fact commit a crime. Second, every major actor involved in the typical defendant's case—the prosecutor, the judge, the defense attorney, and the defendant himself—has strong incentives to avoid a trial.

Judges, who must accept a guilty plea for a trial to be waived, have the easiest incentives to understand. Trial judges often must process hundreds of cases per year. Even a simple trial can take several days of court time. If more than a small percentage of cases go to trial, judges' dockets can quickly become hopelessly backlogged. Guilty pleas help clear dockets.

The incentives for defendants are perhaps the hardest to see at first. After all, by accepting a guilty plea, one forfeits any chance of an acquittal. But the chance of acquittal may be very small, and going to trial carries costs. The most obvious costs are huge legal fees for the minority of defendants who pay for their attorneys. But even the much larger group of defendants who are represented by assigned counsel or public defenders may suffer economic costs, such as lost wages from missed work. Perhaps even more importantly, a trial can mean public humiliation for oneself and one's family. These reasons may be strong enough in themselves for obviously guilty defendants to plead guilty. If an additional incentive is needed, the prosecutor can hold out the prospect of a lighter sentence than the defendant might receive if he went to trial. The prosecutor can do this either by agreeing to recommend a lighter sentence to the judge in return for a plea or by agreeing to drop or reduce the severity of one or more charges. For example, the prosecutor might agree to reduce a felony charge to a misdemeanor charge (which will cause fewer problems for the convicted defendant in the future) in exchange for a guilty plea.

Prosecutors' main reason for welcoming guilty pleas is the same as judges': they have more cases than their offices can handle. The same is true for public defenders. Lawyers also like guilty pleas because they eliminate the chance of a public defeat in the courtroom, something that can damage a private attorney's reputation among prospective clients, a prosecutor's re-election prospects, and any lawyer's ego.

These incentives can operate on attorneys even when they personally would be willing to spend extra time on a case. In the typical case, the attorneys on both sides will have encountered each other over and over again in the same courtroom before the same judge and will know that they are likely to do so many times in the future. Refusing to cooperate in this case may come back to haunt them in a later case where they really want to reach a deal. More subtly, having worked together so much (even if in opposition to each other), attorneys may come to see themselves as members of what scholars sometimes refer to as a courtroom "workgroup" or "community" and to internalize the norms and practices of that community. In most courtrooms, those norms and practices will include plea bargaining.

Another implication of courtroom workgroups is that plea bargaining will often not look much like what its name implies, with attorneys forcefully laying out their positions and exchanging offers and counter-offers. One scholar famously suggested the competing metaphors of a Middle Eastern bazaar and a supermarket, with plea agreements more often resembling shopping at the latter (see Malcolm M. Feeley, *Pleading Guilty in Lower Courts*, 13 LAW & SOCIETY REVIEW 461 (1978)). That is, when it comes to the less serious and more common crimes, such as drug possession, there is often a "going rate" for a particular type of offense, and bargaining—which often takes just a few minutes—is mostly a matter of identifying the type.

For most participants in and observers of the legal system, it is hard to imagine getting by without a high rate of plea agreements. Nevertheless, the facts we have just described raise red flags for many. If lawyers are too ready to reach plea agreements and judges are too ready to accept them, then some defendants will receive more lenient punishments than they deserve, while others will accept unduly harsh sentences or, worst of all, plead guilty despite being innocent. Critics who worry about injustices toward defendants often point in particular to the practice of "overcharging," where prosecutors bring questionable charges only in order to bargain them away later, so that the defendant pleads guilty but ends up with no better a sentence than he probably would have received if he had gone to trial. ■

The Trial

We come at last to the trial, which many believe to be the centerpiece of the American judicial system. This belief is true in one respect and false in another. It is false in the sense that very few civil or criminal cases actually make it to trial. On the other hand, the rarity of trial is due in large part to the fear of what might happen there, a fear that motivates many civil parties to settle their cases before trial and many criminal defendants to plea bargain and ultimately enter a plea of guilty. The prospect of trial looms large in every civil and criminal case, affecting all decisions made in the case from its initial filing up through whether or not to seek an appeal to a higher court if a party loses in the trial court. So even though trials are rare, it is impossible to understand the American judicial system without considering the looming significance of the trial. And it is impossible to understand trials in the American system without considering the role played by ordinary citizens when they serve as jurors in trials.

Trial by Jury

Juries were brought over to the colonies from Britain and have been considered a fundamental part of the American judicial system ever since. The right to a jury trial was written into the Sixth Amendment (criminal cases) and Seventh Amendment (civil cases) of the U.S. Constitution. Juries are so familiar to Americans that it can be easy to take their prominent role in the legal system for granted. But a little thought shows that the need for juries is far from self-evident, that in fact the practice of using juries is even a bit odd. Consider, for instance, how disputes are handled in sports. The contestants in a college basketball game disagree about whether a player traveled before letting a shot go. Do they ask twelve randomly selected Americans to rule on the play? Maybe the idea seems ridiculous only because the call must be made immediately. But what about a claim that one of the players who participated in the game wasn't eligible to do so? It might take weeks to decide that, but we can't imagine the NCAA asking twelve ordinary people to make the decision. One reason is that fans might be biased toward their teams. But we could make sure to disqualify fans of either team or of other teams in their conference. We could even limit the group of decision makers to people who don't care for basketball. "But," you're likely to say, "that's nuts. Those people don't know the rules of basketball and have no experience with this type of issue." Those characteristics—the lack of specialized knowledge and experience—are precisely the characteristics of an ordinary jury in a legal proceeding.

Asking people with limited expertise and experience to make difficult decisions carries obvious risks: that they won't approach the decisions in the right way and that, even if they do, they will have trouble making sound decisions. On the other hand, it's also easy to see the advantages of juries. There is the old adage that two heads are better than one: they are more likely to pick up on important details and to notice and correct mistakes in recall or reasoning. Six heads, or twelve, should be better still. Similarly, multiple decision makers bring more perspectives to a case, increasing the probability that someone will understand some aspect of it that might be difficult for a single decision maker and allowing the worldviews and biases of individuals to cancel each other out in a way that's not possible with just one judge. Judges are already spread thin in many jurisdictions, and to bring a number of them together to decide a case would cause terrible delays in other cases. If we wish to have group deliberation over cases, we have to turn to the general population.

Having ordinary people decide cases brings other advantages, too. Especially in criminal cases, we think of the jury as the voice and conscience of the community, judging the defendant's offense against the community. Choosing a group of people rather than a single person to stand for the community makes it more likely that the decision maker will be representative of the community. Moreover, at least some of those people—unlike the judge—will not be employees of the same state that is seeking to put the defendant in prison. They stand as an important protection against the awesome power of the state.

All of those things in favor of juries being said, the worry that they won't be up to the job is a very real one. This concern is reflected in the fact that no other country in the world employs lay decision makers in its court system as much as the United States does. Japan, for instance, did not use lay jurors at all between 1943 and 2009, and when it reintroduced them, it was as members of combined layperson-judge panels. This practice of having laypeople and professional judges decide cases together is common in continental Europe, too. Regardless of whether lay jurors decide by themselves or as part of a team with judges, in most countries where they participate it is only in trials of the most serious crimes.

The differences between the U.S. and other countries are even starker on the civil side. Most countries never allow juries in civil cases, and they are extremely rare where they are allowed. Even in England—the source of our right to trial by jury—the right is now limited to a fairly small subset of civil cases.[1]

Although Americans stand out from the people of other countries in their embrace of juries, they too have reservations about juries, as reflected in numerous policies and practices that limit the ability of parties to have a case tried by a jury and by the fact that many parties choose to settle or plea bargain their cases before trial. For instance, the Administrative Office of the U.S. Courts reports that nearly 261,000 civil cases filed in federal district courts terminated in the year ending in March 2014 but that only 2157 of these cases went to trial before a jury.[2] Many of these cases were settled by the litigants; in fact, there was no judicial involvement in a quarter of them. Still, of 27,000 cases that made it to pre-trial proceedings, fewer than 10% made it to a jury. It is important to understand that even in the U.S. jury trials are fairly unusual events.

There are several reasons for this. First, the Supreme Court has interpreted the Constitution's guarantees of jury trials to have narrower scope than the Constitution's language might suggest. It has ruled that the Sixth Amendment right extends to prosecutions in both federal and state courts but is limited to trials for "serious crimes," defined as those carrying possible sentences of six months or more in prison.[3] The right to a jury in civil cases is more limited. Most importantly, the Supreme Court has never ruled that the Seventh Amendment right to a civil jury extends to proceedings in state courts, except when state courts hear claims based on federal law. The right to

---

1   Sally Lloyd-Bostock and Cheryl Thomas. 1999. "Decline of the 'Little Parliament': Juries and Jury Reform in England and Wales." *Law and Contemporary Problems* 62:7-40.

2   http://www.uscourts.gov/Statistics/FederalJudicialCaseloadStatistics/caseload-statistics-2014.aspx

3   *See, e.g., Cheff v. Schnackenberg* 384 U.S. 373 (1966).

a jury in a state civil case involving claims based on state law depends on the constitution and statutes of that state.[4]

Second, the numbers reflect the choices of litigants. The right to a jury trial can be waived, with litigants choosing to have the judge decide the case, in what is called a *bench trial*. You might be surprised at how many cases are tried by judges rather than juries. Between April 2013 and March 2014, 943 civil cases filed in federal courts were tried before a judge while 2,157 civil cases were tried before juries. Juries were favored a bit more in criminal cases tried in federal court, with juries trying 2,053 criminal defendants and judges trying 262 criminal defendants.[5]

The third reason why juries decide fewer cases than one might expect is that judges often do not allow juries to decide cases even where there is a right to a jury trial. We discussed in Chapter 3 how parties can use motions for summary judgment to dispose of claims without a trial. Even after the trial has begun, parties may ask the judge to rule that the evidence is insufficient to submit the case to the jury for a decision. A judge can even substitute her own judgment for the jury's *after* all of the evidence has been presented and the jury has rendered its verdict. This happens where the judge had hoped that the jury would issue a verdict consistent with the judge's dim view of the evidence, but the jury failed to do so. In such cases, if the verdict reached by the jury was not, in the view of the judge, reasonably supported by the evidence, then the judge can overturn the jury's verdict and enter a judgment in favor of the party that lost. However, this power to direct a verdict in favor of one party during trial or to overturn the jury verdict is supposed to be used sparingly, reserved for those cases where the judge is convinced that no reasonable jury could find in favor of one of the civil parties or in favor of the prosecution.

Unless you read the last paragraph very closely, it might have escaped your attention that there is an asymmetry to these judicial interventions in criminal cases that is not present in civil cases. In civil cases, the judge can intervene and rule in favor of either the plaintiff or the defendant. But in criminal cases, the judge can only intervene and enter a judgment in favor of the defendant. This asymmetry reflects the much higher burden of proof in criminal cases: a jury can only convict a defendant if the evidence of guilt is

---

4   Recall from Chapter 2 that state courts may decide claims based on federal law unless those claims have been exclusively reserved for federal courts.

5   In these cases, juries acquitted 247 defendants and judges acquitted 95 defendants, and juries convicted 1,806 defendants and judges convicted 167 defendants. To bring home how rare taking a case all the way through trial is, consider that during the same year in the federal courts, 6,977 criminal cases were dismissed with no conviction entered and 80,111 criminal cases were concluded by entry of a guilty plea.

"beyond a reasonable doubt," whereas a plaintiff in a civil case can prevail by showing that the evidence more likely than not favors the plaintiff. Given the high threshold for conviction, it would be inappropriate for a judge to conclude that a jury has acted unreasonably in acquitting a defendant, while there is much room for the judge to conclude that the evidence in favor of conviction is so weak that reasonable doubt obviously exists. Additionally, where a criminal defendant has a right to have the community determine whether he deserves punishment, we do not want a judge substituting her judgment for that of the community—indeed, judges rarely intervene even in weak cases without first giving the jury the chance to acquit. For these reasons, the right to trial by jury is more robust in criminal cases than civil cases. (As we will discuss in the next chapter that covers appeals from trial court decisions, the Double Jeopardy Clause bars the prosecution from appealing a jury verdict in favor of a criminal defendant.)

When the judge takes a case away from a jury and rules for one of the parties, either during the presentation of evidence to the jury or after the jury has issued its verdict, we say that the judge has entered judgment "as a matter of law." The power of the judge to do this illustrates the ambivalence we feel about American juries. On the one hand, we prize the right to a jury so much that it is protected in the U.S. Constitution. On the other hand, we fear that juries may err in their assessments of the evidence, so we give judges some oversight power to decide a case where the facts are very clear or where it appears that the jury has made an egregious mistake about the facts. The idea is that where the evidence is so clear the judge can decide the case by simply applying the law to these clear facts.[6]

The phrase "as a matter of law" points to a traditional distinction in American courts between questions of fact and questions of law. To see the difference, think of a typical first degree murder case. Before we can convict someone of first degree murder, we have to decide whether the defendant killed the victim and, if so, whether he formed the intention to kill before the actual encounter with the victim. These are questions of fact. But you might find yourself asking, "Why are those the particular factual questions we need

---

6   For many years, both federal and state courts referred to a motion asking the judge to rule on the sufficiency of evidence during trial as a "motion for a directed verdict," but in 1991 the Federal Rules of Civil Procedure were amended to refer to this motion as a "motion for judgment as a matter of law." In criminal cases, such a motion is called a "motion for judgment of acquittal." Some state courts and many attorneys still refer to this motion as a motion for a directed verdict in both civil and criminal cases. A motion asking the judge to overturn a jury's verdict on grounds that it cannot be supported by the evidence is called a "renewed motion for judgment as a matter of law" in civil cases (in criminal cases, a motion filed after the jury's verdict retains the label "motion for judgment of acquittal").

to decide?" Legislators issue laws that specify which sets of facts constitute crimes, from first degree murder down to illegal possession of drugs, and these laws supply the factual questions that a jury must answer.[7] The general rule in American courts is that questions about which laws to apply and how to interpret those laws are left to the judge to decide, while questions of facts are for the jury to decide.

Constraining Juries

You can see this division of labor in Judge Martini's instructions to the jury in *Promotion in Motion v. Beech Nut*. The judge determines what law governs the case and then, based on that law, formulates instructions for jurors on what questions of fact they must decide and how to evaluate the evidence to decide which version of the facts to accept. Jury instructions are always given at the close of the trial, after the parties have finished presenting evidence; many judges also give instructions at the beginning of the trial to help the jury evaluate the evidence they are about to see, as Judge Martini did for the Beech-Nut jury.

Using words that might be heard in any courtroom in the U.S., Judge Martini told the jurors:

> It's your duty to accept these instructions of law and apply them to the facts as you determine those facts to be. Again, on legal matters you must take the law as I give it to you. If any attorney has stated a principle of law that's contrary to what my instructions are, it's these instructions that are binding and you must adhere to my instructions...

> Now, you should not be concerned about the wisdom of any rule that I may instruct you on. Regardless of any opinion you may have as to what the law may be or ought to be, it would violate your sworn duty to base a verdict on any other view of the law than that which I give to you.[8]

---

7   We touched on this issue in Chapter 2, when we discussed how civil parties are supposed to allege facts that support the legally-required elements of a civil claim (e.g., the elements of a breach of contract claim), and the prosecutor is supposed to be able to present enough evidence to convince a judge that there is probable cause to believe all of the elements of the criminal charges can be satisfied (e.g., the elements of a first-degree murder charge). Questions about the proper elements of a civil claim or criminal charge are questions of law; whether the civil defendant or criminal defendant engaged in behavior that violated a civil or criminal law are questions of fact.

8   Transcript, Part 3, p. 42.

Jury instructions are one of the main ways that judges try to make sure that jurors decide the right factual questions using the right evidence. The ultimate question in any case is not whether the jurors like one civil party more than the other or whether they think the criminal defendant is a bad person; the ultimate question is whether the law was violated. Jury instructions explain the elements of a civil claim or criminal charge to the jury and direct the jurors how to evaluate the evidence to see if the facts fit these elements.

In addition to jury instructions on the elements of the law relevant to the case, the parties can request instructions on other matters that could affect how the jurors evaluate the evidence. For instance, at Mr. Woodall's sentencing trial to determine whether he should be given the death penalty, Mr. Woodall chose not to testify, as was his right under the Fifth Amendment privilege against self-incrimination. His attorneys asked the trial judge, Judge Cunningham, to instruct the jury that "[a] defendant is not compelled to testify and the fact that the defendant did not testify should not prejudice him in any way." Judge Cunningham refused to give this instruction to the jury because he believed it was neither appropriate nor required by the law. A proposed instruction such as this, if accepted by the judge, can help the parties influence how the jury evaluates the evidence. If the instruction is not accepted, the party has now created an issue that can be used on appeal after the trial is over. Woodall's attorneys knew that if the outcome of the sentencing trial went against him, he could appeal that outcome to a court of appeals, arguing that the trial outcome should be reversed because Judge Cunningham erred in refusing to give the requested instruction.

The other main way that judges constrain jurors and try to focus them on the right questions is through the use of rules of evidence. Anyone who has seen a trial depicted in a TV show or movie, with lawyers leaping to their feet to object to some question or piece of evidence, is familiar at least with the Hollywood version of the rules of evidence. The rules of evidence are a type of procedural law governing what evidence can be used at a trial. Many of the rules of evidence are designed to prevent the parties from using irrelevant or unreliable evidence to win a case. For instance, you have surely seen a TV lawyer object to evidence as "hearsay." The hearsay objection is used to prevent a witness from repeating in court something that someone else said out of court, on the theory that, since the jurors did not see the speaker when the statement was made, they will have difficulty evaluating the meaning and credibility of that statement. So the hearsay rule aims to prevent the use of potentially misleading evidence in court. An example of an evidence rule aimed at preventing jurors from basing their decision on the wrong reasons is the character evidence rule, which prevents parties from putting on evidence that a party in the case was a good or bad person. Although there are some exceptions, in general we do not allow the prosecutor to argue that the jury should convict a criminal defendant because he is obviously a mean person with a criminal disposition. Rather, we want the prosecutor to put on evidence that the criminal defendant committed the specific crime charged. If the prosecutor does not have sufficient evidence that the defendant committed this crime, then he should be acquitted, even if he is a very bad person.

Hearsay

The technical definition of hearsay is evidence of a statement made outside of the courtroom that is offered for the truth of the matter asserted in the statement. Suppose a police officer at Woodall's trial testified that a friend of Woodall's told the officer that he saw Woodall murder Sarah Hansen. If that statement was offered to prove that Woodall did in fact murder Hansen, the police officer's repetition of the friend's out-of-court statement would violate the hearsay rule. However, this evidence would nevertheless be admissible if an exception to the hearsay rule applied, and there are many exceptions to the hearsay rule. For instance, if the police had reached Sarah Hansen just before she died and she told the police who had attacked her, her statements would fit under the "dying declarations" exception to the hearsay rule.

Other rules of evidence prevent the jury from hearing evidence, not because the evidence is unreliable or misleading, but because allowing the evidence to be used would interfere with some public policy that is considered just as important as reaching the correct result at trial. A prominent example of an evidence rule like this is the attorney-client privilege, which prevents an opposing party from using evidence from communications between a client and her attorney. If you are accused of a crime and you confess to your attorney that you did in fact commit the crime, allowing the jury to hear about that confession would surely help the jury make the correct decision in the case. But thanks to the attorney-client privilege, the prosecuting attorney will not be allowed to put your attorney on the witness stand and ask whether or not you confessed to the crime. The idea behind the attorney-client privilege is that the attorney and client need a zone of privacy in which they can candidly discuss the facts and law so that the attorney can offer good advice on how to handle the case.

Judges also sometimes exclude evidence because it was obtained improperly. The exclusion, or "suppression," of evidence happens mostly in criminal cases, where suppression protects a criminal defendant's constitutional rights, especially the Fourth Amendment right to be free of unreasonable searches and seizures and the Fifth Amendment right not to be compelled to be a witness against oneself. (The famous "Miranda warning" about the right to remain silent and the right to an attorney comes from *Miranda v. Arizona*, where the Court concluded that the Fifth and Sixth Amendments require such a warning).[9] If a police officer obtains evidence through an illegal search or by asking questions of someone in custody without first administering the Miranda warning, then the judge can exclude the evidence to vindicate the criminal defendant's rights and to deter future misconduct in violation of these constitutional amendments.

Although some questions about the admissibility of evidence are handled in the midst of the trial, making for great drama, many important evidentiary questions are resolved right before the trial by agreement of the parties or through what is called a *motion in limine* (meaning a motion on the threshold of trial). With a motion in limine, a party asks a judge to decide whether or not a piece of evidence will be admissible at trial. Motions in limine are usually used with very important pieces of evidence and for evidentiary issues that the judge may need additional time to consider. The judge's ruling may determine whether the parties are willing to settle the case before the trial rather than incur the risk and expense of trial. And if a question about evidence requires the reading of many legal cases and serious deliberation on the judge's part, it would be inefficient to wait on the question and then interrupt the trial for an extended period while the judge deliberates. Efficiency concerns encourage the resolution of important and complicated evidentiary questions before a trial starts.

A pretrial order worked out by the parties and the judge paves the way for a more efficient trial by setting out the parameters of the case: what the key issues are, what facts the two sides agree and disagree about, what witnesses will be heard from, and what physical evidence will be offered (e.g., the murder weapon, or correspondence between the parties). The facts that the two sides

---

9   Rules of evidence apply in jury trials and *bench trials* (or trials where the judge serves as the fact finder), but most judges apply the rules less stringently in bench trials out of a belief that they are less susceptible to misleading evidence than a jury of laypersons.

agree on are set out in what are called stipulations. These stipulations are read to the jury during the trial, and the jurors are told that they may rely on these stipulated facts as evidence when making their decision. You might imagine it would be nearly impossible to get the two sides to stipulate to anything important. But in reality it is not unusual for the parties to be fairly cooperative, if only to avoid antagonizing the judge now and the jury later. As you will see if you review the full pre-trial order from the Promotion in Motion case (available on the book's website), there were forty-seven stipulated facts in the pretrial order from the Fruit Nibbles case, and a number of them concerned important facts. For instance, Stipulations 31 through 34 described complaints from customers that the jury could now accept as true. Stipulation 35 stated, "The Fruit Nibbles product complained of as described above did not satisfy the warranties in the purchase orders." In other words, Promotion in Motion conceded before the trial started that some of the Fruit Nibbles were of unacceptable quality. (What Promotion in Motion denied was that the inadequate Nibbles were numerous enough to "substantially impair the value" of all the Fruit Nibbles sold to Beech-Nut.)

Preparation of the pretrial order requires attorneys to crystallize the issues in a case and specify the evidence they plan to use. This crystallization process, along with rulings the judge makes on motions in limine, will often reduce uncertainty about case outcomes. The more closely the two sides agree about the probabilities of various outcomes, the more likely they are to agree on a resolution and spare themselves the expense of a trial. For this reason, settlements are commonly reached at the pre-trial order stage.

Still, parties' predictions do not always converge, and sometimes emotions, principles, or long-term strategy push parties toward trial even though a settlement was possible. If the parties do insist on going forward after the pre-trial order is issued, then unless the case is to be decided by bench trial, the next step is to select a jury.

Jury Selection

Most people, when they think of an American jury, picture twelve people. Twelve is the traditional size of a jury, and criminal cases in federal courts and many state courts are indeed heard by twelve-person juries. Twelve people served on the jury that recommended the death penalty for Woodall. However, smaller juries are not unusual. In federal court and in many state courts, parties can agree to a jury as small as six. In 1970, the Supreme Court ruled that the right to a jury trial, even in a criminal case, is not violated so long as at least six people sit on the jury.[10] The Woodall jury consisted of twelve people, but Beech-Nut and Promotion in Motion agreed to a jury of eight.

The selection of six to twelve jurors begins with the random drawing of names from a jury pool, the set of all people in a community who are eligible for jury service. Nowadays we expect the jury pool to be made up of all adults in the community, excepting only those who are physically or intellectually incapable of serving or those who are excluded because of their occupations or criminal history. (In states where felons are not allowed to vote, they usually are not allowed to serve on juries either.) For much of America's history, much stricter limitations were placed on jury duty. Until well into the 20th century, minorities and women were frequently prevented from serving on juries. The use of what was called the "key man" system operated to further restrict who could serve on a jury.[11] In the key man system, the jury pool was created through a selection process reminiscent of a gentlemen's club's. The clerk of the court (i.e., the person in charge of administrative matters for a court) would invite members of the community who were thought to possess integrity and sound judgment to join the jury pool. Those people would in turn nominate others until there were enough names in the pool to serve the community's purposes. The key man system persisted in many federal courts until 1968, when Congress banned it, and in some state courts until 1975, when the Supreme Court ruled that the 6th Amendment guaranteed a "jury drawn from a fair cross-section of the community."[12]

Today all jurisdictions define their jury pool as the general population located within the federal judicial district (for federal court trials) or county (for state court trials). Names of potential jurors are drawn from voter registration lists, driver license records, and tax returns. The exact methods used vary across jurisdictions, as do rules about what occupations are excluded from jury duty and the reasons for which one may be excused from jury duty.[13] For these reasons, the jury pool is never perfectly representative of the community, and it is less so in some places than in others. Still, it is reasonable to think of those called for jury duty as a random sample of the adult population.

---

10   *Williams v. Florida*, 399 U.S. 78 (1970)

11   Described in Irving R. Kaufman. 1967. "A Fair Jury——The Essence of Justice." Judicature 51:88-92

12   *Taylor v. Louisiana*, 419 U.S. 522 (1975)

13   For example, government officials, members of the armed forces, firefighters, and police officers cannot serve on juries in federal courts. See http://www.uscourts.gov/services-forms/jury-service/juror-qualifications

What happens once they report for duty, though, is far from random. Instead, the people who serve on the jury in a particular case are selected through a process of questioning and challenges called *voir dire*.

The purpose of voir dire, as the judge and legal system see it, is to produce a jury that is open-minded, fair, and conscientious. From the attorney's point of view, the purpose of voir dire is to produce a jury that is favorably disposed toward the attorney's client. Good lawyers and savvy litigants take this opportunity to shape the jury seriously and may even hire expensive jury consultants to help decide what kind of people would be best for the jury. Still, it is important to understand that lawyers do not have as much control over the composition of the jury as popular culture sometimes suggests. In fact, even the term "jury selection" is misleading, as the only power lawyers have is a negative one: to exclude—or seek to exclude—potential jurors.

Exactly how much influence lawyers have on the makeup of the jury depends on a number of things, including the particular jurisdiction's rules on voir dire and the attitude of the presiding judge. During voir dire, prospective jurors are quizzed about their backgrounds, possible relationships to the parties, and attitudes to determine whether there is any reason they should not serve on the jury. Often jurors will have filled out a questionnaire providing basic information about themselves, or the judge will begin jury selection with a set of basic questions designed to eliminate people who have an obvious connection to the case or whose work or family situation will not permit them to serve for the whole trial. The judge will then ask additional questions submitted by the attorneys or will allow the attorneys to question the potential jurors themselves. Questions will typically be asked of the whole group, with follow-up questions for individual jurors, depending on how they respond to the general questions. Some prospective jurors might even be interviewed privately if the judge permits, usually to avoid unnecessary embarrassment or to prevent other potential jurors from hearing something that might bias them against one of the parties.[14]

Let us use the Woodall case to illustrate the jury selection process. There voir dire began with seventy-four potential jurors, to be whittled down to fourteen (twelve jurors and two alternates, who would serve if one or two of the first twelve had to drop out). Each potential juror was questioned individually by

---

14   For more on variation in voir dire practices, see Valerie P. Hans and Alayna Jehle. 2003. "Avoid Bald Men and People with Green Socks–Other Ways to Improve the Voir Dire Process in Jury Selection." *Chicago-Kent Law Review* 78:1179-1201.

the judge and attorneys for both sides.[15] Here is an excerpt from the questioning of one prospective juror. It revolves around a crucial issue for voir dire in any capital case: whether the prospective juror is willing to impose the death penalty. Note that in court, the jurors were addressed by name; we omit their names here to protect their privacy. When the transcript refers to "the Court," it indicates a question or statement by the trial judge.

> THE COURT: Ms. H, if you find beyond a reasonable doubt the existence of certain aggravating factors there will be a range of penalties for you to consider . . . Would your personal beliefs prevent you or substantially impair you from considering and imposing any of these five punishments if instructed to do so by the court and you found it was warranted by the evidence? Do you understand the question?
>
> Ms. H: Yeah, I think so.
>
> THE COURT: Will you be able to consider each of these penalties involved in this case?
>
> Ms. H: I think so.
>
> THE COURT: Would you automatically vote for any of these particular penalties?
>
> Ms. H: Yes.
>
> THE COURT: You would automatically vote for one of them?
>
> Ms. H: Yes, I would.
>
> THE COURT: And what penalty would that be?
>
> Ms. H: I'd say maybe 25 years.
>
> THE COURT: Alright, You're saying that you would vote for 25 years--
>
> Ms. H: Without parole.

---

15   John Lucas. "Panel Picked for Woodall Sentencing." *The Evansville Courier.* July 15, 1998.

...

THE COURT: Alright. Are you telling us that that's what you would vote for if you had to determine a sentence right now based on what the charges are and what he's pled guilty to? Is that what you're saying.

Ms. H: Yeah.

THE COURT: If you're selected as a juror and each side presents evidence and the Court instructed you that you are to consider all these different penalties, would you be able to consider all those penalties and not automatically at the time impose the sentence of life without parole for 25 years?

Ms. H: It could be considered.

THE COURT: Alright, but do you think you could consider the entire range of penalties based--and make your determination based upon the evidence?

Ms. H: Yes.

THE COURT: In other words, when I say you would not automatically or would you automatically set a certain sentence, I want to know that if you heard the evidence that was presented to you by both sides in this case would you be willing to not set a sentence automatically, but consider the entire range of penalties?

Ms. H: I think it should be considered, the entire range.

THE COURT: Did any of this that you've read about cause you to formulate this opinion--you indicated that you had a notion it should be life without parole for 25 years I think. That's a notion we're talking about. Was this based upon what you read and heard about this case?

Ms. H: Yes.

THE COURT: And would you be able to disregard anything you may have read or heard and decide this case solely on the evidence and consider this entire penalty range? Would you be able to do that?

Ms. H: Well, if it comes up, it all depends.

THE COURT: Depends on what?

Ms. H: The evidence.

…

PROSECUTOR: Do you have any religious beliefs or feelings against any of those range of punishments?

 MS. H: I don't like capital punishment.

THE PROSECUTOR: Pardon me?

Ms. H: Not capital, not you know, not the chair.

THE PROSECUTOR: I'm sorry?

Ms. H: I couldn't go for the chair.

THE PROSECUTOR: Are you opposed to--does your belief, your feelings inside you prevent you from really considering the death penalty?

Ms. H: No, I wouldn't consider that.

THE PROSECUTOR: You could not consider that.

Ms. H: Uh-uh.

Shortly after this exchange, out of the presence of Ms. H, the prosecutor moved to dismiss Ms. H from the jury panel. The conversation between the attorneys and judge went like this:

THE PROSECUTOR: The Commonwealth moves to have Ms. H struck for cause. I'd like for the record to reflect that on each occasion she was sitting in the chair she did not look at the questioner unless you asked her to. She was looking in the opposite direction and thought she was talking to --I know when she started talking to --she was looking at Mr. B when you were talking to her and that Mr. B was talking to her and looked the same way as well. She's 78 years of age and she did say that she was opposed to the death penalty and could not impose it.

THE COURT: Any response?

DEFENSE COUNSEL: Judge, she is an elderly black woman, but she--under questioning by counsel she said that she could follow the law as you--as you instructed her to do and could consider the death penalty, and I don't see much difference in her and Ms. P and a couple of others that we've---she seemed to understand all the questions also, your honor. She did respond. So we would motion that she stay on.

THE COURT: This juror has problems. I don't know what they were, but she--as Mr. Vick indicated she either didn't see--she didn't perceive where the questions were coming from. She was looking at people that were not asking her questions. I think she's going to have problems following the evidence first. She's 78 years old. Something wasn't right about her. I think she's not--arguably she has a pretty good recall of what she read, but she wasn't connecting here some way or another, and I think she would have said almost anything. She basically answered the questions I asked the way she thought I wanted to when she said she could not consider the death penalty, she said it with conviction, and I think that she is not qualified to serve. So I'm going to grant the motion over the objection of defense counsel.

This is an example of a successful *challenge for cause*. In a challenge for cause, an attorney argues that the prospective juror cannot be trusted to decide the case fairly or with a sufficiently open mind. Perhaps the case involves a car accident and the prospective juror was once in a serious accident or had a memorably unpleasant experience with an insurance company. Or perhaps the prospective juror is friendly with a defendant or a member of the defense legal team. It may even be that the prospective juror displays hostility toward one of the parties in language or demeanor. But as the judge's questions to Ms. H indicate, judges give jurors every chance to say they will keep an open mind so that the judge can avoid dismissing them for cause.

If Ms. H had said that she knew the victim well and would have difficulty fairly evaluating the evidence in the case, her dismissal would have been unremarkable. A dismissal for opposition to capital punishment is more controversial. There are many people in the U.S. who, like Ms. H, oppose the death penalty. The routine removal of such people from juries in death-penalty-eligible cases necessarily results in a jury that is not representative of the entire community in its views on capital punishment. You might even wonder whether a jury composed only of people who accept the death penalty is representative of the community's views about crime and punishment more generally. The Supreme Court considered a challenge to the exclusion of opponents of the death penalty from juries and concluded that such exclusions were proper because blanket opposition to the death penalty could "prevent or substantially impair the performance of [someone's] duties as a juror."[16] Therefore, Woodall's rights were not infringed by the exclusion of Ms. H from the jury that would recommend whether or not he should be put to death for his crimes.

Attorneys are allowed an unlimited number of challenges for cause, but there is an important catch: the judge decides whether to exclude the challenged juror. Many challenges for cause are not successful. Woodall's attorneys had at least six challenges rejected by the judge. (There may have been more, but it was only these six for which we have a record, since they were the ones raised in his appeal to a higher court.) One unsuccessful challenge was of someone who, for several months between the murder and the trial, worked in the store from which Sarah Hansen had been abducted. Woodall's lawyers claimed that she had heard the case discussed by other employees while there and could not approach his case with an open mind as a result. Another woman unsuccessfully challenged by Woodall's attorneys had a daughter who had been in the high school band with Sarah Hansen and a sister who had been raped by someone who was never apprehended.

The first of these women ended up on the jury, but the second did not. Woodall's lawyers were able to keep her off the jury by exercising a second type of challenge called a *peremptory challenge*. Unlike challenges for cause, peremptory challenges are limited in number. In the Woodall case, each side had ten.[17] In the numerical sense, then, peremptory challenges are more limited than challenges for cause. But peremptory challenges are more expansive in

---

16   *Wainwright v. Witt*, 469 U.S. 412 (1985).

17   States vary in their treatment of peremptory challenges. Each side in a federal civil trial gets three peremptory challenges, but the judge may grant more in cases involving many parties or for other reasons. In a federal criminal trial, the presumptive number of peremptory challenges depends on the nature of the crimes charged: when a federal prosecutor seeks capital punishment, each side gets twenty peremptory

that they can be exercised for any reason at all (with a few important exceptions that we will explain shortly) and ordinarily do not need to be explained to the judge and do not require the judge's approval.

You can easily see why attorneys value peremptory challenges: they allow parties to exclude potential jurors who worry them but who are not so obviously biased against one of the parties that they can be excluded for cause. This makes sense from society's point of view as well. After all, we want jurors to be fair and impartial, and the judge may sometimes miss something about people that makes them poor choices to serve on a particular jury. This risk exists even though jurors answer questions during voir dire under oath and are theoretically subject to perjury charges if they lie. The reality is that potential jurors often give misleading if not outright false information during voir dire[18] but are rarely indicted for perjury. Peremptory challenges can help eliminate jurors who seem deceptive or appear to be biased in some way that was not clearly brought out through the voir dire process. Allowing parties the right to construct a jury they are comfortable with should also increase acceptance of the jury's verdict. Peremptory challenges can therefore be seen as an important way of making the right to a trial by a jury more meaningful to the parties.

But peremptory challenges have a serious downside, too. Because they do not have to be justified unless there is an objection, there is no way to ensure that they are being used to eliminate problematic jurors rather than jurors who are perfectly fit to serve but are not the type lawyers want to see on their jury. In other words, peremptory challenges allow attorneys to manipulate the composition of the jury based on their views or stereotypes of whole groups of people rather than on what a particular potential juror said during voir dire. (Of course, challenges for cause are also directed at people lawyers don't want to see on the jury, and lawyers try to save favored jurors who are challenged by the other side. But remember that the judge ultimately makes the call with challenges for cause after the parties explain their concerns.) For instance, perhaps an attorney has the idiosyncratic view that men with long hair are not to be trusted and thus always exercises peremptory strikes against long-haired men. Or perhaps an attorney believes that women are always biased in favor of the plaintiff in sexual harassment cases and uses peremptory challenges to

challenges; in non-capital felony cases, the prosecutor gets six peremptory challenges and the defendant gets ten; in misdemeanor cases, each side gets three peremptory challenges.

18   For instance, one study based on interviews conducted after voir dire found that over a quarter of the jurors had been a victim of a crime or had family members who were victims of crime but didn't disclose this information at voir dire when asked. Seltzer, Richard, Mark A. Venuti, and Grace M. Lopes. 1991. "Juror Honesty During the Voir Dire." *Journal of Criminal Justice* 19:451-62.

exclude as many women as possible from the jury. Should we allow the use of peremptory challenges that are based on views about whole groups of people?

In a series of decisions between 1986 and 1994, the Supreme Court considered the use of peremptory challenges based on the sex or race of potential jurors and ruled that such challenges violated the Constitution.[19] In particular, the Court ruled that it violated the rights of the potential jurors, not the parties, to be excluded from juries because of their race or sex. The Court reasoned that citizens should have an equal right to serve on a jury and that when a trial court grants a peremptory challenge that was based on a potential juror's race or sex, it endorses illegal discrimination against that person. After these rulings by the Supreme Court, it is impermissible to exclude persons from juries based on their race or sex. Some lower courts have extended the Court's ruling to apply as well to a juror's ethnicity and religion. Note, though, that potential jurors with biased views can be excluded from a jury for cause even if their views originate in some way in their sex, race, ethnicity, or religion. And since hair length is not a protected characteristic under the Constitution, peremptory challenges can be based on idiosyncratic views about the trustworthiness of long-haired males, at least so long as that is not just a pretext for keeping males off the jury.

The decisions by the Supreme Court and lower courts that peremptory challenges cannot be used to exclude certain groups from juries raise a difficult question for trial judges and trial attorneys: since parties do not have to justify their peremptory challenges, how can judges tell when these challenges are improperly motivated? A wily attorney who excluded all of the males from a jury using peremptory challenges might claim that it was their baldness, not their sex, that motivated the use of the challenges. It will be up to the opposing party to object and show that the challenges used by the other party show a pattern of discrimination (e.g., perhaps women giving the same answers as men during voir dire were not excluded from the jury), at which point the judge will have to decide whether there is sufficient evidence to suggest improper motives. If so, then the attorney who exercised the challenges will be given a chance to offer an explanation of them that is not based on race, sex, ethnicity, or religion. If the judge finds the explanation convincing, then the judge will overrule the objection and honor the peremptory challenges. If the judge finds the explanation unconvincing, then the judge will either reject the challenges or restart the whole jury selection process.

---

19   *Batson v. Kentucky*, 476 U.S. 79 (1986); *Edmonson v. Leesville Concrete Company*, 500 U.S. 614 (1991); *J. E. B. v. Alabama ex rel. T. B.*, 511 U.S. 127 (1994).

During jury selection in the Woodall case, Woodall's attorneys objected to the prosecution's use of a peremptory challenge to exclude an African-American woman from the jury. This woman, who was the only African-American left among the potential jurors, had indicated during voir dire that she had not heard previously about the case, was not fundamentally opposed to the death penalty, and was willing to consider all of the evidence from both sides before reaching a decision on the proper penalty. Her answers left little to argue about on a challenge for cause, and indeed she was not challenged for cause. In response to Woodall's objection to the peremptory challenge, the prosecution indicated that this juror had been excluded because she wrote on her juror questionnaire that "she did not trust anyone" and made "several other responses of negative statements" during voir dire. Ultimately, Judge Cunningham rejected Woodall's objection without explanation.

This episode illustrates that while parties often object to the use of peremptory challenges on grounds that a challenge was sex- or race-based, it is difficult to prevail on such an objection. Because the trial judge has considerable discretion in evaluating whether the peremptory challenge was race- or sex-neutral, and because any neutral reason can suffice no matter how illogical it may be, objections to peremptory challenges rarely succeed. This limitation on the use of peremptory challenges is thus important but difficult to enforce. As a result, it does not greatly restrict the leeway given to lawyers to remove jurors—though just a few—for any reason, good or bad, usually without ever having to disclose the reason.

The Burden of Proof

Once all challenges have been made and the jury is empaneled, the trial is ready to begin. Often the judge will begin with a brief speech to the jury about what their tasks are and how they are expected to approach them. In the Fruit Nibbles case, Judge Martini began by explaining to jurors what was coming next:

> The first step in a trial would be, after our break, what's called the opening statements of the attorneys. Each of the attorneys will have an opportunity to address you and tell you an outline of what they expect the evidence will prove or not prove, depending on their respective positions. Again, what you should understand about comments or opening addresses by attorneys, that's not evidence, the same way summations are not evidence. The evidence is what's here under oath or

in a document that's admitted into evidence. However, what they have to say is important because usually it gives you a framework of what they expect to prove or not prove, and then at the end, the summations are a summary of what they contend the evidence does prove. But the comments of counsel are not evidence.

Judge Martini went on to describe different types of evidence, offer guidance on how to evaluate the testimony of witnesses, and explain the *burden of proof* in the case.

The burden of proof is a crucial concept that deserves greater attention than we have given it so far. In a typical civil trial, whichever party is seeking relief—that is, whichever party is trying to win something, such as money, as Beech-Nut was trying to do against Promotion in Motion—has the burden to prove all of the elements of its claim(s) by a "preponderance of the evidence." Here is how Judge Martini described this burden in his instructions to the jury in the Beech-Nut case:

> Now, this is a civil case, and Beech-Nut is the party whose claims must be decided. [Promotion in Motion, or "PIM"] is the party against which the claims have been made. Beech-Nut has the burden of proving its case by what is called the preponderance of the evidence. That means Beech-Nut has to prove to you, in light of all the evidence, that what it claims is more likely so than not so. To say it differently, if you were to put the evidence favorable to Beech-Nut and the evidence favorable to PIM on opposite sides of the scales, Beech-Nut would have to make the scales tip somewhat on its side. If Beech-Nut fails to meet this burden, your verdict must be for PIM. If you find, after considering all the evidence, that a claim or fact is more likely so than not so, then the claim or fact has been proved by a preponderance of the evidence.

In a criminal trial, the prosecutor always has the burden to prove beyond a reasonable doubt the elements of the crimes charged against the defendant as well as any facts necessary to impose the death penalty. If Woodall had not changed his pleas to guilty, then the prosecutor at the guilt trial would have had to prove all of the elements of the murder, kidnapping and rape charges. Because Woodall pled guilty, this was unnecessary, but the prosecutor still had to prove that the crime was committed in a way that justified imposition of the death penalty. Here is how Judge Cunningham instructed the jury in Woodall's case with respect to the prosecution's burden of proof:

But you cannot fix the sentence at death, or at confinement in the penitentiary without benefit of probation or parole, or life in the penitentiary without benefit of probation or parole until he has served a minimum of twenty-five years of his sentence, unless you are satisfied from the evidence beyond a reasonable doubt that one or both of the aggravating circumstance or circumstances [that were previously explained] are true in their entirety, in which event you must state in writing, signed by the Foreperson, that you find the aggravating circumstance or circumstances to be true beyond a reasonable doubt.

If you have a reasonable doubt as to the truth or existence of one or both of the aggravating circumstance or circumstances [necessary for these penalties], you shall not make any finding with respect to it. If upon the whole case you have a reasonable doubt whether the Defendant should be sentenced to death, you shall instead fix his punishment at a sentence of imprisonment.

Judge Cunningham did not further define the reasonable doubt standard, and he was not constitutionally required to do so. However, other courts sometimes offer a fuller definition of the standard. For instance, the federal trial courts located within the Sixth Circuit of the United States (which encompasses Tennessee, Kentucky, Ohio, and Michigan) use the following standard instruction on the burden of proof in criminal cases:

1. As you know, the defendant has pleaded not guilty to the crime charged in the indictment. The indictment is not any evidence at all of guilt. It is just the formal way that the government tells the defendant what crime he is accused of committing. It does not even raise any suspicion of guilt.

2. Instead, the defendant starts the trial with a clean slate, with no evidence at all against him, and the law presumes that he is innocent. This presumption of innocence stays with him unless the government presents evidence here in court that overcomes the presumption, and convinces you beyond a reasonable doubt that he is guilty.

3. This means that the defendant has no obligation to present any evidence at all, or to prove to you in any way that he is innocent. It is up to the government to prove that he is guilty, and this burden stays on the government from start to finish. You must find the defendant not guilty

unless the government convinces you beyond a reasonable doubt that he is guilty.

4. The government must prove every element of the crime charged beyond a reasonable doubt. Proof beyond a reasonable doubt does not mean proof beyond all possible doubt. Possible doubts or doubts based purely on speculation are not reasonable doubts. A reasonable doubt is a doubt based on reason and common sense. It may arise from the evidence, the lack of evidence, or the nature of the evidence.

5. Proof beyond a reasonable doubt means proof which is so convincing that you would not hesitate to rely and act on it in making the most important decisions in your own lives. If you are convinced that the government has proved the defendant guilty beyond a reasonable doubt, say so by returning a guilty verdict. If you are not convinced, say so by returning a not guilty verdict.

What this all means is that civil cases start with a presumption in favor of the party being sued and criminal cases start with a presumption that the person accused of a crime is innocent. The presumption favoring the defending party is harder to overcome in a criminal case than a civil case. Put simply, the criminal jury is supposed to be very sure that the defendant committed the crime, while the civil jury just needs to believe that the evidence slightly favors the plaintiff.

These presumptions also mean that the party *without* the burden of proof may put on no evidence at all and still win. In fact, criminal defendants often present little or no evidence of their own, with their main defense being that the prosecution has failed to come forward with sufficient evidence to meet its high burden of proof. (Although they are not required to, civil defendants almost always choose to put on evidence, since the burden of proof for civil claims is so much lower.)

> ### Another Standard of Proof
>
> Occasionally something other than the preponderance burden of proof applies in civil cases. For instance, in cases where the state attempts to remove a child permanently from a parent's custody, the state must come forward with "clear and convincing evidence" that child has been permanently neglected. *Santosky v. Kramer*, 455 U.S. 745, 748-49 (1982). This standard is higher than the preponderance standard, but lower than the reasonable doubt standard that applies in criminal cases. The clear and convincing standard is less common than the preponderance standard but has been applied to a range of claims, from paternity to patent invalidity to claims for punitive damages.

The choice of different burdens of proof for civil and criminal trials reflects society's assessment of the relative costs associated with incorrect verdicts. For civil cases, where the parties have primarily money at stake, we tend to think that the harm of incorrectly holding a party liable is not much greater than the harm of incorrectly allowing a party to escape liability. Basically, the preponderance standard provides that if the evidence does not favor either side, then the tie goes to the defending party. But in criminal cases, where the criminal defendant may lose his freedom or even his life as a penalty, we have a much higher burden of proof because we want to minimize the risk of falsely convicting an innocent person. This higher standard means that sometimes criminal trials will allow guilty persons to go free where prosecutors could not marshal enough evidence to prove guilt beyond a reasonable doubt. Those errors are seen as less harmful than punishing an innocent person.

The specific claims and criminal charges in a case dictate the facts that the parties need to prove, and the burden of proof determines how strong a case each needs to put before the jury (or the judge in a bench trial). All of Beech-Nut's claims against Promotion in Motion boiled down to the same question: Were the defects in the Fruit Nibbles made by Promotion so severe or pervasive that they substantially impaired the value of the Fruit Nibbles product? If so, then Beech-Nut was justified in rejecting the product and demanding compensation from Promotion. To win, Beech-Nut had to put on enough evidence of the defects and their harms to convince the jury that it was more likely than not true that the defects substantially impaired the value of the product. Promotion in Motion could in response put on evidence casting doubt on the severity or pervasiveness of the defects, but it had no obligation to do so.

Since Robert Woodall pled guilty to all three of the crimes in his indictment—first-degree murder, rape and kidnapping—all that was left was a trial to set the penalties for these crimes. Because the prosecution sought the ultimate sanction of death, it had to prove that Woodall's crimes were committed under one or more of the circumstances that Kentucky law specified as sufficient to impose the death penalty. In particular, the prosecution had to prove, beyond any reasonable doubt, that Woodall intentionally killed Sarah Hansen while he was engaged in the act of raping her or that he committed the act of kidnapping so that he could rape Ms. Hansen, physically injure her, or terrorize her. Woodall could put on evidence of mitigating circumstances that might, in the eyes of the jury, reduce the heinousness of his crimes, but he had no obligation to do so.

WHEN IS THE DEATH PENALTY APPROPRIATE?

A series of decisions in the 1970s and 1980s by the U.S. Supreme Court established that when the prosecution seeks the death penalty against a criminal defendant, a special trial must be held in which the prosecution presents evidence of aggravating factors that justify imposition of capital punishment and the defendant has the opportunity to present evidence of mitigating factors that weigh in favor of leniency. Aggravating factors involve either the nature or manner of the crime (e.g., the victim was a police officer or the murderer also raped the victim) or the victim's record (e.g., the defendant has committed prior violent offenses). Mitigating factors involve evidence suggesting diminished responsibility due to the defendant's history or condition (e.g., no prior criminal offenses, a history of abuse, or diminished mental capacity) or the circumstances under which the crime occurred (e.g., the defendant was pressured by someone else or the victim willingly participated in the events that led up to the crime). The sentencer must identify the relevant aggravating and mitigating circumstances and weigh them against each other.

In 2002, the U.S. Supreme Court held that aggravating factors other than a defendant's criminal record must be determined by a jury rather than a judge. So today a jury must play at least some role in imposing a death sentence, unless the defendant waives his right to a jury. Although this rule was not in place at the time of Woodall's sentencing hearing, Kentucky was one of many states that already required juries to make recommendations regarding the death penalty. At Woodall's sentencing trial, the prosecution emphasized the circumstances surrounding Woodall's crime, including his brutal attack on and rape of Ms. Hansen and his leaving Ms. Hansen to die submerged in water. Woodall's defense emphasized Mr. Woodall's intellectual disabilities, his youth and immaturity, and a history of deprivation and abuse.

In 2002, the Supreme Court ruled that executing intellectually disabled persons violated the Eighth Amendment's prohibition on cruel and unusual punishments (*Atkins v. Virginia*, 536 U.S. 304 (2002)), but the Supreme Court left it to the states to define the point at which a person is so intellectually disabled that he cannot be executed. In 2014, the Supreme Court ruled that Kentucky's death penalty statute (as well as Florida's) too narrowly defined the category of intellectual disability (*Hall v. Florida*, 134 S.Ct. 1986 (2014)). Thus, the state statute under which Woodall was sentenced to death did not adequately protect intellectually disabled persons from execution. Woodall is presently seeking a reversal of his death sentence due to this deficiency in the Kentucky statute. (Woodall's IQ was measured at 78. In 1998, Kentucky law provided that persons with an IQ lower than 70 could not be given the death penalty.)

The website maintained by the Death Penalty Information Center (http://www.deathpenaltyinfo.org) is a good resource for students interested in gathering more information about the law on capital punishment and about the imposition of capital punishment in the United States.

The Main Event: Opening Statements, the Presentation of Evidence, and Closing Arguments

As in the Beech-Nut case, the trial often begins with jury instructions. If the judge does not give prefatory jury instructions, then the jury's introduction to the claims or crimes at issue in the case will come through the parties' opening statements, which are delivered by the attorneys if the parties have legal counsel.[20] Each side will be given a specified period—sometimes as long as a few hours in complicated cases—to walk the jurors through its theory of the case and to preview the evidence that will be offered to support that theory. The party with the burden of proof always goes first, and the party defending against the claim or criminal charge goes second.

---

20   It is not entirely correct to say that the opening statements are the first introduction to the claims or crimes in a case. At the start of the voir dire process for jury selection, judges always give a synopsis of the case for which a jury is about to be selected. The opening statements are usually the first detailed introduction to the questions that the jury will have to decide.

A good opening statement creates a story or narrative that fits the coming evidence and suggests an explanation of events that favors the party offering the story. In *Beech-Nut v. Promotion in Motion*, for instance, Beech-Nut's attorney began her opening statement by comparing what happened to Beech-Nut to a common consumer experience:

> What happened in this case is very straightforward. In fact, I bet it has happened to all of us at some point. This case is about buying a product thinking you were getting something that you paid for but ending up with something broken and you just want your money back so you can go someplace else and get the product that you wanted from the very beginning. That's exactly what we have here.

Beech-Nut's attorney went on to explain the deal between Beech-Nut and Promotion in Motion and the incidents leading up to the lawsuit, but she kept returning to this theme of a defective product that caused Beech-Nut much damage:

> As you will hear in greater detail from the witnesses, Beech-Nut had faced a steadily mounting avalanche of complaints. Beech-Nut concluded that the problems could not be isolated between one particular lot or shipment. So the evidence will show that Beech-Nut was left with no choice but to withdraw the product from the market and revoke its acceptance of the product from PIM. Beech-Nut allowed its retailers to cancel orders, it refunded them payments, and it paid additional fees to those retailers to take those products off the shelf. As a result, Beech-Nut suffered significant financial losses; lost revenues, profits, out-of-pocket costs, and suffered a "black eye" in the market. Beech-Nut is entitled to recover the damages for its losses.
>
> . . . .
>
> At the end of the day, PIM is stuck with the consequences of making a bad product. PIM promised a product it did not deliver. PIM must accept its responsibility.

In response, Promotion's attorney offered a counter-story that admitted some problems with the product but contended that Beech-Nut over-reacted before it knew the true extent of the problems:

> Promotion In Motion has never denied the fact that some of the product had issues with it. But that's not the question. The question is: Of the

230,000 cases that were shipped to Beech-Nut, can Beech-Nut meet its burden of proof and show that there's a material breach that substantially all of the product was nonconforming and was of no value to them, and therefore they had a right to terminate the contract? We maintain they didn't.

In tennis there's an expression: Foot fault. A foot fault isn't the end of the day. There's no one hundred percent guarantee in life. There's no one hundred percent guarantee in the four purchase orders that counsel referred you to and that I'm going to talk about in a moment. "Some problems" does not equate with liability to my client.

. . . .

One of the stipulated facts is that 230,000 cases of Fruit Nibbles were manufactured. That's a lot of cases. The question I want you to focus on when you hear evidence from Beech-Nut, or even when you hear my clients speak, is, how many of those 230,000 cases—I'll speak in English—were defective, had problems, or which you wouldn't give to your kid or your grandchildren or, you know, put out for Halloween for trick-or-treat... Can Beech-Nut tell you that 5 percent of the 230,000 cases had a problem? Can they tell you that 10 percent? ... And let me suggest an answer: They can't, because they haven't been able to do it up to date as we've asked them that question. No one from Beech-Nut has been able to say: Here is the total number of cases of Fruit Nibbles where there was a problem, or here's a percentage in which there's a problem...

The reality—and you'll hear this in from Kennedy, one of their senior officers when he testifies—is that Beech-Nut did not examine the product when my client shipped it to them. They didn't take out the knife and open up the cases and they didn't pull random samples. Beech-Nut did not examine the product when it came off the shelves, Kroger, Walmart, and some of the other retailers that it sold it to.

So, yes, Beech-Nut can tell you 230,000 cases. This is a product for toddlers. We had no choice. I disagree. And I hope you do also. The choice was for them, before they ask you to award a lot of money—and that's what they're asking for, you'll hear that, they're asking for a lot of money here—the choice was for Beech-Nut to take out one of those carton knives, open up the boxes and start looking at samples to see, what is the problem? How widespread is the problem? Is there a problem? So as the Judge has instructed you, think about whether or not the substantial nonconformance can be established. "Some problems" is not the standard. That's not the payday for Beech-Nut. It's the substantial nonconformance standard.

With these competing opening statements, we see the parties and their attorneys framing the questions in an effort to influence how the jury evaluates the evidence that is about to be presented. Beech-Nut wanted the jurors to imagine how they would feel and behave if they had bought a product that turned out to have defects, asking them to consider how far they would go before rejecting the product. It hoped they would look at the big picture and conclude that Beech-Nut acted appropriately given the marketing and consumer satisfaction problem that it was confronting. Promotion in Motion, on the other hand, wanted the jurors to focus on the details. Because it had conceded that there were defects in some of packages of Fruit Nibbles sold to Beech-Nut, it was in the details that Promotion had its best chance of winning.

An opening statement can provide a great story or framework for evaluating the evidence, but if the evidence actually presented at the trial does not support the story, the opening statement can backfire. Trial lawyers believe that one of the worst errors a lawyer can commit is making promises in the opening statement that cannot be honored when the evidence is presented. For instance, if it turned out that Beech-Nut had in fact performed a random check of the Fruit Nibbles before rejecting the product, the jury would likely lose trust in anything Promotion in Motion's attorney had told them. A good opening statement makes promises that will be kept.

After opening statements, it is time for the parties to try to honor those promises. The party with the burden of proof puts on its evidence first. Evidence comes in two basic forms: testimony from witnesses and physical evidence. Witnesses answer questions posed by the attorneys (or by the parties if the parties do not have attorneys), first from the attorney who called the witness to testify—this is called the "direct examination" of the witness—and then by the attorney for the opposing party—this is called the "cross-examination." Cross-examination is usually limited to questions about what was said during the direct examination, as opposed to questions about new topics. Cross-examination is optional, but if there is a cross-examination, the attorney who conducted the direct examination may be given a chance for "redirect" or follow-up questions and then other attorney may be given a chance for "re-cross."

(This process usually ends with redirect or re-cross, but it theoretically could go on much longer if the trial judge allowed it). Witnesses must testify under an oath or affirmation that their testimony will be truthful, and a witness who gives false testimony can be prosecuted for perjury.

You may have heard that good lawyers do not ask witnesses questions at trial unless they already know the answers to them. This is an excellent strategy, designed to prevent the inadvertent disclosure of information that could benefit the other side and to avoid undermining the jury's confidence in the lawyer asking the question. But how can lawyers be sure that they know the answers to questions in advance? For that matter, how can they be sure that the promises they make about evidence in their opening statements can be honored? The answer to both questions is discovery. Through careful examination of physical evidence during discovery and thorough questioning of the opposing party and other potential witnesses in depositions, lawyers can develop a detailed knowledge of the facts of the case prior to trial, allowing them to make promises and ask questions during trial without fear of embarrassment. Perhaps paradoxically, attorneys in criminal cases are in a worse position than attorneys in civil cases, because of the greater limitations on discovery in criminal cases. (Recall that prosecutors cannot compel criminal defendants to answer questions, defense counsel often operate on very limited budgets, and courts must approve the use of depositions in criminal cases and generally only do so where the witness may not be available to testify at trial).

Witnesses come in two varieties: fact witnesses and expert witnesses. Fact witnesses are people who have some personal knowledge of the events at issue in the case. For instance, in Woodall's sentencing trial, Sarah Hansen's mother testified about the last time she saw her daughter and about the impact of her death on the Hansen family. Expert witnesses are people who, through their education, training, or experience, have some special knowledge or abilities that can be used to help the jury understand the evidence. For instance, most jurors do not have the special training needed to examine an X-ray and understand what it shows. The parties in a medical malpractice case may call radiologists to testify as expert witnesses to explain to the jury what a reasonable doctor should or should not have seen in the patient's X-rays.

Courts use different criteria to decide whether an expert witness should be allowed to testify, but in general every American court will require that the expert base his or her testimony on reliable methods and principles. Whether an expert is relying on reliable methods or principles is easy to assess in many cases. (An expert astronomer who testifies based on principles from physics will be allowed, but an astrological expert who testifies based on horoscopes will not be allowed.) However, it can be more difficult in areas of new scientific inquiry where the methods and principles are developing. For example, forensic scientists regularly testify nowadays about whether the defendant's DNA matches DNA recovered from the crime scene test results, but in the early days of DNA testing many such experts were not allowed to testify. Opponents of emerging areas of expertise often call the new evidence "junk science," while proponents emphasize that every scientific method and principle is novel at some point and that the body of scientific knowledge is constantly expanding. Trial judges find decisions on the admissibility of novel scientific evidence some of the most challenging they must make.

The other variety of evidence, physical evidence, is anything that can be presented in physical form, such as documents, computer files, photographs, videos, weapons, drugs, or bloody clothes. Physical evidence, which the jury is typically allowed to take into the jury room and examine closely during deliberations, can be quite powerful because it often comes into being at the same time as the events in question and provides insight into what was happening as events unfolded. For instance, Beech-Nut presented to the jury two e-mails that came to its attention during discovery and that contained statements apparently quite harmful to PIM's case. The first was written by PIM's quality control manager to the scientist in charge of product development:

> I believe we are making a serious mistake continuing to ship Beech-Nut product produced with white grape juice concentrate. We all know the only reason the product in our warehouse had an acceptable appearance is that it's less than two weeks old. The flavor and smell were already not to standard. In a very short time that product will taste and smell bad and appear ugly. In my opinion, if that product reaches the marketplace the complaints will be astronomical. I feel we should recall all product produced with white grape juice concentrate before it destroys ours and Beech-Nut's reputations. Should we discuss this with Michael [Rosenberg, the president of the company,] in our meetings on Tuesday?

(By the time of the trial, this employee no longer worked for Promotion in Motion.) The reply appears on its face to be equally damning (as well as prophetic):

> It may sound simple, but it is not. Our failure to detect the problem sooner may end up costing us over a million dollars. I wish we had a million dollars to give Beech-Nut for recalling the product, but we don't.

Michael is aware of the situation. By bringing it up again we will only anger him about our incompetence.

The effect on the jury of physical evidence like this—which seems to fall into the metaphorical category of "smoking guns"—can be very difficult to overcome.[21]

When evidence is being presented at trial, the parties and their attorneys must be on their toes, ready to object to any evidence that may be inappropriate.[22] For example, if a party tries to use hearsay as evidence, then the opposing party must object and ask the judge to prevent the use of the evidence. Deciding what evidence will be admitted into the trial is a central duty of the trial judge. But the judge is a passive gatekeeper: unless a party objects to a piece of evidence, the judge will generally allow the evidence to be admitted. (The judge can interject to prevent egregious errors in what evidence is used, but such interjections are fairly rare.) It is up to the parties and their attorneys to be familiar with the rules of evidence and attentive to their application at the trial.

Making objections to evidence is crucial not just to prevent "bad" evidence from being used against one's side of the case; it is also crucial to preserve any complaint a party may have about the evidence used at trial. In general, unless a party (or its attorney) objects to a piece of evidence, that party cannot complain in a post-trial motion or in an appeal to a higher court that the trial judge erred by admitting it into the trial. The idea is that one's concerns about a piece of evidence must be raised so that the trial judge has a chance to avoid an error in the first place; otherwise, parties might wait and see whether they win at trial and then, if not, raise all sorts of complaints that could have been avoided had they objected when the evidence was offered.

Some Common Objections at Trial

Irrelevant: Only relevant evidence is admissible at trial. A piece of evidence is relevant if it makes a fact that is of consequence to the case more or less likely to be true. For instance, if a witness for the prosecution says that she saw the criminal defendant shoot the victim, that identification testimony is relevant because it makes it more likely that the defendant

---

21   The scientist in charge of product development, who was still employed by Promotion in Motion, testified that the quality control manager had over-reacted.

22   The propriety of evidence depends on the rules of evidence followed by the particular court. The rules of evidence followed in American courts, whether at the federal or state level, tend to be quite similar, but the content of these rules is beyond the scope of this book.

committed the crime. Likewise, if on cross-examination the witness admits that she was not wearing her glasses at the time of the shooting, that testimony is relevant because it makes it less likely that the witness correctly saw who the shooter was. But if on cross-examination, defense counsel asks the witness whether she likes to play golf, that question seeks irrelevant information because the answer cannot make it more or less likely that the defendant was the shooter.

Hearsay: A statement made outside of court that is offered as evidence for the truth of the facts asserted in the statement should be objected to on grounds of hearsay.

Improper Character Evidence: Evidence of the character of a person offered to prove that the person acted in accordance with that character in the events at issue in the trial should be objected to on grounds of improper character evidence. Although there are exceptions, in general trials turn on whether a person committed a particular act rather than whether a person has a good or bad character.

Lacks a Foundation: Physical evidence offered without proof that the evidence is what it is claimed to be should be objected to on grounds of lack of foundation. For instance, if the prosecution offers a handgun at trial as the murder weapon, the prosecution needs to be prepared to put on a witness who can link this particular gun to the scene of the crime.

Outside the Scope of Direct Examination: Cross-examination is generally limited to questions about topics discussed during the direct examination of a witness or topics relating to the credibility of the witness' testimony. If the question goes beyond these domains, then the question should be objected to as outside the scope of direct examination.

Improper Leading Question: During the direct examination of a witness, questioning is generally not supposed to presume or suggest the proper answer to the question. For instance, the attorney conducting direct examination is supposed to ask, "Did you see who shot the victim?" rather than, "it is true, isn't it, that you saw the defendant shoot the victim?" Questions of the second kind are "leading questions" that should be objected to if asked during direct examination. Leading questions can be used with hostile witnesses (i.e., witnesses who are being evasive or difficult) and on cross-examination.

This rule that errors at trial must be preserved by making an objection and giving the trial judge a chance to consider the party's concerns extends to the trial judge's instructions to the jury. Before instructing the jury, the judge provides the parties an opportunity to object to the instructions the judge plans to give and to request additional instructions. Recall, for instance, that Woodall asked Judge Cunningham to instruct the jury that he had a constitutional right not to testify at this trial, but Judge Cunningham refused to give that instruction. Because Woodall requested the additional instruction, he preserved for appeal any error that Judge Cunningham might have made by not giving the requested instruction.

After all of the evidence is presented, the parties can ask the judge to enter a judgment rather than allow the case to go to the jury for a decision. As discussed above, if the key facts are so clear that no reasonable jury could disagree about them, then the judge has the power to direct a verdict in favor of either party in a civil case or in favor of the defendant in a criminal case. Usually, though, the judge will deny motions for a directed verdict and will let the jury decide the case.

If the judge allows the case to go to the jury for its decision, then the parties are given a chance to make what are known as "summations" or "closing arguments" to the jury about how to evaluate the evidence and decide the case. As Judge Martini described the summation process to the Beech-Nut jurors, closing arguments are the attorneys' "account[s] as to what they believe the evidence demonstrates or has proven or not proven." The party with the burden of proof is traditionally given the opportunity to make the last closing argument to the jury. Sometimes, that party will go first and then offer a rebuttal closing argument after the defending party's closing argument. Other times the defending party will go first and then the party with the burden of proof will offer its summation.

Closing arguments typically mirror opening statements thematically. For example, Promotion in Motion's attorney returned to the theme that Beech-Nut did not investigate the problems sufficiently in his closing argument: "There are really two key phrases to focus upon and that we ask you ask yourselves and discuss among yourself the following: Did Beech-Nut show a substantial impairment of the entire contract? Not, did Beech-Nut show that some of the bags out of 230,000 cases had a problem. It's the totality of the circumstance. Did Beech-Nut meet its burden?" He then went through the evidence that had been admitted showing how Beech-Nut had failed to take steps to investigate the scope of the problems in the Fruit Nibbles, asking why Beech-Nut had failed to call certain people to testify and suggesting the answer: their testimony would not have helped Beech-Nut's case.[23]

Attorneys also use closing arguments to remind the jury of evidence that may be particularly helpful to a case. Thus, it should not surprise you that Beech-Nut's attorney, during her summation, reminded the jury about Promotion in Motion's internal e-mails in which the quality control manager recommended a recall of Fruit Nibbles and the scientist in charge of the product development expressed fear that the incident would cost Promotion more than a million dollars.

Once the closing arguments are complete, the judge gives the jury final instructions on the applicable law and explains the decisions the jury will have to reach by going over the verdict form that the jury will be given when it retires to the jury room to deliberate. The judge also instructs the jury that the first thing it should do on retiring to the jury room is to elect a foreperson, whose duty it will be to ensure that the jury reaches a verdict based on the required number of votes and to fill out the verdict form reflecting this vote.

Typically unanimity is required for a jury to reach a verdict, though states can choose to allow non-unanimous verdicts (e.g., ten out of twelve jurors) and the parties can agree to permit a non-unanimous verdict even when the default rule is that a verdict must be a unanimous. The jury is supposed to continue its deliberations until it reaches the required number of votes in favor of answering each question on the verdict form in a particular way. For instance, if the jury is given a general verdict form in a criminal case, the jury may be given only one question: Did the prosecution prove, beyond a reasonable doubt, that the defendant committed the crime charged? Until the required number of jurors agrees that the prosecution did or did not carry its burden, the jury is supposed to continue its discussion and continue to take votes. If after an extended period of deliberations without success a judge is convinced that there is no reasonable probability of a verdict from the jury, then the judge can declare the jury deadlocked, discharge the jury, and order a new trial with a different jury. Deadlocked, or "hung," juries are fairly rare, however. Most jury trials end with the jury's foreperson reading the verdict in court, an event

---

23   This sort of argumentation, in which the attorneys encourage the jury to draw adverse inferences from the absence of evidence, is proper and common in American trials: the one exception is that the prosecution, in its closing argument in a criminal trial, is not supposed to encourage the jury to draw an adverse inference from the defendant's failure to testify. Indeed, in the guilt phase of a trial, a criminal defendant is entitled to an instruction to the jury that the jury cannot use the lack of the defendant's testimony against him. Woodall argued that he was entitled to a similar instruction at his sentencing trial, but, as noted above, Judge Cunningham disagreed.

that is just as dramatic as it is portrayed in TV and movies. Lives and fortunes can depend on a jury's verdict.

Verdicts and Post-Verdict Motions

The juries in both of the cases we have been following returned verdicts. In fact, it only took the jury in the Beech-Nut case one hour to reach a verdict in favor of Beech-Nut. The verdict form signed (illegibly) by the foreperson of the Beech-Nut jury is reproduced on page 127. As you can see, the jury was presented with a single yes/no question: Did defects in the Fruit Nibbles produced by Promotion in Motion substantially impair the value of the product? Because the jury answered "yes" to this question, the jury then had to set the amount of damages, or monetary compensation, due to Beech-Nut. The jury set that amount at $2,222,000 based on its evaluation of the evidence presented during the trial.

Unfortunately, we cannot know what happened in the jury room for that hour. The general rule is that jury deliberations are secret and are not recorded. What is more, even if a juror wanted to complain about the process—say the juror was coerced by the others into voting in favor of Beech-Nut—the rules of evidence do not permit the juror to do so in most jurisdictions. Most courts bar jurors from giving any evidence about how the jury arrived at its verdict, including evidence of physical or mental intimidation among the jurors. (A few courts make exceptions for certain kinds of internal actions that are deemed particularly inappropriate, such as racial animus on the part of the jurors in a case where the plaintiff is seeking relief for racial discrimination). In one infamous case, the U.S. Supreme Court even ruled that evidence that jurors were intoxicated during deliberations could not be considered in support of a motion to overturn the jury's verdict because it would intrude on the secrecy of internal jury deliberations.[24]

Questions about how the jury interacted and deliberated to arrive at its verdict are strictly off limits because the courts do not want to encourage second-guessing of jury deliberations and do not want to encourage the parties who lost to try to intrude on the jury deliberation process to find evidence of questionable behavior. After a trial is over, jurors can discuss in the media how they reached a decision, but those disclosures will not be used by a court to

---

24   *Tanner v. U.S.*, 483 U.S. 107 (1987).

overturn a jury's verdict, no matter how outrageous the jury's decision process may have been.

In stark contrast to this off-limits attitude toward internal dynamics, all courts allow jurors to testify after a verdict about external influences on that verdict. For instance, say one party engaged in illegal jury tampering by secretly paying jurors to vote in its favor or threatening them harm if they voted for the other party. Such external influences fundamentally undercut the independence of the jury and the integrity of the trial's result. If the party who lost at trial obtained evidence of jury tampering, then a new trial would be ordered. But jury tampering, or at least evidence of it, is very rare.

Losing parties can make other attacks on a jury's verdict using two kinds of post-trial motions. We have already discussed a renewed motion for judgment as a matter of law, in which the losing party argues that the facts and law clearly favored it yet the jury somehow failed to see that or just ignored the evidence. Sometimes such behavior by a jury is motivated by improper factors, such as a personal dislike of one of the parties. However, there are also times when juries disregard the facts and the law because they believe that following the law would result in an injustice. When a jury feels this way and enters a verdict in favor a party that it knows should lose under the law, the jury has engaged in what is called "jury nullification."

Jury nullification is a controversial practice. Some people feel that it serves a valuable purpose and that juries should be told that they are free to disregard unjust laws or unjust applications of good laws. For instance, a number of attorneys and legal scholars have argued that American drug laws are draconian and racially biased in their impact and, therefore, that juries should nullify prosecutions under these laws, at least in cases where the criminal charges seem disproportionate to the crime committed. Others argue that nullification places the jury in the role of the judge, a role it is not qualified to fill, and so should be discouraged as strongly as possible. But even strong opponents of nullification recognize that nothing can be done to prevent it entirely. This is because, under long-established law, jurors cannot be punished for their votes, even if the judge thinks those votes utterly unjustified and blatantly inconsistent with the law. (A juror can be punished for behavior related to a vote—taking a bribe, for instance—but not for the vote itself.)

If a jury in a criminal case engages in jury nullification and acquits a defendant who, under the law and facts, should have been convicted, there is nothing the prosecution can do because the Double Jeopardy Clause of the U.S. Constitution prevents a retrial on the charges. However, jury nullification in a civil trial can be addressed by the judge. If the judge grants a renewed motion for judgment as a matter of law, the verdict is vacated and judgment is entered in favor of the party that lost at trial.

An alternative post-trial motion, which is less radical in its effects, is a motion for a new trial. In a motion for a new trial, the party filing the motion enumerates supposed errors in the first trial that caused the jury to reach an erroneous verdict. Whoever lost a civil trial, plaintiff or defendant, can file a new trial motion, but in a criminal trial only the defendant can seek a new trial after losing. A motion for a new trial can be based on an argument that the verdict is against the great weight of the evidence, that the judge erred somehow during the trial, or that one of the parties or jurors engaged in misconduct that was discovered only after the trial. In general, any supposed error by the judge that is the basis for the new trial request needs to involve an event at trial (such as the admission of evidence) to which one of the parties objected or a request by a party that was denied by the judge. Woodall, for example, could file a new trial motion asking Judge Cunningham to reconsider his refusal to instruct the jury not to hold Woodall's silence against him, since Woodall had asked for that instruction earlier.

In Woodall's case and in the Beech-Nut case the trial judges refused to grant new trials. With the rejection of the losing parties' new trial motions, there was nothing further to be done in the trial courts. The only option remaining for the losing parties was to seek relief from a "higher" court, with higher here simply meaning a court with power to review the decisions of trial courts. Both of the losing parties did pursue appeals to higher courts.

For Beech-Nut and its attorneys, the jury's verdict was a tremendous victory and relief, and for Promotion in Motion and its attorneys, the verdict was a great loss and disappointment. And the jury's decision in Woodall's case was surely upsetting to Woodall and his family and perhaps some small solace to Ms. Hansen's family. But the relief felt by the winners and the unhappiness felt by the losers in these cases were both blunted by the reality that the cases were far from over. All of the parties knew that winning in the trial court was just one battle victory in the long, often very long, war that litigation in American courts can be. In the next chapter, we introduce you to the appeal processes used to correct errors that occurred in the trial court by examining the appeals taken by Promotion in Motion and Woodall. As you will see, winning a case at the trial court level, even when that win comes through a jury's verdict, is no guarantee of ultimate victory in the case. ■

Case 2:09-cv-01228-WJM-MF   Document 52   Filed 09/12/12   Page 1 of 1 PageID: 1399

9/12/12
11:50 AM

UNITED STATES DISTRICT COURT
DISTRICT OF NEW JERSEY

BEECH-NUT NUTRITION CORPORATION,	Civil Action No. 2:09-CV-1228 WJM-MF
Plaintiff,	Honorable William J. Martini, U.S.D.J.
v.	
PROMOTION IN MOTION, INC., PIM BRANDS, LLC.	
Defendants.	**JURY VERDICT FORM**

Substantial Impairment

1)   Do you find from a preponderance of the evidence that there were defects in the Fruit Nibbles such that those defects substantially impaired the value of all the Fruit Nibbles purchased by Beech-Nut and could not be cured by PIM?

Yes   ✓   No   _____

If your answer is "No," please hand in this verdict form. If your answer is "Yes," please proceed to the next section.

2)   What amount of damages do you award Beech-Nut?

$ 2,222,000   .

Please hand in this verdict form.

September 12, 2012

[signature]

CHAPTER 6

Appeals

When a trial is over, a litigant who is dissatisfied with the outcome usually has the right to appeal to a higher court to undo part or all of the trial court's decision. This general rule is subject to a variety of small exceptions and one very big exception: the prosecution's right to appeal is significantly restricted by the Double Jeopardy Clause of the Fifth Amendment to the U.S. Constitution. That clause commands that no person shall "be subject for the same offense to be twice put in jeopardy of life or limb." The defendant has not been placed "in jeopardy" until a jury has been selected and sworn in or, if the case is to be decided by a judge alone, the judge has begun to hear evidence to reach a decision on the merits of the case. So the prosecution can appeal decisions made before this point, such as a trial judge's order to dismiss an indictment or to suppress evidence.[1] It can also appeal a trial judge's order granting the defendant a new trial after a jury has voted to convict the defendant.[2] However, aside from these instances, the Double Jeopardy Clause means that the prosecution cannot appeal any decision made once the defendant has been placed in jeopardy, including, of course, a verdict of not guilty.

In some states, one can appeal the decision of a court of limited jurisdiction to the major trial court (court of general jurisdiction), where a new trial will be held. But this is the exception. Normally a trial court decision is appealed

---

1   A federal statute, 18 U.S.C. § 3731, authorizes appeals from orders that would suppress the prosecution's evidence against the defendant so long as the U.S. attorney overseeing the prosecution certifies that the appeal is not being taken just to delay the case and that the evidence would be substantial proof of a fact material to the trial. States have passed similar statutes that authorize appeals by state prosecutors in similarly limited circumstances.

2   Appeals from these two kinds of orders would not violate the Double Jeopardy because, in the first instance, the judge did not consider the merits of the case against the defendant and, in the second instance, overturning the new trial order would not call for a second trial because the appellate court would just reinstate the verdict in the first trial, which the prosecution won.

to a special court set up only to hear appeals. Appellate courts differ from trial courts in some very important and noticeable ways. No witnesses appear in appellate courts, and rarely is new evidence introduced there. Furthermore, there are no juries in appellate courts. And although a trial is usually presided over by a single judge, an appeal is heard by a team of judges. In supreme courts, it is typical for all the judges of the court to participate in each case (with the exception of those judges who *recuse* themselves because of a conflict of interest). This is called sitting en banc. The alternative is to have a case heard by a subset of a court's membership, called a panel. Panels are typically employed as an efficiency measure by courts with large caseloads, including supreme courts in some countries; more cases can be heard if the judges divide them up. The U.S. Courts of Appeals—the first level of appellate courts in the federal system—decide most cases in panels of three randomly assigned judges, only rarely sitting en banc.

■ JUDICIAL RECUSAL

Imagine that you apply for a job with a major corporation and are turned down. About the same time you receive your rejection letter, you are contacted secretly by an employee of the corporation who tells you that you were the best-qualified candidate but were rejected because of your gender, in violation of federal and state law. After consulting with an attorney, you file a lawsuit against the corporation. The judge issues a summary judgment for the defendant. Shortly afterwards, you learn from your attorney that the judge owns $500,000 stock in the company you sued. Imagine how you would feel about the judge and the legal process.

Rules concerning recusal are intended to keep such situations from occurring. They require judges to refrain from participating in cases where they have a conflict of interest that could undermine their impartiality. A financial stake in one of the parties is the quintessential conflict of interest. Another common example is having a family member or former professional partner serving as an attorney for one of the parties. A litigant who feels that a judge is not impartial can bring a motion asking the judge to step aside, but judges are also supposed to recuse on their own initiative when they recognize a possible conflict of interest.

The rules tend to be strict on paper. For instance, federal law requires judges to "disqualify" themselves from any case where their "impartiality might reasonably be questioned." But the stringency of those rules is somewhat undermined by the fact they are largely self-enforced. In federal courts and most state courts, it is the judge himself who makes the decision whether or not to remain on the case, even though it is his impartiality that is being questioned.

Judges' decisions not to recuse themselves sometimes seem to fly in the face of basic logic and fairness. Take the case of *Commonwealth v. Williams*, 105 A.3d 1234 (Pa. 2014). There the Pennsylvania Supreme Court reviewed a lower court ruling that Williams was entitled to a new death-penalty sentencing hearing because the prosecutor's office engaged in serious misconduct, including withholding key exculpatory evidence from the defendant (recall that in Chapter 4 we discussed the prosecution's disclosure obligations). The district attorney who had supervised the prosecutor's office at the time of the original hearing was Ronald Castille. By the time the case made it through the system and this appeal reached the Pennsylvania Supreme Court, Castille had become chief justice of that court. Williams asked the chief justice to recuse himself on the grounds that he could not impartially decide whether his own office had violated the law. He refused, and his court unanimously reversed the lower court decision and reinstated the death sentence.

Judges' denials of motions to recuse can be appealed, though rarely successfully. As of the writing of this book, the U.S. Supreme Court has agreed to review the Williams case but has not yet decided it. It seems likely that the Court will rule that Chief Justice Castille's refusal to recuse himself violated the Due Process Clause of the Fourteenth Amendment. Harder to predict is whether it will order a new sentencing hearing or allow the execution to proceed on the grounds that Castille's vote was not decisive. You might wish to think through the issue on your own before checking on what the Supreme Court did.

In recent years, debates about recusal have been especially heated in states where judges are elected. Judges in those states frequently raise money to help them campaign for reelection. Campaign funds occasionally come from individuals or organizations who appear before them as litigants; very often they come from the attorneys who practice before them. Reformers have proposed that recusal motions be decided by another judge, not the one being challenged. For now, though, most litigants must simply hope that a judge who has received a campaign donation from someone involved in a case will recuse voluntarily or decide the case without being influenced by that donation.

Promotion in Motion was the appellant in the Fruit Nibbles case, challenging in a single appeal both the summary judgment ruling that dismissed its claims against Beech-Nut and the jury's verdict in favor of Beech-Nut on Beech-Nut's claims against Promotion in Motion. A three judge-panel of the U.S. Court of Appeals for the Third Circuit affirmed the district court in a brief opinion written by Judge Thomas Ambro. Judge Ambro took only two sentences to reject Promotion in Motion's challenge to the summary judgment and one paragraph each to dispose of its two main challenges to the trial verdict, both concerning the judge's decision to disallow certain evidence. You can read the relevant portions of Judge Ambro's opinion explaining the decisions in the box below.

Afterwards, the Court of Appeals issued an official document called a mandate, closing the case at the Court of Appeals and directing Promotion in Motion to pay the costs of the appeal. When the mandate was received in the district court, the judgment in favor of Beech-Nut became final and not subject to further appeal. If Promotion in Motion had appealed to the U.S. Supreme Court (it did not) and the Supreme Court had taken the case, then the mandate would not have been issued by the Third Circuit Court of Appeals until after the Supreme Court had ruled. (We explain the process of appealing to the Supreme Court in detail in the next chapter.)

Excerpt from Third Circuit Opinion resolving the appeal by Promotion in Motion:

The District Court correctly dismissed PIM's claims against Beech-Nut. Among other things, PIM did not allege that Beech-Nut breached the terms of the purchase orders, which are the only enforceable contracts between the parties.

PIM argues that the District Court erred by excluding evidence tending to indicate that there were no specifications as to the Fruit Nibbles' appearance, color or texture, and that, as a result, the jury was asked to rule on whether PIM breached certain specifications without ever being told what the specifications might have been or why there were none. However, Beech-Nut does not argue that the Fruit Nibbles were non-compliant for being the wrong color, taste or texture, and the jury was not asked to make such a narrow determination; rather, it was instructed to consider the broader issue of whether they were merchantable or fit for their intended purpose. Given the language of the purchase orders that the Fruit Nibbles would be "fit for the purpose intended, merchantable and free from defects of material and workmanship," and PIM's stipulation that the product "did not satisfy the warranties in the purchase orders," the District Court correctly found that PIM had conceded warranting merchantability and a violation thereof, and that arguments as to color, taste and texture were irrelevant.

The purchase orders provide that they are "the only contracts between the parties," that "their express terms governed the parties' financial responsibilities for any defective Fruit Nibbles," and include the express warranty already noted. PIM nonetheless attempted to introduce extrinsic evidence of negotiations underlying an un-ratified co-pack agreement as a "course of dealing" reflecting the parties' understanding that there were no warranties. The parties' exchange of drafts and failure to agree to the terms of the co-pack agreement do not constitute a "sequence of previous conduct ... fairly to be regarded as establishing a common basis of understanding." The District Court correctly found that the purchase orders were never modified, that they governed the rights and obligations of PIM and Beech-Nut with respect to the Fruit Nibbles, and that the extrinsic evidence was inadmissible.

Finally, the jury verdict should not be overturned as unsupported by the weight of the evidence. Given that PIM did not file post-trial motions for judgment as a matter of law or for a new trial before the District Court, we cannot review this claim. Even if we could review the jury verdict, there is no indication in the record that the jury's verdict in Beech-Nut's favor was against the weight of the evidence.

For these reasons, we affirm.

Although disappointing to the appellant, a straightforward affirmance of the kind that occurred in the Promotion in Motion appeal is the norm. Woodall's case eventually took a very different turn, but there too the first appeal resulted in an affirmance. Woodall's case presented a far more complicated and interesting appeal, though, and will be the focus of this chapter. Recall that Woodall pled guilty in a Kentucky trial court to multiple crimes, a jury recommended that he be sentenced to death for murder, and the trial judge accepted the jury's recommendation. As is frequently the case in states that employ the death penalty, Kentucky gave capital defendants the right to appeal directly to the state supreme court. This is what Woodall did, in a case now renamed *Woodall v. Commonwealth of Kentucky* to reflect the fact that it was Woodall's decision to pursue the case further. (The original title, *Commonwealth of Kentucky v. Woodall*, reflected the state's decision to prosecute Woodall.)

Appellate Procedure

Whatever the type or substance of the appeal, it begins with the filing of a *notice of appeal* by the dissatisfied party, who becomes the *appellant*. This notice must be filed with the trial court and sent to the other party (the *appellee*) within a certain time frame. (Thirty days from the judgment or order being appealed is common, but each jurisdiction has its own rules on when the notice of appeal has to be filed.)

The next step for the appellant—also subject to time limits—is to submit a trial record, or *record on appeal*, and a *brief.* The record on appeal includes a transcript of the trial (taken by a court reporter) as well as documents that the parties introduced into evidence or sought to introduce into evidence at the trial. Physical evidence offered at the trial (such as a weapon or clothes) is usually not sent to the court of appeals, but it is kept available in case the judges wish to see it. A trial transcript can be costly, and the appellant is not normally required to send the entire transcript to the court of appeals. But the appellant has to be careful, because the court of appeals won't consider arguments referring to parts of the trial that are missing from the transcript.

The brief is a highly formalized argumentative essay in which the appellant describes the case to the appellate court and tries to convince the appellate court that the trial judge made one or more important mistakes in presiding over and/or deciding the case. Typically, the appellant asks the appellate court to *reverse* the trial court decision—that is, to declare that the trial court made a mistake and to nullify its judgment or order—and either to enter a judgment for the appellant or to send the case back (*remand*) to the trial court with orders to fix the mistakes. The appellee submits a reply brief defending the trial court's actions and asking the court of appeals to affirm the trial court's decision.

Woodall's attorneys, public defenders provided for him by the state, submitted a brief that was 136 pages long, not including a 19-page appendix that included key material from the trial. The brief included twenty-eight separately headed arguments, some of which involved multiple issues. This kitchen-sink approach to briefs is not uncommon, especially in criminal appeals with extremely high stakes. Attorneys do not want to be left with regrets, wondering whether they neglected the one line of attack that might have convinced the appellate court to side with their client. So, even at the risk of distracting or irritating the judges reading the brief, they often include every argument that strikes them as even remotely plausible. That appears to have been the strategy of Woodall's brief. It is doubtful that his lawyers thought all twenty-eight of their arguments were strong or were surprised when the Kentucky Supreme Court rejected many of them in just a few sentences.

The issue that would turn out to be the most important for Woodall was in fact the first raised in the brief. The Fifth Amendment to the U.S. Constitution states that "No person...shall be compelled in any criminal case to be a witness against himself." The Supreme Court has long understood this to mean (among other things) that a defendant in a criminal case cannot be forced to testify if he would prefer not to. But what about in a situation like Woodall's, where guilt has already been established? Does the right extend to the sentencing hearing as well? If so, what protections does it provide? We will explain how his lawyers addressed these questions and how the Kentucky Supreme Court responded to them after concluding this discussion of the basic appellate process.

After briefs are submitted, the next step in many cases, usually several weeks later, is oral argument. At oral argument, attorneys for each side appear before the judges in the appellate courtroom and take turns defending their side. The litigants may attend oral arguments, but unless serving as their own attorneys, they do not participate in any way. Nor are there any witnesses to testify or be questioned.

The precise role played by judges and lawyers in oral argument has changed over time and still varies across courts and across cases at the same court. But the common thread running through contemporary oral arguments is that judges are not relegated to a passive role. Occasionally they may listen patiently as a lawyer makes a speech, but typically this is not what happens. Instead, the judges set the agenda, interrupting lawyers frequently with questions and challenges that the lawyers are expected to do their best to respond to, no matter how inconvenient or distracting.

Oral argument is a regular part of the appellate process at the U.S. Supreme Court and many state courts. It used to be in the U.S. Courts of Appeals as well, but there the frequency of oral argument has declined dramatically in recent years.[3] According to the administrative office of the U.S. Courts, 80% of all cases decided in the Courts of Appeals between September 2013 and September 2014 were decided on the briefs alone, without oral argument. The figure is over 90% for two circuits. A large majority of cases were decided without oral argument in every circuit except the District of Columbia, which

---

3   William M. Richmam & William L. Reynolds, *Injustice on Appeal* (Oxford University Press, 2013).

has its own appellate court because so many cases challenging federal laws are filed in the federal district court for Washington, D.C.[4]

Once judges have had a chance to read and/or hear all the attorney's arguments, they must make and announce their decision. Usually the first step toward doing so is for the judges to meet together and take a preliminary vote after some discussion of the case. One of the judges will then be assigned to draft the opinion of the court, a written statement explaining why the court decided the case as it did.

Opinions

Strictly speaking, there is no absolute requirement that a court issue a written opinion. It could simply announce a decision and give its reasons orally. Or it could announce its decision without giving reasons at all. Sometimes the arguments for one side are so weak that judges are obviously tempted to dispense with explanations, and opinions can be quite curt. Still, judges usually feel that deciding without any explanation at all would show too much disrespect for litigants and could leave them wondering whether the judges even considered their arguments. Providing reasons demonstrates to litigants and other readers that the judges took a case seriously.

But the most important reason for the practice of issuing written opinions has little to do with the parties to the case. Rather, it is done with future litigants, lawyers, and judges in mind. Imagine Congress passes a major statute imposing new regulations on banks and the first court to confront the statute must decide whether a certain bank practice violates the new law. Say it decides that the practice violates the law but does not write an opinion describing the facts of the case or explaining its decision. Now other banks in that jurisdiction will know they are in danger of violating the law but will have no idea what constitutes a violation, aside from what they might be able to piece together from the bank that lost its case. Lawyers who advise banks whether their activities are legal will be in the same position. And think about the next judges to confront the statute. They find its language confusing and would gladly draw on the thinking of the only other judges to interpret the statute so far. But with no written opinion, there is no help there.

It would be much better for everyone if the first court wrote something down. People and entities covered by the law would have an easier time deciding

---

4   http://www.uscourts.gov/uscourts/Statistics/JudicialBusiness/2014/appendices/B10Sep14.pdf

whether actions they are engaging in or thinking about would be legal, and judges hearing later cases would have some additional help in thinking through the issues. In short, written opinions allow decisions to serve as useful *precedents* to guide future behavior and decisions.

An opinion can provide at least some useful guidance simply by describing the central facts of the case and noting the court's decision. Imagine you are a judge in the second case involving the banking statute. The opinion from the first case tells you that the bank there performed actions A, B, and C without performing action X. In your case too the bank did A, B, and C without doing X. You can be pretty sure that the first court would have decided against your bank too. But say your bank did only A and B, not C. Or say it did A, B, and C, but it also did X. Now there are potentially important differences between the two situations and it is less clear whether the precedent really applies.

There are two ways we could alter the scenario to make your position more comfortable. First, we can let your case be the tenth to involve that statute, not the second. Now there is a whole series of cases where banks acted in somewhat different ways. Perhaps some of these had different outcomes, or perhaps the bank lost in all of them. Either way, you now have more data to work with to help you figure out what constitutes a violation under this statute—at least, as other judges have interpreted the statute. Even more helpful, though, would be if other judges explained the rationales behind their decisions. For instance, the first court might opine that the purpose of the statute was to protect borrowers from being locked into harsh repayment conditions without sufficient warning. Provided you agree, it will now be that much easier for you to choose the right outcome for your case. Just as importantly, the first court's account of its reasoning can help you determine whether you agree with it in the first place. Perhaps you'll say, "I don't think that's a correct reading of the statute's purpose and therefore don't think a bank that acts in that way really does violate the law."

One of the problems the Kentucky Supreme Court had to deal with was that Woodall was claiming the protection of the Fifth Amendment at his sentencing hearing, which might or might not be understood to be part of the "criminal case" referred to in the amendment. The court's job here was made easier by the fact that the U.S. Supreme Court had spoken directly to the question in a case from 1981, *Estelle v. Smith:* "We can discern no basis to distinguish between the guilt and penalty phases of respondent's capital murder trial so far as the protection of the Fifth Amendment privilege is concerned. Given the gravity of the decision to be made at the penalty phase, the State is not relieved of the obligation to observe fundamental constitutional guarantees."[5]

So you can see why a written opinion is important. You can also see why it is especially helpful for that opinion to represent the views of the court as a whole. It was once common practice for judges to deliver their opinions seriatim—each judge writing (or orally delivering) his or her own opinion. One still sees this in some other countries and even sometimes in the U.S. For instance, in the first major Supreme Court case on the constitutionality of the death penalty, *Furman v. Georgia*[6], each of the nine justices wrote an opinion. But seriatim opinions leave lawyers and other judges to tease out common ideas and understandings from various statements rather than laying out a single set of reasons. For this reason, American courts moved long ago to the practice of issuing one opinion of the court where possible.

But that is not always possible. The judge given the task of writing the opinion of the court will do her best to secure majority support for it by circulating a draft, receiving feedback from the other judges, and responding to their concerns in revised drafts. However, the other judges in the majority are under no obligation to "join" her opinion–that is, to agree that her opinion speaks for them. Unless enough of them do so for the opinion to speak for a majority, then in the end it will not be the opinion of the court; it will just be an opinion—entitled to no special respect from later courts.

In fact, the majority opinion writer's challenge is even more difficult than this suggests. For the other judges in the majority are not even obliged to vote for the side they said they were going to vote for in conference. A vote is not final until the court publicly announces its decision, and all judges are free to change their votes at any point up until the announcement. This means that the judge drafting the opinion of the court can actually lose her majority.

One thing that might encourage judges to change their minds is reading a more persuasive competing opinion. If the initial vote is not unanimous, one or more judges will be planning to *dissent*. While the opinion of the court is being drafted, circulated, and revised, these judges will likely prepare a dissenting opinion(s) that will also circulate to the other judges. Even other judges in the majority might choose to write opinions. These are called concurring opinions, or *concurrences*. A particularly important type of concurrence, sometimes called a "special concurrence" is written by someone who agrees with the outcome

---

5   451 U.S. 454, 462-63 (1981)

6   408 U.S. 238 (1972)

favored by the judge drafting the opinion of the court but not with the reasoning behind that opinion. If enough other judges join a special concurrence or a dissenting opinion, it will become the opinion of the court.

We do not have enough inside information about the writing of the Kentucky Supreme Court's opinion to illustrate the writing process through Woodall's case. So let us look instead at one of the U.S. Supreme Court cases that was to become central to the debate in Woodall's appeals. Some Supreme Court justices are diligent about taking notes and preserving documents and are willing to share these with the public after they retire. Typically, a justice's papers are embargoed until his or her death or even later—sometimes until all the justices who served with that justice have left the bench. So they are always somewhat dated by the time we get to look at them—telling us what went on in the Supreme Court twenty or thirty years ago, rather than last year. Still, they are a wonderful source of insight into an appellate court's inner workings.

We have Justice Lewis Powell to thank for an inside look at *Carter v. Kentucky*.[7] The Fifth Amendment of the U.S. Constitution commands that "No person… shall be compelled in any criminal case to be a witness against himself." Sixteen years before *Carter*, in *Griffin v. California*[8], the Supreme Court held that this clause of the Constitution is violated if a prosecutor says anything to the jury about a defendant's refusal to testify at trial or a judge instructs the jury that the defendant's silence can be seen as evidence of guilt. The logic behind this ruling was that holding the defendant's silence against him would be a form of punishment for invoking his right and that someone who knows he can be punished for exercising a right is, in a sense, being compelled to waive that right. The key question in *Carter* was whether the Court should extend this "no adverse inference" rule to require that judges instruct the jury not to draw any inferences from the defendant's silence if the defense requested such an instruction.

Three of the justices on the Court in 1981 had participated in deciding *Griffin*. Justice Brennan had joined the majority opinion, and Justice White had joined a dissent written by Justice Stewart. The other six justices in 1981, including Powell, were facing the question for the first time.

Justice Powell's notes on the Court's conference tell us each justice's preliminary vote and, in some instances, a bit of the justice's reasoning. From

---

7   450 U.S. 288 (1981). Justice Powell donated his papers to the Washington and Lee University School of Law, which has graciously provided the files reproduced in this book.

8   380 U.S. 609 (1965)

his notes we learn that the initial vote was 8-1 to reverse—that is, to rule in favor of the defendant, who had lost in the lower court. Notably, the justice in the minority was Rehnquist. Stewart and White, although having dissented in Griffin, now voted in favor of the defendant, and Powell's notes give us no indication that they struggled much with their decision. For instance, his summary of Justice White's remarks reads, "Prior cases point to requirement that this instruction be given if counsel requests it. Would not go on D/P [Due Process] ground. The privilege not to self-incriminate—as Court has construed it—applies." Curiously, Justice Brennan, who regularly ruled in favor of defendants and had been in the majority in *Griffin*, was more hesitant about extending *Griffin*, saying that he was "[n]ot inclined to constitutionalize a rule in this case" and would prefer to decide for Carter on the "specific facts of this case." However, after all the justices had had a chance to speak, he did say that he might change his mind about this. And indeed he did, as we know from the fact that he later joined the opinion of the Court.

Justice Powell's files do not indicate how many drafts Justice Stewart circulated, but it is clear from the timeline that he made quick progress. The conference was on January 16, 1981, and by February 19, he had already received at least two memos from other justices indicating that they would join his opinion. (In the memo from Justice Marshall reproduced on pages 143-146 you can see the curious language the justices most often employ when they agree to join another justice's opinion: "Please join me.")

In the Supreme Court, this preliminary conference vote is the basis for assigning the opinion of the Court. If the chief justice is in the majority, then he assigns the opinion, either to himself or another justice. If the chief is in the initial minority, then the justice in the majority with the greatest seniority assigns the opinion of the court. Here, Chief Justice Burger was in the majority and wound up assigning the opinion to Justice Stewart. Had Burger voted with Justice Rehnquist in the minority, the prerogative of assigning the opinion would have fallen to Justice Brennan, the justice in the majority who had been on the Court for the longest time

Justice Powell's Conference Notes for *Carter v. Kentucky*

Reverse 8-1

80-5060 Carter v. Kentucky   Conf. 1/16/81

The Chief Justice *Await decision, ~~voted to~~ Reverse*
In Fed Cts & 42 states, rule is that
if Δ — requests an instruction on silence
of accused, it should be given. —
Also held prosecutor was out of bounds
in her comments.
Griffin reserved this Q. See *Lakeside*
See ABA Standards. But most defense lawyers
prefer no instruction & no reference to subject.

Mr. Justice Brennan *Reverse - only on D/P ground.*
Not inclined to Constitutionalize a rule
in this case. Should not impose this
type Q on a state. This is properly
left to Rule making
But on special facts of this case,
~~simple case this~~ court should have
given instruction on matter of D/P.
              x x +
After discussion, W J B said he
may change mind on Const. Q

Mr. Justice Stewart *Reverse*
This is a Const Q, & the 5th amend
applies - self-incrimination:
Reasoning of *Taylor v Ky*, as well
as *Griffin*, requires a Const. rule.

Mr. Justice White *Reverse*

    Prior cases point to requiring
that this instruction be given
if counsel request it.
    Would not go on D/P grounds
    The privilege not to self-
incriminate — as Court has
construed it — applies.

Mr. Justice Marshall *Revd*

Mr. Justice Blackmun *Reverse*

Mr. Justice Powell *Reverse*

    I may have voted differently in *Griffin* as our law unduly handicaps the prosecution, & the one person a jury should be entitled to hear is the Δ.

    But *Griffin* is the law & its rationale controls here. Agree with P.S & B.R.W.

Mr. Justice Rehnquist *Affirm*

    . Would overrule *Griffin* — a weakly reasoned decision

    Should leave to States — not a Court rule.

Mr. Justice Stevens *Reverse*

    Not sure how would have voted in *Griffin*

    But *Griffin* now substantially controls this case.

    Const. right <u>only</u> if instruction is requested.

    agree

Supreme Court of the United States
Washington, D. C. 20543

CHAMBERS OF
JUSTICE THURGOOD MARSHALL

February 19, 1981

Re: No. 80-5060 - Carter v. Kentucky

Dear Potter:

Please join me.

Sincerely,

T.M.

Justice Stewart

cc: The Conference

Justice Marshall's Memo to Justice Stewart Regarding
Carter v. Kentucky

At this point, Justice Rehnquist distributed a memo saying that he would be writing a dissenting opinion, and Justice Powell began drafting a concurring opinion. It would have been obvious to both justices that their opinions had no chance of becoming the opinion of the court, and so you might wonder why they would bother writing them. There are many reasons. A dissent, or a special concurrence taking issue with the majority's reasoning, is often intended as an appeal to the future, the hope being that readers of the opinion will be persuaded by its reasoning and that other courts or even the deciding court itself will end up rejecting the majority view. Some concurrences attempt to put a spin on the opinion of the court, suggesting that it be interpreted in a certain way. Some are meant to counter the arguments in dissenting opinions. But probably the most common function served by any concurring or dissenting opinion is self-expression: a judge wants to go on the record explaining his or her thinking about a case. We can see this clearly in Justice Powell's concurrence, where he expresses his discomfort in joining the majority and explains that he does so because he thinks it proper to follow precedent, not because he agrees with the precedent.

```
lfp/ss 2/19/81

80-5060 Carter v. Commonwealth of Kentucky.

        JUSTICE POWELL, concurring.

        In joining the opinion of the Court, as I do, I

write briefly to make clear that for me this is required by

precedent, not by what I think the Constittuion either

requires or should require.
```

From a Draft of Justice Powell's Concurring Opinion in *Carter v. Kentucky*

Whoever writes it, if an opinion is joined by a majority of judges and therefore becomes the opinion of the court, it stands as the authoritative statement of the court's reasons for its decisions and is the primary source other judges will look to when considering that case as a precedent. As you have surely gathered by now, precedent is integral to the operation of the U.S. judicial system. Furthermore, it is complicated. Exactly how a court will understand and use a precedent depends on a number of things, including the nature of the cases, the content of the precedential opinion, the predilections of later judges, and the relationship between the court setting the precedent and the court deciding the later case. Let us explore precedent in a little more depth, while recognizing that entire books are written on the subject and we cannot do it justice here.

More on Precedent

The most important precedents to any court are those set by its superiors—that is, by courts that have the authority to reverse that court's decisions. Lawyers call these precedents binding, meaning that a lower court is professionally obligated to follow them when deciding relevant cases. Say a state supreme court rules for an insurance company in a dispute over policy coverage. When a trial or appellate court in that state faces a subsequent case involving a very similar situation and very similar policy provision, it is supposed to interpret the policy to favor the insurance company, even if it feels that the outcome is unjust. If the court were to do otherwise by ignoring or defying the supreme court's precedent, it could expect not only to have its decision reversed on appeal, but also to be criticized by much of the legal community.

The U.S. Supreme Court has the authority to reverse any court in the country on a question of federal law. (Recall that it has no authority to reverse a state court on a question of state law.) Therefore, any U.S. Supreme Court decision interpreting the federal constitution, federal statutes, or federal regulations is binding precedent for every court in the country. In citing *Estelle v. Smith* and other U.S. Supreme Court precedents to the Kentucky Supreme Court, Woodall's attorneys understood that even though the Kentucky justices might chafe at some U.S. Supreme Court rulings, they would almost certainly feel professionally obligated to respect them.

The Kentucky Supreme Court, like any state supreme court, sets binding precedent on all other courts any time it interprets the law of its own state. When it comes to federal law, its power is more limited. It has the authority to reverse a Kentucky court's ruling on federal law, but not a federal court's ruling. Therefore, its decisions on federal law are binding precedent only on state courts. Similarly, the U.S. Court of Appeals for the Sixth Circuit, which covers Kentucky (along with Michigan, Ohio, and Tennessee) can hear appeals only from federal courts in the Sixth Circuit. So its rulings are binding precedent for all federal courts in the Sixth Circuit but not for state courts there and not for federal courts elsewhere.

A precedent from another court that is not one's superior has no formal status and is often referred to as persuasive precedent, the idea being that a later court is under no obligation to follow it and will only do so if it thinks the earlier decision is correct, or persuasive. Even though they are not binding, persuasive precedents can play an important role in the judicial process. Especially when judges face a novel and tricky legal problem, reading about how other judges approached the problem can help guide their own thinking. Or if they feel uncertain for whatever reason, knowing that another court—or, better, several other courts—decided in a certain way can help them make a choice. Still, there is nothing unprofessional in rejecting or simply ignoring a persuasive precedent.

There is thus a dramatic difference in the status of precedents from a superior court and from another court that is not one's superior. But what about precedents from one's own court? In some courts these are binding. For instance, in some federal circuit courts one three-judge panel's decision is considered binding precedent on all subsequent panels in that circuit unless the court meets en banc and overrules the first panel's decision. More commonly, though, precedents from one's own court have a status somewhere between that of binding and persuasive precedent. It would be considered professionally improper to ignore precedents from one's own court or to reject them casually, but it is not considered wrong to *overrule* them—that is, to declare that they were decided incorrectly and are no longer valid statements of the law—provided there are strong reasons to do so.

Because judges can usually be counted on to give respectful attention to precedents from any court, lawyers tend to cite any precedents that favor their position. But they understand that the precedents that will carry the most weight with the court are those decided by the court itself or by its superiors. This is reflected in the Woodall brief, where citations of U.S. and Kentucky Supreme Court cases far outnumber citations to any other courts.

You may have noticed that we have written about "following precedent" without explaining precisely what that means. Defining the term turns out to be tricky. To illustrate, let us return to *Estelle v. Smith*, an important precedent in Woodall's case. In *Estelle*, a psychiatrist who had interviewed the defendant, Smith, testified at the sentencing phase of Smith's capital murder trial. The Court ruled that admission of the psychiatrist's testimony was unconstitutional because Smith hadn't been told of his right not to speak with the doctor.

At the most basic level, to follow a precedent means to make the same decision when confronted with a case that's substantially the same as the first one. Of course, no two cases are absolutely identical. (If nothing else, the actions occur at a different time or place.) So by "substantially the same" we mean having essential facts in common. Imagine the prosecution in Woodall's case had tried to introduce a psychiatrist's testimony about Woodall's statements at his sentencing. Woodall's crime was somewhat different from Smith's, but no judge would think that mattered. Being bound to follow *Estelle*, the trial judge would have known that the prosecution could not be allowed to use that testimony.

Now imagine a slightly different scenario: the state tries to force Woodall to take the stand at his own sentencing hearing. The analysis would be a bit more complicated, for forcing a defendant to testify is quite different in some ways from allowing someone else to testify about what a defendant said. Are those differences important enough to render the precedent inapplicable? After even a little thought, you would no doubt conclude that this is an impossible question to answer in the abstract. And you would be right. Deciding whether an earlier case actually serves as a relevant precedent requires us to go beyond the facts and consider the logic of the decision in light of the facts. What was wrong with allowing the psychiatrist to testify? Presumably, the problem was that it allowed Smith's own words to be used against him—he became a witness against himself. If that is right, then it readily follows that the state could not force Woodall to testify, because that is an even more direct way of compelling someone to be a witness against himself.

Here the logic of the precedential decision seems obvious. But that won't always be the case. Imagine, for instance, that the Supreme Court had ruled for the state in *Estelle*. Knowing only the facts and the outcome, one might wonder if Smith lost because (a) allowing someone else's testimony about what you said doesn't turn you into a witness against yourself, (b) that clause of the Fifth Amendment only protects defendants up to the point of conviction, not at post-conviction sentencing, or (c) some other reason entirely. The court setting the precedent can make things easier on later courts by providing an explicit rationale for its holding. That's what the Supreme Court did in *Estelle*, when it explained that it could see no difference between the guilt and penalty phase of a murder trial "so far as the protection of the Fifth Amendment privilege is concerned."

Unfortunately for judges and lawyers, the inclusion of an explanation for a holding is not a foolproof solution. To see why, think about giving reasons in an ordinary situation. Imagine you are considering attending a concert and ask a friend's opinion. The friend says, "I like her music but felt she lacked energy in the concert I saw and didn't engage much with the crowd." Compare that to this response: "Concerts are noisy, and the traffic is always terrible, so you shouldn't bother." The first response would undoubtedly strike you as more helpful than the second. The second just seems too sweeping, making it less obviously relevant to the question you are trying to answer, and raising doubts about the basis for it and the quality of analysis that went into it.

Our distrust of overly sweeping statements is captured by the traditional distinction in common law countries between holdings and dicta (a shortened version of the Latin *obiter dicta*), where dicta are statements thought to be unnecessary to the court's decision. Holdings are entitled to much more weight than dicta. When we say a lower court is bound by precedent, we mean by the holding of the higher court; it is considered acceptable for lower courts to disregard dicta.

Now, you may be wondering how exactly one determines when a statement becomes too broad and crosses the line between holding and dicta. There is no answer to that question, and there is often considerable controversy about what constitutes dicta and whether courts are applying the dicta/holding distinction properly. But the key point to understand is that it complicates one's analysis of precedent. Although determining where precedent points is often a fairly easy matter, interpreting and applying precedent can sometimes present a real challenge, requiring careful and sophisticated consideration of the facts of earlier cases, the logic that appears to underlie them, and the language used to explain them. This can be for the reasons just discussed, because there are multiple plausibly relevant precedents with different results (e.g., some decided for the state, some for the defendant) or because a question in a case has not been directly addressed by previous cases.

In Woodall's case, the two sides disagreed about whether the key issue was already settled by precedent. Recall that at the trial, Woodall's attorneys asked the judge to instruct the jury not to take Woodall's silence into account when deliberating on his sentence. As we have seen, there is support for Woodall's request in the Court's 1965 and 1981 decisions. The problem for Woodall was that the Court had not yet explicitly held that the jury instruction he requested was available in the sentencing phase, after the defendant had pled guilty. So his attorneys were forced to make a somewhat more creative argument: not that the Supreme Court had already decided the issue in his case, but that the logic of the Court's precedents, considered together, showed that Woodall was entitled to the jury instruction he asked for.

In addition to the cases already mentioned, there was one more that looked helpful to Woodall. This case, *Mitchell v. U.S.*[9], was decided after Woodall's trial but before his appeal reached the Kentucky Supreme Court. In *Mitchell*, the U.S. Supreme Court first reaffirmed *Estelle*'s holding that the right to remain silent extends to the sentencing phase of a trial and made it clear that it is irrelevant whether the defendant pled guilty or was convicted after a trial. It also reiterated the "normal rule in a criminal case...that no negative inference from the defendant's failure to testify is permitted" and "decline[d] to adopt an exception for the sentencing phase of a criminal case with regard to factual determinations respecting the circumstances and details of the crime." On the other hand, near the end of its opinion the Court added this somewhat cryptic language: "Whether silence bears upon the determination of a lack of remorse...is a separate question. It is not before us, and we express no view on it."

Woodall's attorneys argued that these cases, read as a group, established that when it comes to the right to remain silent and not to have adverse inferences drawn from one's silence, there is no difference between the trial phase and sentencing phase of a trial and no difference between a sentencing phase that follows a guilty plea and one that follows a trial. Therefore, the trial judge should have instructed the jury not to read anything into Woodall's silence when Woodall's lawyer requested that. Because the trial judge didn't, the Kentucky Supreme Court should send the case back to the trial court for a new sentencing hearing.

Only one justice on the Kentucky Supreme Court accepted Woodall's adverse inference argument.[10] The majority of the justices distinguished the key precedents Woodall relied on (i.e., explained why those opinions were not binding in this situation), stating that they were not sufficiently similar to Woodall's case to require that his be decided the same way. "The factual situation in *Estelle*," the majority wrote, "is different from that presented in this case because it involved the use of an out-of-court statement the defendant made to a government expert. The statement in that case was in regard to a psychological examination by the government prosecutors which

---

9   526 U.S. 314 (1999)

10   *Woodall v. Commonwealth*, 63 S.W.3d 104 (2001)

was used against the defendant without warning in the penalty trial." As for *Mitchell*, there

> the defendant pled guilty to federal charges of conspiring to distribute five or more kilograms of cocaine…The amount of the cocaine would determine the range of penalties. She only admitted that she had done "some of" the conduct charged. She did not testify. Three other codefendants did testify as to the amount of cocaine she had sold. Ultimately, the U.S. Supreme Court ruled that it would not permit a negative inference to be drawn about her guilt with regard to the factual determination respecting the circumstances and details of the crime. Here, Woodall did not contest any of the facts or aggravating circumstances surrounding the crimes.

In its rather terse analysis, the court did not explain why it felt these factual differences were important. And, notably, it did not mention the statement in *Estelle* about the Court's inability to see a difference between guilt and penalty phases when it came to the self-incrimination clause—even though the statement was quoted in *Mitchell*. It didn't reference the language about remorse, either, although that would turn out to be crucial to the case by the end.

The one justice who agreed with Woodall about the adverse inference instruction wrote a dissenting opinion explaining why and noting that she also accepted two of Woodall's arguments concerning the voir dire. Another judge joined this opinion except as to its discussion of Woodall's adverse inference argument. Thus the final vote was 5-2 against Woodall.

A 5-2 vote was a slightly better result than Promotion in Motion achieved in its appeal (Woodall convinced two judges his appeal had some merit, while PIM convinced none), but still the appellant in both cases lost decisively. At most appellate courts, this is the expected outcome. There are several reasons for this. One is that substantial deference is built into the rules of appellate judging. Most court cases turn on the interpretation of facts—which witnesses are telling the truth or remembering things correctly, what is revealed by certain documents or physical evidence. So the most likely source of disagreement between trial and appellate judges is over what actually happened in a case. However, the traditional rule in American courts is that appellate judges will be highly deferential to a trial court's (whether judge's or jury's) findings of fact, rejecting them only if they are clearly erroneous. In other words, an appellate court cannot say the trial judge or jury misread the facts simply because the appellate judges find another reading more plausible; they must have a "definite and firm conviction that a mistake has been committed."[11]

Of course, trial judges make many legal rulings in the course of a trial, and those can be grounds for reversal by a higher court. But for many of those rulings—for instance, most rulings involving voir dire and the admission or exclusion of evidence—the *standard of review* is the highly deferential *abuse of discretion* test. It is unnecessary to get into the details of the abuse of discretion standard here. Just know that it is quite similar to the clearly erroneous standard in requiring considerably more than mere disagreement with a trial judge's ruling before it can be reversed by the court of appeals.

Now, there are plenty of rulings by the trial judge—summary judgments and other judgments as a matter of law, for instance—that are reviewed *de novo* by the appellate court. Under the de novo standard, the appellate judges are to act as if they were the first judges to rule on the contested issues, beginning with no presumption that the trial judge got it right. Yet even where review is de novo, agreement is more common than disagreement. For one thing, appellate and trial judges, as colleagues with very similar training, are likely to view legal questions the same way much of the time. Furthermore, the legal questions presented to them will often be fairly easy ones. True, appeals are expensive, and litigants who recognize that the other side has a much stronger argument will frequently decide against an appeal as a waste of money. But people are not wholly rational, and litigants and lawyers are quite capable of fooling themselves about the prospects for success. In addition, there are times when a litigant feels compelled to appeal even with the odds stacked against a win. Perhaps most importantly, there is a large class of potential appellants for whom the cost-benefit analysis almost always favors an appeal: criminal defendants. The payoff from a successful criminal appeal is tremendous, of course—new proceedings with the possibility of a reduced sentence or even freedom. And most criminal defendants, being indigent, are entitled to free counsel for an appeal. This calculus means that many criminal appeals, especially, have little merit.

For all these reasons, affirmance is the typical outcome in most appellate courts. Also typical was what happened at the next stage of Woodall's case. His lawyers were, of course, dismayed at the Kentucky Supreme Court's rejection of this argument along with all the other arguments they raised. There was still one court further up the hierarchy to which they could appeal—the U.S. Supreme Court. But in the vast majority of cases, Woodall's included, there is

---

11   *United States v. United States Gypsum Co.* 333 U.S. 364, 395 (1948).

no right of appeal to the U.S. Supreme Court; you have to ask it to hear your case. That is what Woodall's lawyers did, but on October 7, 2002, the Court announced that it would not hear his case.

"Wait!" we hear you saying, "you told us at the beginning of the book that Woodall's case did make it to the Supreme Court." Very true, but you might also remember that it didn't get there for another decade or so. The way it did is through a process that looks a lot like an appeal but technically is not. It began with Woodall's filing of an application (or petition) for a writ of habeas corpus. Habeas corpus is as controversial as it is important, and no account of the American judicial system can be complete without a description of it.

Habeas Corpus

The writ of habeas corpus, sometimes referred to by lawyers as the Great Writ, originated in the common law of England long before the colonies were founded and was considered a fundamental part of American law by the time the Constitution was ratified. Article 1, Section 9 of the U.S. Constitution says nothing about how exactly habeas corpus should operate but highlights its importance with the command that "The Privilege of the Writ of Habeas Corpus shall not be suspended, unless when in Cases of Rebellion or Invasion the public Safety may require it."

At the most basic level, habeas corpus protects against being incarcerated without a trial. If the police were to arrest someone and hold him in jail without charging him with a crime, his lawyer would go to court and ask that it command the state to either release his client or immediately implement proper procedures—charges, arraignment, bail hearing, etc. The court would issue this command through a writ of habeas corpus. Prisoners held at the military base in Guantanamo, Cuba since the second Gulf War have applied for writs of habeas corpus in U.S. courts and are using the writ precisely in this traditional way, saying that they should either be charged and tried or released. Their cases are complicated by the fact that they are foreign nationals alleged to be involved in warlike activities against U.S. citizens and are being held outside the U.S. But the underlying claim is a simple one.

The bulk of habeas corpus cases, including Woodall's, involve more complex claims—not that the prisoner is being held without trial, but that there were serious legal flaws in the trial where he was convicted or sentenced. Although this extends the reach of habeas corpus, one can easily see the logic of it. Imagine being seized by a police officer in a one-party state, charged by a prosecutor from that party on the basis of trumped-up evidence, brought to a court presided over by another party official, and tried in front of jury members who are warned by the prosecutor that they should do "justice" if they do not wish to see their family members suffer. The fact that certain procedures are observed would be no consolation to you. Nor should a just society be prepared to accept your imprisonment. From either perspective, there is no important difference between imprisoning someone after a farcical trial and imprisoning someone without trial.

Imagine a less extreme example: the prosecutor, judge, and jury all act in good faith, but the police fabricate the evidence against you. Here, too, most people would feel that the conviction could not stand and that a court that became aware of the fabrication of evidence should order the prisoner released. To go one step further, how much difference would it make if the conviction was based on proper evidence but fabricated evidence was introduced at the sentencing phase? There would be no need to overturn the conviction in this case, but there is a strong argument that the sentence should be vacated and redone. Our intuition seems to be that habeas corpus should be available not just for people who are held without any trial at all, but also for those imprisoned after an illegitimate trial, whether at the guilt or sentencing phase.

This intuition has been incorporated into habeas corpus law for many years and in fact has been codified by Congress. According to current federal law, "The Supreme Court, a Justice thereof, a circuit judge, or a district court shall entertain an application for a writ of habeas corpus in behalf of a person in custody pursuant to the judgment of a State court only on the ground that he is in custody in violation of the Constitution or laws or treaties of the United States."[12] The "only" near the end of that sentence is an important limitation. It means that not every problem with a trial is grounds for a successful habeas challenge. For instance, say an innocent defendant knew that an important prosecution witness had lied at his trial. As long as the prosecution was unaware that the witness was lying, this would not normally succeed as a habeas claim. Still, the broad language of the statute does open the door to a variety of claims.

This breadth is one reason why habeas is controversial. There are many ways in which U.S. law can be violated in the course of a police investigation, prosecution, and trial. For instance, the police pull over and arrest a driver because they think his license plate matches that of a car reported stolen. They find a gun and drugs in his jacket and large quantities of drugs in his car. It turns out that the police misread the license plate, and the car really

---

12   28 U.S.C. § 2254.

belonged to the driver. This makes the initial seizure of the driver and the subsequent search illegal under the Fourth Amendment. But many people would think it wrong to free the obviously guilty driver on the basis of this "technicality." Furthermore, even unsuccessful habeas petitions can take years to make it through the system, tying up judicial resources and delaying the final resolution of cases.

You may have spotted the other reason why habeas is controversial in the quoted language from the statue. The statue authorizes all federal courts, not just the U.S. Supreme Court, to undo *state court* convictions or sentences. Recall from Chapter Two that while state courts (as well as lower federal courts) are subordinate to the Supreme Court when it comes to interpretations of federal law, state courts are not subordinate to other federal courts. The equal standing of state and federal courts is a core tenet of the federalist system. The habeas process appears to violate that tenet. True, an application for habeas is technically a new (civil) case, not a direct appeal. But in practice the result of a successful habeas petition is indistinguishable from the result of a successful appeal: one court tells another that it got the law wrong and that it has to start over. In the most dramatic departures from the norm, as in Woodall's case, it is a federal trial court telling a state supreme court that it messed up.

Congress's decision to give all federal courts habeas authority over state courts was not unreasoned. Unlike federal judges, few state court judges hold their positions for life. If they want to continue in office they must be reappointed—or, more often—reelected when their terms expire. Ordering retrials or resentencing of defendants, especially if they look guilty, is rarely a popular action. State judges who want another term in office may sometimes hesitate to take such an action even when it is warranted. Federal judges, with complete job security, don't have to worry as much about such pressures. Federal habeas corpus provides another line of defense against injustice. Because there are far too many habeas cases each year for the Supreme Court to handle, lower federal courts must be allowed to hear them if it is to be an effective line of defense. (For example, between October 1, 2013 and September 30, 2014, just under 20,000 habeas petitions were filed in federal district courts.)

Nevertheless, concerns about the abuse of habeas corpus by guilty prisoners and about the relationship between state and federal courts have troubled many people over the years. One longstanding response to these concerns is a requirement that the prisoner take all available steps to get the conviction or sentence overturned in state court before petitioning a federal court for habeas corpus. (This requirement is referred to as exhaustion of remedies.) Woodall, for instance, could not have simply skipped his appeal to the Kentucky Supreme

Court and gone right to a federal district court with a habeas petition; the district judge would have refused to consider it.

Even so, some critics have called for more restrictions on habeas corpus. The most important of those critics have been on the U.S. Supreme Court and in Congress. The Court issued a series of opinions in the 1970s through 1990s making it more difficult for prisoners to succeed in their habeas petitions.[13] Congress continued this trend through amendments to habeas corpus law in the 1996 Anti-Terrorism and Effective Death Penalty Act. It imposed new time limits on habeas applications and, very importantly, added the following condition:

> An application for a writ of habeas corpus on behalf of a person in custody pursuant to the judgment of a State court shall not be granted with respect to any claim that was adjudicated on the merits in State court proceedings unless the adjudication of the claim—
>
> (1) resulted in a decision that was contrary to, or involved an unreasonable application of, clearly established Federal law, as determined by the Supreme Court of the United States; or
>
> (2) resulted in a decision that was based on an unreasonable determination of the facts in light of the evidence presented in the State court proceeding.

In the end, as we will see, the first criterion played a crucial role in Woodall's case.

Other Important Personnel

The habeas petition that was presented to Chief Judge Thomas Russell of the U.S. District Court for the Western District of Kentucky was about the same in scope and length as the brief to the Kentucky Supreme Court. You may be thinking that that's a lot to work through for a judge juggling many other cases at the same time (and, as chief judge, some important administrative responsibilities). You would be right. For this reason, judges are provided with different kinds of assistants to help manage their work.

---

13   John H. Blume. 2006. *AEDPA: The "Hype" and the "Bite."* CORNELL LAW REVIEW 259-301.

Even in the earliest years, judges had administrative help. The oldest supporting position is the clerk of court. Every court, whether trial or appellate, state or federal, has a clerk supported by a staff. Clerks' offices range from two or three employees in the smallest courts to dozens of employees in the busiest metropolitan courts. Whatever their size and whatever the nature of the court, the clerk's office is the place where lawyers and litigants file pleadings, motions, and other papers in the cases brought in the court. The clerk's office keeps a file on each case and maintains the docket book and the official record of the court's actions in all of its cases. Its personnel work closely with the judges in setting cases for hearing or trial and in generally managing the court's docket to keep the cases moving. An effectively functioning clerk's office is essential to a smoothly functioning court.

In addition, individual judges have long had secretarial help for writing/typing and other clerical chores. In fact, administrative staff far outnumber judges. For example, in the Virginia court system there are over 2,800 employees, but only 419 are judges; in the California judiciary there are over 21,000 employees, of whom only 1,660 are judges.

Still, for much of U.S. history, judges were on their own when it came to their core tasks. They researched the law, analyzed the issues, reached decisions, and wrote opinions without assistance from anyone else (except for other judges on the panel in appellate cases). This began to change in the late nineteenth century when law clerks were introduced into the U.S. Supreme Court. The idea spread to the federal appellate courts in the 1920s and to state courts and federal trial courts after that.

A law clerk—not to be confused with the clerk of the court, a long-term administrative officer—is usually a recent and exceptionally successful law school graduate. For nearly all clerks, a clerkship is the first job after graduation, and typically a clerk serves only one year, at most two. The clerk is a personal legal assistant to the judge. The clerk's office or working area is usually immediately next to the judge's office, and there is frequent daily contact. Judges use their clerks in various ways. In general, clerks do legal research, prepare memos summarizing and analyzing the facts and issues in a case, edit drafts of opinions written by the judge, and serve as a sounding board and discussion partner for the judge. It has become increasingly common for judges to have their clerks prepare initial drafts of opinions, a practice that has sometimes been criticized as an undue delegation of judicial responsibility.

Today all federal judges are entitled to at least two clerks and have at least one. Appellate judges in both state and federal courts universally employ clerks. Judges in many appellate courts, including all the U.S. Courts of Appeals, can also call on staff attorneys for assistance. Staff attorneys serve much the same function as law clerks, except that they serve the court as a whole, not individual judges. Furthermore, they tend to serve for longer, with some making a career of it. Staff attorneys often screen cases for panels, recommending against oral argument in cases that they feel can be decided easily. They can even recommend dispositions of cases and draft opinions for the judges.

The work of law clerks in trial courts differs somewhat from that of law clerks in appellate courts. Appellate clerks spend much time working on the opinions that their judges are assigned to prepare for the court. Trial clerks also draft some memoranda and short opinions, but in addition they assist the judge with motions of all sorts and in pretrial conferences and hearings. They often deal directly with parties' lawyers to assist the judge in managing his docket. To a considerable extent these differing duties reflect the difference between the work of a trial court and that of an appellate court.

Even with the help of clerks, the complicated business of trials can be too much to handle. Legislatures have responded by authorizing the appointment of quasi-judicial officers to help process cases. "Special masters" or just "masters" have been around since the country was founded and are still used today. A master's position is typically part-time, filled by court appointment on an ad hoc basis for a specific purpose. Masters are often practicing lawyers appointed to assist the court in particularly complicated or protracted matters. For example, in a civil action involving an elaborate financial accounting the trial judge might designate a lawyer as a master to conduct the accounting and report the results to the court. In cases requiring the testimony of numerous widely scattered witnesses, the court could appoint a master to preside over the taking of the testimony and to transmit that testimony to the court with recommendations for factual findings. Masters, however, are the exception and not the rule, and their actions are in the form of recommendations to the judges, who exercise the final decision-making authority.

By far the most important assisting officers in the federal system today are magistrate judges. Unlike traditional federal judges, who are appointed by the president with the consent of the Senate, magistrate judges are appointed by the court, and they hold office for terms of eight years, with the possibility of reappointment.

Federal magistrate judges perform two kinds of functions. First, they hold hearings on a variety of motions and make recommendations to the district judge as to the disposition of those motions. Assistance of this sort enables district judges to take care of matters like oversight of discovery without having to conduct hearings themselves; they can simply accept the magistrates' recommendations. Magistrate judges also hold hearings on habeas corpus petitions and make recommendations to the district judge. Second, magistrate judges are authorized to conduct trials in civil cases and in criminal misdemeanor cases if the parties consent. In other words, the parties can choose to go to trial before a magistrate judge instead of a district judge. If the parties exercise this option, the magistrate judge is empowered to decide the case and enter final judgment in the name of the district court.

You may be troubled to learn that so much important work in the federal courts is done by little-known people chosen by judges rather than those vetted by and chosen by the president and Senate. If so, you are not alone. But understand that this practice is a response to large caseloads and that there are not many plausible alternatives. Probably the most important alternative to consider is significantly increasing the number of positions for Article III judges (those appointed by the president and confirmed by the Senate, as described in Article III of the Constitution). Congress can do this any time it wishes, as the number is set by statute, not the Constitution. The idea of increasing numbers is not popular with many sitting judges (who would become somewhat less unique and influential), nor does it appear to have a great deal of support among lawyers.[14] That is not to say that it is not worth considering, though.

Woodall's Habeas Petition

In any case, the system we have is one where many people aside from Article III judges play an important role in the judicial process. When Woodall's application for habeas corpus was filed in the district court, Judge Russell referred it to Magistrate Judge W. David King. (Because a habeas petition is technically filed against the official responsible for incarcerating the prisoner, the case was now called *Woodall v. Simpson*. Simpson was the warden of the prison where Woodall was being held.) In addition to the lengthy petition, Judge King read a response brief from the state and a reply brief from Woodall. In a 45-page opinion, Judge King rejected all of Woodall's arguments and recommended that the petition be denied. Woodall, naturally, objected to that recommendation. As a result, Judge Russell was required to review the petition.

---

14   There are exceptions. For instance, many lawyers and judges believe the Ninth Circuit Court of Appeals should have more judges because it is so busy. Others argue that it should be split into two circuits with more collective judges to handle the large caseload.

Judge Russell agreed with the magistrate judge about almost all of Woodall's arguments, though in some instances his reasons were different. But he disagreed about two: Woodall's adverse inference argument and one of his complaints about voir dire. (The complaint was that he should have been able to challenge the prosecution's peremptory challenge of an African-American juror as a possible violation of constitutional law.) Finding that the Kentucky trial court had misapplied clearly established federal law in these two respects, Judge Russell granted Woodall's application for a writ of habeas corpus in part, ordered his sentence vacated, and remanded the case to the Kentucky trial court for resentencing.

VI. ORDER

The court **ADOPTS** the Magistrate Judge's Report and Recommendation with the modifications discussed above.

IT IS ORDERED that Petitioner Robert Keith Woodall's application for a writ of habeas corpus (DN 1) is **GRANTED IN PART** and **DENIED WITH PREJUDICE IN PART**. The application is **GRANTED** as to 1) Petitioner's claim that the trial court's failure to give a no adverse inference instruction as requested by Petitioner violated his Fifth Amendment right to remain silent and his Fourteenth Amendment right to a fair trial and 2) the trial Court's failure to recognize that Petitioner had a right to make a *Batson* challenge to the exclusion of an African-American juror violated the due process and equal protection clauses of the Fourteenth Amendment. The application is in all other respects **DENIED**.

IT IS FURTHER ORDERED that Petitioner Robert Keith Woodall's sentences of September 4, 1998, to death and life in prison for the rape, murder, and kidnapping of Sarah Hansen are **VACATED**, and this matter is **REMANDED** to the state trial court for further proceedings.

IT IS FURTHER ORDERED that a certificate of appealability shall issue with respect Petitioner's claim that the jury instructions impermissibly implied required unanimity with respect to mitigating circumstances.

Date: February 23, 2009

Thomas B. Russell

Thomas B. Russell
Chief Judge, U.S. District Court

Judge King's Order Granting Woodall's Application for a Writ of Habeas Corpus

In the last paragraph of his opinion, Judge Russell issued a "certificate of appealability… with respect to Petitioner's argument that the jury instructions impermissibly implied required unanimity with respect to mitigating circumstances." The certificate of appealability is another outgrowth of concerns about prisoners' abuses of the habeas process. Under the federal habeas corpus statute, state prisoners do not have an automatic right to appeal the denial of a habeas petition. In order to appeal, the petitioner must be given a certificate of appealability from either the district court or the court of appeals indicating that a reasonable judge could believe that the prisoner had a plausible claim to have been denied a constitutional right.[15] Here Judge Russell was saying, with admirable professionalism, "I believe my decision on this issue is correct, but reasonable judges might disagree with me, so Woodall should be allowed to appeal it."

This certificate could have played a major role in later proceedings if Judge Russell had denied Woodall's petition entirely. As it was, the more immediately important question was whether the U.S. Court of Appeals for the Sixth Circuit would agree with Judge Russell's rulings in favor of Woodall. The answer came after several rounds of briefs and an oral argument: the court of appeals affirmed Judge Russell's ruling on the adverse inference instruction by a 2–1 vote. Because that was enough to necessitate a new trial, the appeals court refrained from ruling on any of the other disputed issues.

The Sixth Circuit's order could have led to Woodall's release from prison if Kentucky did not begin new sentencing proceedings within a certain time. But Kentucky told the court that it intended to appeal the decision to the U.S. Supreme Court and asked the Sixth Circuit to put its order on hold until the Supreme Court had decided whether to hear the case. The Sixth Circuit agreed to do this by issuing a "stay of mandate." As promised, Kentucky did go to the U.S. Supreme Court, and this time the Court agreed to hear the case. We take up the story of how the case reached the Supreme Court and what happened there in the next chapter, where we also expand on some important topics that we have only touched on so far. ■

---

15   *Slack v. McDaniel*, 529 U.S. 473 (2000).

CHAPTER 7

The Supreme Court

I
f we have succeeded in our task to this point in the book, you should now be well aware that an awful lot of what happens in American legal systems takes place somewhere other than the U.S. Supreme Court. It may have occurred to you that the amount of attention the Supreme Court gets from the media relative to other courts is far disproportionate to the share of the work it shoulders. Certainly that is what we think. So you may be wondering why we would devote an entire chapter to the Supreme Court.

There are two reasons, and those reasons are in some tension with each other. One is that we simply know a lot more about the Supreme Court than any other court. This is because it receives disproportionate attention from scholars as well as the media. With better access to information about the Supreme Court, we can use examples from it to flesh out some discussions of process from the last chapter. The other reason is the Court's uniqueness. While almost every characteristic that makes it interesting is shared with at least some other courts, the combination of characteristics it possesses ensures that things work differently there—differently enough that someone who only knew about the Supreme Court would have a drastically distorted view of how courts in general operate.

The upshot of this is that we can learn a lot by focusing on the Supreme Court but that we need to think carefully about how what we learn applies to other courts and how it does not. Let us begin by considering the set of characteristics that make the Court special. First, the Court's pronouncements set federal law for the country as a whole and are not subject to reversal by any higher court. Second, the Court has almost complete discretion in choosing its *docket*—which cases it will hear and decide. Third, the U.S. Constitution provides that the justices of the Court serve for "good behavior," meaning that they can stay on the Court as long as they wish, provided they do not commit "treason, bribery, or other high crimes and misdemeanors" that could lead to their being impeached by the House of Representatives and convicted by a two-thirds vote of the Senate.

All federal district and circuit judges enjoy the same job security as the Supreme Court justices, as do judges in a handful of states. Control of its docket is not unique to the Supreme Court, either; many state supreme courts have considerable discretion in choosing cases. And just as the Supreme Court has the final say when it comes to federal law, each state supreme court is the ultimate authority in interpreting the law of that state. Furthermore, the phrase "final say" is not quite accurate. Any Supreme Court interpretation of a federal statute or administrative regulation can be overturned through ordinary legislation. Even constitutional decisions can be overturned through constitutional amendments, though those are much more difficult to pass. (Amendments to the U.S. Constitution must be proposed by a two-thirds vote of each house of Congress or at a convention called for by at least two-thirds of the state's legislatures and then must be ratified by three-fourths of the states.)

So it is not that the Supreme Court is different in all ways from all other courts in the system. But its characteristics, taken together, do make it easily distinguishable from other American courts, both in how it operates and in what it produces.

Certiorari

From a litigant's perspective, the most important difference between the Supreme Court and lower federal courts, aside from the fact that Supreme Court precedents have greater authority, is that there is typically no right of appeal to the Supreme Court. That is, if you want the Supreme Court to hear your case, with very few exceptions, you must convince it that your case is important enough to be considered by the top court in the land. This was not always true, but as the country grew the justices began to feel overwhelmed with cases and felt they could not give adequate attention to the most important ones. Congress responded in 1925 and then again in 1988 with legislation relieving the Court of the duty to hear most cases. A sprinkling of cases get to the Supreme Court by other routes even today, but the vast majority depend on the Court's acquiescence and get there through what is called a *writ of certiorari*. A request for such a writ is formally called a petition for a *writ of certiorari*, or "cert petition" for short.

The Supreme Court is not in session through the entire year. It begins a term on the first Monday in October and usually finishes the term around the end of the following June, with the exact date determined by how long it takes the Court to wrap up business. The term is dated according to when it starts, with the odd result that most of the Court's work in a given term is labeled with the wrong year. For instance, the 2013 term of the Court (more formally, the 2013 October Term) began on October 7, 2013 and concluded on June 30, 2014, with most of the work occurring in 2014. In that period, the Supreme Court decided seventy-nine cases with the full appellate-process treatment—reading of briefs, oral argument, and an opinion explaining the outcome. The Court disposed of an additional seventy-two cases without oral argument, but many of these were simply sent back without an opinion to lower courts to reanalyze in light of opinions the Court had issued. These numbers are typical for recent years. In the previous four terms, the number of cases decided fully by the Court was 77, 79, 86, and 82.[1]

That's a total of 403 cases across the last five terms. In that same period, according to annual year-end reports submitted by the chief justice, the Supreme Court received 38,614 cert petitions, an average of 7,723 per year. The math is easy to do: the Court grants about 1% of the cert petitions submitted to it.

This number is slightly misleading, for there are two types of cert petitions. Ordinarily, a litigant asking the Court to hear its case must pay a $300 filing fee and submit forty copies of the cert petition, formatted and bound according to strict guidelines.[2] Such "paid" petitions are the minority. The Court receives several times as many *in forma pauperis* (ifp) petitions. These petitions, requiring a signed statement that the litigant cannot afford the filing fee, are allowed to be filed without the fee, with ten copies rather than forty, and with slightly relaxed printing rules. The vast majority of ifp petitions are from inmates, desperate to be freed from prison and with little to lose by petitioning the Court. As a result, many lack merit, and as a whole, these are far less likely to be granted than paid petitions. But even for paid petitions the success rate is only about 5%. And we have no way of knowing how many potential cases drop out when the parties decide against the expense of a petition to the Supreme Court in light of the low probability of a grant. The fundamental fact is that a litigant's chances of getting a case to the Supreme Court are extremely slim.

---

1   http://www.uscourts.gov/uscourts/Statistics/JudicialBusiness/2014/appendices/A01Sep14.pdf

2   http://www.supremecourt.gov/ctrules/2013RulesoftheCourt.pdf

This is not because the formal rules of the Court are stacked against petitioners. In fact, it only takes four of the nine justices to grant certiorari. The process, once a petition has been filed, begins with the justices' clerks. This was not always the case. In early years justices read cert petitions themselves, and Justice William Brennan continued to handle many cert petitions himself even after the volume of petitions had grown immensely.[3] However, as far as we know, Justice Brennan was the last justice to process a significant number of petitions directly; all other justices for the past several decades have relied on their clerks to screen petitions for them.

Even divided among a justice's four clerks, several thousand petitions a year is a lot to keep up with. In the early 1970s, several justices addressed this problem by creating a "cert pool."[4] Each justice who is a member of the pool contributes clerks to it. The clerks in the pool take turns reviewing and preparing memos about cert petitions for all the justices in the pool.

The cert pool is highly efficient; instead of several different clerks each writing separate memos for their justices, a single clerk acts for all, allowing the other clerks to work on other things. But the practice also carries a risk—that the one clerk will miss something that makes a case worthy of being heard by the Court. Perhaps for this reason, there has never been a time when all nine justices have participated in the pool. (As of this writing, Justice Alito is the sole justice outside of the pool.) Having at least one justice outside the pool ensures that at least two clerks will review the petition with some care. In addition, justices typically have their own clerks review and, where appropriate, respond to cert memos.[5] And, naturally, justices will themselves read petitions if something in a clerk's memo catches their eye.

In the vast majority of cases, the pool clerk summarizes the issues and recommends that certiorari be denied, the other clerks readily agree, nothing jumps out at any of the justices, and cert is in fact denied. In the exceptional cases, at least one justice concludes that the petition deserves serious consideration and asks the chief justice to place it on the "discuss list." At the next conference, the justices briefly discuss this case and any others that made it on the list and take a vote. If four justices agree to hear the case, cert will be granted.

---

3   H.W. Perry, Jr. 1991. Deciding to Decide: *Agenda Setting in the United States Supreme* Court. (Harvard University Press).

4   David M. O'Brien. 1997. "Join-3 Votes, the Rule of Four, the Cert. Pool, and the Supreme Court's Shrinking Plenary Docket." *Journal of Law and Politics* 23:779-808.

5   Todd C. Peppers. 2006. *Courtiers of the Marble Palace: The Rise and Influence of the Supreme Court Law Clerk.* (Stanford University Press).

Justice Powell's file on *Carter v. Kentucky*, which we visited in Chapter 5, offers a glimpse into the cert process. The first document in that file is the cert pool memo—written, notably, by John Roberts, then a clerk to Justice Rehnquist and now Chief Justice of the U.S. Supreme Court. Roberts indicates that he thinks Carter's argument is weak, though he doesn't offer an explicit recommendation to grant or deny. Toward the bottom of this copy of the pool memo we see handwritten comments from Paul Cane, one of Justice Powell's clerks, noting that he sees the question raised by the petition as "significant" but is "undecided" about whether the Court should grant cert. At the top of the memo are a few lines in Justice Powell's handwriting summarizing the main issue and indicating that, like his clerk, he thought it might make sense to put off deciding the issue.

The next document, a docket sheet, tells us that cert was granted. Justice Powell and four other justices voted to deny cert, while Justices Brennan, Marshall, and Stevens voted to grant cert. Justice Stewart cast a Join-3 vote, a somewhat odd practice in which a justice says he doesn't feel strongly that a case should be heard but is willing to cast a fourth vote for cert if three other justices want to hear the case.[6] That made four votes, and the Court issued an order shortly afterwards informing the parties that the case would be heard.

Reasons for Granting Cert

What do Carter and other litigants who beat the odds and persuade the Court to hear their case have in common? What makes a case special enough for the Supreme Court to take it? The Supreme Court's own published rules as well as empirical studies by scholars agree in pointing to two key things that matter most and one that matters less than you might expect.

Let us begin with the factor that is less important than you might think. As the justices themselves have often said in public statements, the Court sees its primary function not as correcting errors in lower court decisions, but as making law or policy. As the Court sees it, the first level of appeal is there to ensure that the lower court got things right. The second level of appeal is meant to serve the needs of the judicial system, not the individual litigant. This is not to say that the justices will never agree to hear a case simply to rectify a serious injustice. And unlike the typical appellate court, the Supreme Court actually reverses lower court rulings more often than it affirms, indicating that the

---

6   For a fuller discussion of the practice, see the O'Brien article cited in footnote 4 of this chapter.

justices are somewhat more likely to take cases when they disagree with the lower court decision. Still, the fact is that disagreement with the lower court is not a driving force in their choice of cases. They frequently take cases even though they agree with the lower court and refuse to hear cases even though they might have voted differently in the lower court's place.

There is an important corollary to this point that is often overlooked in media coverage of the Court.[7] Although a cert denial has the same effect as an affirmance for the parties to the case, it is not the equivalent of an affirmance as far as the law is concerned. When the justices affirm a lower court decision, they say that lower court decision was right, thereby setting a precedent that can guide lower courts. When they deny certiorari, all they are saying is that they don't want to hear the case. They do not tell us whether they think that the lower court was right, and we cannot assume they thought it was, so no new precedent is set. The law is the same after a cert denial as it was before it.

What matters most to the justices in choosing cases is their importance in the larger scheme of things. A case can be important in the sense that the resolution of it will have a direct and major impact on society. *Bush v. Gore* (deciding the 2000 presidential election) and *U.S. v. Nixon* (requiring Richard Nixon to turn over the Watergate tapes and hastening his exit from the presidency) are examples. A decision declaring a major statute unconstitutional would be important in this sense too. But more often what makes a case important is that it raises a legal issue likely to arise in many other cases. Whether or not Woodall would be executed was, of course, a very serious question, but it seems likely that only a small number of people cared deeply about the outcome and felt that their lives were directly affected by it. What made his case important from the Supreme Court's perspective was that the question of the proper jury instructions on adverse inference was likely to come up at many sentencing hearings in the future.

The fact that a case raises an important legal issue makes it more likely that the Court will hear it, but it is no guarantee. Even a major legal question can sometimes be easy to answer, and if lower courts appear to be having little trouble with it, the Supreme Court may see no point in intervening. Recognizing this points us to the other most important criterion in the Court's selection of cases—whether the law in an area needs to be clarified. A complicated statute, a terse and vague provision of the Constitution, ambiguity or inconsistency in Supreme Court precedents: all of these can cause lower courts

---

7   Elliot E. Slotnick and Jennifer A. Segal. 1998. *Television News and the Supreme Court.* Cambridge University Press, chapter 6.

to struggle in their efforts to make sense of federal law. As chief interpreter of federal law, the Supreme Court has the responsibility to help lower courts through these difficulties by providing authoritative answers.

The clearest signal that lower courts are experiencing difficulty is disagreement among them about the answer to a legal question. The most dramatic manifestation of disagreement is an inter-circuit conflict, where two or more federal courts of appeals, each supervising a multi-state circuit, address the same legal issue and reach decisions that cannot be reconciled with each other. The presence of an inter-circuit conflict makes it considerably more likely that the Supreme Court will agree to hear a case.

To see why, consider the circumstances behind *EC Term of Years Trust v. United States.*[8] If the IRS informs a taxpayer that he has underpaid his taxes and the taxpayer refuses to pay the amount due, the IRS can seize and sell a portion of the taxpayer's property to get the money owed. Sometimes, as with property that has been placed in a trust, someone other than the taxpayer claims an interest in the property and can challenge the IRS seizure. In the *EC Term of Years* case, the litigants challenging the IRS seizure argued that there were two different methods they could use to challenge the seizure. The U.S. Court of Appeals for the Fifth Circuit disagreed with them, ruled that the method they chose was the wrong one, and dismissed their claim against the IRS. Several years before this, another federal court of appeals—the Ninth Circuit—had ruled the other way, allowing litigants to use the alternate method later rejected by the Fifth Circuit.

This inter-circuit conflict caused two major problems. First, although federal law should be the same for everyone in the country, here property owners in one large region of the country had a resource against the IRS that was not available to property owners in another large region of the country. Second, the federal government, which operates in all regions, faced the administrative inconvenience of adapting its operations to different laws in different places. Thus circuit conflicts can raise serious issues of fairness and efficiency. The Court does not resolve every circuit conflict it encounters; the issue involved may be too minor, or the Court may wish to give lower courts more time to work out possible solutions. But it takes conflicts seriously, and the combination of an important issue and inter-circuit conflict make it highly likely that cert will be granted.

The Woodall case does not fit perfectly with this account of certiorari, reminding us that the real world is always too messy to reduce to a few simple

---

8   550 U.S. 429 (2007)

rules. The Supreme Court, after briefs and oral argument, wound up ruling against Woodall, reversing the court of appeals. Here is a key passage from the opinion of the court, written by Justice Scalia: "Perhaps the logical next step from *Carter, Estelle*, and *Mitchell* would be to hold that the Fifth Amendment requires a penalty-phase no-adverse-inference instruction in a case like this one; perhaps not. Either way, we have not yet taken that step, and there are reasonable arguments on both sides—which is all Kentucky needs to prevail in this AEDPA case." In other words, after making Woodall's case one of the very few it considered that year, the Court didn't actually answer the question at the heart of the case!

Its refusal to do so does not rule out the possibility that it took the case in the first place because it saw an important issue that was causing some problems for lower courts. But it is hard to escape the conclusion that some of the justices were at least partly motivated by the feeling that the court of appeals (and district court) had made a misstep. That said, the justices still focused on a bigger issue than what happened to Woodall—namely, how federal courts should approach habeas petitions and how much deference they should show to state courts. The thrust of the majority opinion is that the federal courts here were too willing to substitute their judgment for that of the state court and failed to pay adequate attention to the requirement that they only grant a habeas petition if the state court failed to follow "clearly established law." (The three Supreme Court justices who dissented agreed with the lower federal courts that the Kentucky courts had disregarded clearly established law that favored Woodall.) The Court's action here was meant to provide guidance to other federal courts in the future, not just to resolve Woodall's case.

Judicial Review

When we think about the Supreme Court, the cases most likely to come to mind are politically controversial ones that raise people's hackles and are exciting to debate. Most involve the federal Constitution. On the other hand, legal matters in general are frequently technical and, to those not directly affected by them, boring. And most do not involve the Constitution. If the Supreme Court's chief criteria for choosing legal issues to decide are that the issues are in need of clarification and are likely to come up in other cases, then we should expect the Court's docket to be populated by non-constitutional cases that put people to sleep as well as ones that send their blood pressure skyrocketing. Look at the box on pages 173-174 and you will see that this is indeed true. Each of the cases there was decided in the Court's 2013 Term. Some might strike you as interesting if you know something about the issues underlying them; others couldn't interest anyone who wasn't paid to be interested in them. Only two raise questions about the Constitution. But all were deemed important enough to take up one of the scarce spots on the Court's docket. And these are just a small sample; a fair number of other cases from that term look much the same. One cannot fully understand the Court without recognizing that cases of that sort make up an important part of its workload.

Issues from Selected Cases in the Supreme Court's 2013 Term

■ *U.S. v. Woods:* "whether the penalty for tax underpayments attributable to valuation misstatements, 26 U. S. C. §6662(b)(3), is applicable to an underpayment resulting from a basis-inflating transaction subsequently disregarded for lack of economic substance."

■ *Atlantic Marine Construction Co. v. U.S. District Court:* "concerns the procedure that is available for a defendant in a civil case who seeks to enforce a forum-selection clause."

■ *Heimeshoff v. Hartford Life & Accident Insurance Co.* "A participant in an employee benefit plan covered by the Employee Retirement Income Security Act of 1974 (ERISA), 88 Stat. 829, as amended, 29 U. S. C. §1001 et seq., may bring a civil action under §502(a)(1)(B) to benefits due under the terms of the plan . . . ERISA does not, specify a statute of limitations for filing suit under §502(a)(1)(B). Filling that gap, the plan at issue here requires participants to bring suit within three years after 'proof of loss' is due . . . The question presented is whether the contractual limitations provision is enforceable."

■ *Daimler AG v. Bauman:* "concerns the authority of a court in the United States to entertain a claim brought by foreign plaintiffs against a foreign defendant based on events occurring entirely outside the United States."

■ *Mississippi ex rel. Hood v. AU Optronics Corp.:* "whether a suit filed by a State as the sole plaintiff constitutes a "mass action" under [the Class Action Fairness Act] where it includes a claim for restitution based on injuries suffered by the State's citizens."

■ *Medtronic. v. Mirowski Family Ventures:* "when a licensee seeks a declaratory judgment against a patentee to establish that there is no infringement, the burden of proving infringement remains with the patentee."

- ■ *Burrage v. U.S.:* "The Controlled Substances Act imposes a 20-year mandatory minimum sentence on a defendant who unlawfully distributes a Schedule I or II drug, when 'death or serious bodily injury results from the use of such substance.' We consider whether the mandatory-minimum provision applies when use of a covered drug supplied by the defendant contributes to, but is not a but-for cause of, the victim's death or injury."

- ■ *Sandifer v. United States Steel Corp.:* "The question before us is the meaning of the phrase "changing clothes" as it appears in the Fair Labor Standards Act of 1938, 52 Stat. 1060, as amended, 29 U. S. C. §201 et seq."

- ■ *Walden v. Fiore:* "whether a court in Nevada may exercise personal jurisdiction over a defendant on the basis that he knew his allegedly tortious conduct in Georgia would delay the return of funds to plaintiffs with connections to Nevada."

At the same time, while only a minority of the Court's cases are the kind that generate big headlines, they make up a far higher proportion of the caseload at the Supreme Court than at any other American court. The Supreme Court spends more time than any other court does on cases raising fundamental questions about the relationship between government and governed, the relative powers of different parts of the government, and even the basic values of society. Among these cases, one type in particular stands out in terms of controversy and consequences: cases involving *judicial review*. Although the term "judicial review" is sometimes used more broadly to encompass less controversial powers, in the U.S. it usually refers to a court's power to declare a statute null and void because it conflicts with a constitution. In some countries this is called constitutional review.

Sometimes judicial (or constitutional) review is described as an invention of the Supreme Court. This is not wholly misleading when it comes to federal courts, for the U.S. Constitution says nothing at all about the power. However, judicial review had already been practiced in a number of states (and colonies) prior to the ratification of the Constitution, and there is evidence that at least some of the Framers assumed courts would have the power to review the constitutionality of federal laws.[9] For instance, Alexander Hamilton famously wrote in Federalist 78:

---

9   Elliot E. Slotnick. 1987. "The Place of Judicial Review in the American Tradition: The Emergence of an Eclectic Power." *Judicature* 71:68-79.

A constitution is, in fact, and must be regarded by the judges, as a fundamental law. It therefore belongs to them to ascertain its meaning, as well as the meaning of any particular act proceeding from the legislative body. If there should happen to be an irreconcilable variance between the two, that which has the superior obligation and validity ought, of course, to be preferred; or, in other words, the Constitution ought to be preferred to the statute.

There were dissenting voices then and have been ever since, but judicial review has been here to stay since the Supreme Court's 1803 decision in *Marbury v. Madison.*

In 1803, the U.S. was the only country with judicial review. Since then, and with increasing speed in recent decades, the practice has spread to other parts of the world and now is found in countries as diverse as Germany, Colombia, South Africa, and Russia. Typically, the power of judicial review is assigned exclusively to a single court with the designation "Constitutional Court." This is not the case in the U.S. As just noted, the practice predates the Supreme Court. Furthermore, there is nothing in the reasoning or language of *Marbury* to suggest that the power is limited to the Supreme Court. Accordingly, the power of judicial review has always been understood to pervade the American court system, and any court of general jurisdiction, state or federal, can rule that a law violates the U.S. Constitution. (However, note that only state courts have the authority to declare a state statute void under their state constitution.)

Of course, a given court's ruling only counts as law in that court's jurisdiction and only so long as the ruling is not undone by a higher court. For that reason, the Supreme Court is far more important when it comes to judicial review of federal statutes than any other court is. Nevertheless, the ubiquity of the power makes it easy for litigants to raise challenges to laws. The result is that virtually any major piece of legislation that is thought to infringe on individual rights will be tested in some court. In this way, judicial review operates as an important safeguard against governments' exceeding their powers. Many people today view judicial review as essential to legitimate government.

Judicial review also has a troubling side, though. For a government to be considered legitimate in our time, it is not enough that it adhere to limits on its powers; most people would also insist that it be, at some level, democratic. This does not necessarily mean that the people must participate directly in lawmaking, but it does at least require that those responsible for making policy be accountable to the public, who must be able to punish those responsible for unpopular or ineffective policy choices by running them out of office at the next election. Judicial review of state statutes in states where judges are elected presents no serious problems for democracy. But review of federal statutes always does. State judges ruling on federal laws are accountable, if at all, only to the people of one state, and federal judges, who hold office for life, are not accountable to any voters. When the Supreme Court strikes down a federal law, nine—or fewer—unelected officials negate the work and reject the judgment of several hundred elected members of Congress and one elected president.

JUDICIAL REVIEW OF EXECUTIVE AGENCIES

As important and attention-grabbing as judicial review of congressional legislation is, courts spend far more time judging the actions of the executive branch. Most suits involving the executive are directed at specific actions of individual employees or offices; common examples are claims for denial of disability, unemployment, or veterans' health benefits, or claims against police officers for violations of an arrestee's civil rights. But there are also many cases that look a lot like judicial review of legislation, involving claims that a law is invalid because it conflicts with a higher law. The difference in these cases is that the contested law is a rule or regulation passed by an agency (e.g., the IRS issues many tax regulations that are binding on taxpayers), not a statute passed by a legislature, and the higher law is usually a statute passed by a congressional body instead of a constitution.

Cases of this sort begin with delegation of power from the legislative branch to the executive. Many years ago, governments in the U.S. (and most other democracies) began taking on a huge range of responsibilities, from regulating the economy and the environment, to fostering education and health, protecting consumers, workers, and companies against unfair business practices, and providing income support for the poor and elderly, along with more traditional tasks such as defending borders and protecting trade. Rules must change with changes in conditions, public preferences, and scientific knowledge and with the emergence of new problems and possible solutions. No legislature has the time or institutional capacity to keep specific rules up to date in even a single one of these areas, let alone all. Nor would legislators relish making all the specific rules and regulations even if they could. Any new regulation necessarily makes someone unhappy. Why make someone unhappy yourself, if you can foist that unpleasant task off on someone else?

The result is that legislatures delegate a great deal of law making to executive agencies, which have far larger staffs and greater expertise and don't have the option of passing the buck. Delegation often comes in broad terms, sometimes incredibly broad. For instance, the federal Clean Air Act instructs the Environmental Protection Agency (EPA) to set "ambient air quality standards the attainment and maintenance of which in the judgment of the Administrator [of the EPA] . . . are requisite to protect the public health." When agencies exercise tremendous discretion to make highly controversial policies, litigation challenging those policies often follows.

Usually, the challenges are based on allegations that, in making (or not making) a rule or regulation, the agency either misinterpreted its mandate from the legislature or failed to follow proper procedures. In either case, the core claim is that the agency has not acted as a faithful agent of the legislature that entrusted it with power. This marks the most crucial difference between this type of judicial review and constitutional review of legislation: Instead of sitting in judgment of the work of an elected legislature, the court is tasked with preventing the legislature's goals from being undermined by unelected agency officials.

The fact that the Supreme Court is unaccountable to the public gives judicial review more bite. If the justices had to worry about displeasing voters every time they ruled on the constitutionality of statutes, we would expect the Court to provide only the feeblest of checks on Congress and the president. Furthermore, the fact that the justices are appointed by the president and Senate and that they are themselves U.S. citizens, exposed to the same news stories and subject to the same restrictions as others, ensures that the Court will rarely be far out of step with public opinion for very long. Still, there is no denying that judicial review is in tension with democracy. Questions about how the Court—and other courts—can responsibly exercise the power of judicial review have provoked intense debate among scholars and practitioners for years and will undoubtedly continue to do so as long as we have courts and legislatures.

As challenging and consequential as they are, cases involving judicial review follow the same basic process as any other. Furthermore, once certiorari has been granted, the process at the Supreme Court looks quite similar to the process in any other appellate court. There are some differences, however. We discussed opinion assignment and opinion writing in the previous chapter. The remainder of this chapter is devoted to a closer look at briefs and oral argument followed by some observations on how the justices go about making decisions.

Amicus Curiae Briefs

In addition to the usual briefs from the petitioner (what the appellant is called when a case reaches the Court on certiorari) and respondent (appellee), the justices in Woodall's case had five other briefs they could have read if they wished to. Two were submitted by fifteen U.S. states—fourteen combining forces on a single brief, with Texas going its own way on another. The states did not stand to gain or lose anything directly from the resolution of Woodall's case, but a precedent in Woodall's favor would naturally place the states in more difficult positions in some later cases. They wrote asking the Court to reverse the lower court decision. The other three briefs were from organizations. The Criminal Justice Legal Foundation, which, according to its brief, "seeks to bring the constitutional protection of the accused into balance with the rights of the victim and of society to rapid, efficient, and reliable determination of guilt and swift execution of punishment," also argued against Woodall in its brief. The National Association of Criminal Defense Lawyers, as you would imagine, wrote in support of Woodall. So did the Los Angeles County Public Defender's Office, which described itself in its brief as "the largest criminal defense firm in the nation" and noted its "strong interest in protecting the fairness and accuracy of criminal sentencing proceedings, especially in capital cases."

Briefs like these, submitted by individuals or organizations who care about the outcome of a case but technically are not parties to the case, are called amicus curiae (Latin for "friend of the court) briefs. Such briefs are allowed at most American courts, but, because the stakes at the U.S. Supreme Court are so high, they are far more common there than anywhere else.

Nothing obliges either the justices or their clerks to read amicus briefs, so there is no real cost to allowing them. This may explain why the requirements for submitting a brief are fairly minimal: the organization or individual need only obtain the permission of both parties or the Court itself. (The submitters are required to explain their interest in the case in their briefs; hence, the passages quoted earlier describing the organizations' interests in the Woodall case.) At the same time, you might think that knowing their briefs are unlikely to be read by the justices would dissuade groups from filing them. But the preparation and filing of a brief is not a heavy expense for a financially healthy organization, and even the slight chance that one will influence the justices' thinking might be enough to justify the cost. Furthermore, amicus briefs can be very good advertising for groups, a way of showing donors that the groups are fighting actively for their beliefs. The amicus brief is a popular enough option that at least one is filed in the majority of Supreme Court cases. Sometimes the Court is flooded with them. For the recent Hobby Lobby case[10], which involved questions about a corporation's religious right to deny its employees insurance coverage for contraceptives, eighty-two amicus briefs were filed[11], many signed by more than one organization.

The label "friend of the court" implies that the briefs are submitted for the court's benefit. That may have been largely true long ago, but today the term is something of a misnomer. Every one of the eighty-two briefs in *Hobby Lobby* clearly favored one side or the other. (This is even true of the two briefs claiming to be "in support of neither party.") So did each of the five briefs in Woodall's case. That is the norm today.

Most one-sided briefs simply restate points that the justices have already read elsewhere and are, therefore, of little value to the justices beyond signaling how different advocacy groups feel about a case. However, a supporting amicus brief occasionally introduces a novel line of argument, and sometimes it can substitute for a poorly written main brief. Most helpful from the justices' perspective is a brief that provides them with information or a perspective not available in the parties' briefs. Good examples can be found in *Grutter v. Bollinger*[12], a case involving affirmative action in higher education. The opinion of the Court specifically referenced amicus briefs from a number of corporations and from "high-ranking retired officers and civilian leaders of the United States military," not for a legal argument, but for their opinion as employers that a racially diverse and well-educated workforce was essential to their organizations' effective functioning.

In *Daubert v. Merrell Dow Pharmaceutical*[13], where the Court struggled to construct an effective test for the admissibility of scientific evidence at trial, several briefs focused primarily on the processes of scientific research and publication, explaining how scientists understand and evaluate their own work. Briefs like these, even if they end up giving more support to one side or the other, come close to the ideal of a friend of the court brief, intended to educate the justices and help them reach a well-informed decision.

---

10   *Burwell v. Hobby Lobby Stores, Inc.*, 134 S. Ct. 2751 (2014).

11   The authors' count comes from a listing of the amicus briefs on the Scotusblog website, http://www.scotusblog.com/case-files/cases/sebelius-v-hobby-lobby-stores-inc/.

12   539 U.S. 306 (2003).

13   509 U.S. 579 (1993).

There is one particular litigant that the Court looks to more than any other for helpful input, to the extent that it regularly invites it to submit amicus briefs, even at the certiorari stage. This litigant is the government of the United States, as represented by the U.S. Solicitor General.

The Solicitor General

The Solicitor General ("SG") is a high-ranking Justice Department official who oversees a staff of attorneys (sometimes the term is used as shorthand to refer to the entire office). The SG is appointed in the same way as a federal judge—by the president with the consent of the Senate. Unlike a judge, though, the SG serves at the pleasure of the president, meaning that the president can fire the SG at any time for any reason. On a day-to-day basis, the SG operates independently of the president, but this job insecurity ensures—as it is meant to—that the SC is at least somewhat responsive to views that the president feels strongly about.

The lawyers in the SG's office represent the federal government in the Supreme Court. Not only do they write the briefs and conduct oral argument in the cases that make it to the Court, but they screen out cases, deciding which government losses should be appealed to the Court. The federal government is far and away the most frequent litigator before the Court. It is also the most successful. In a typical year, the U.S. government wins upwards of 60% of the cases in which it participates. Its success at the certiorari stage is even more impressive. Recall that only about one in twenty paid cert petitions is granted. For the SG, the rate is usually around *fifteen* out of every twenty.[14]

In the extensive literature on the SG, there is a robust debate about the reasons for these high success rates. We find three explanations most plausible and suspect that each plays at least some role in the SG's success. The first is the identity of the SG's client. The SG serves at the pleasure of the president and represents the federal government. When the SG speaks, it is at least with the voice of the executive branch and sometimes with the voice of the entire government. The justices are themselves part of that government and will naturally share its perspective sometimes. Even when they don't, they may feel that constitutional propriety or simple prudence dictates deference to the

---

14   Ryan C. Black & Ryan J. Owens, *The Solicitor General and the United States Supreme Court.* (Cambridge University Press, 2012). Other excellent books on the Solicitor General are Lincoln Caplan's *The Tenth Justice* (Knopf, 1987), Rebecca Mae Salokar's *The Solicitor General* (Temple University Press, 1992), and Richard Pacelle's *Between Law and Politics* (Texas A&M University Press, 2003).

government's views. To the extent this explanation holds, the win is the federal government's more than the SG's.

The second reason has more to do with the SG's office: it is the high level of mutual respect between Solicitor General and Supreme Court. In any close working relationship, one can gain the confidence and trust of others by consistently producing high-quality work. Not only are the attorneys in the SG's office capable of this, but they understand the value of the Court's trust and work to maintain it. We see this in several ways. Recall that the SG decides what government losses to appeal to the Court. There may be hundreds of these in any given year, but the SG will submit only a few dozen petitions for certiorari, disregarding the sometimes loud protests of the many disappointed federal agencies. The logic behind this is that the Supreme Court will be aware of and appreciate the SG's selectivity and so will look favorably on those petitions it does receive from the federal government. More dramatically, the SG sometimes agrees with the party it beat at the lower court that certiorari should be granted, even though the government risks ending up worse off if the Court takes the case and reverses. You will almost never see another litigant do that. The SG will even go so far as to "confess error," conceding that the government should not have won in the lower court in the first place!

Finally, and most simply, the attorneys in the SG's office are unusually good at what they do. This is partly because the office, with its combination of exciting work, unparalleled prestige, and career-launching potential (former SG attorneys are highly sought after by law firms and paid very handsomely), attracts exceptionally talented young lawyers. It is also because the high volume of government litigation before the Court provides them with a wealth of experience. They quickly come to understand the most effective way to write petitions and briefs. And while they may not ever become entirely comfortable with it, they quickly learn the ways of that odd practice known as oral argument.

Oral Argument

In the early days of the Supreme Court, oral proceedings looked little like anything we would call an "argument." With fewer cases to handle and written briefs not yet standard, the justices were content to allow lawyers to speechify for hours at a time.[15] Today, in contrast, the label fits; the Court is an excellent

---

15   William H. Rehnquist. 1999. "From Webster to Word-Processing: The Ascendance of the Appellate Brief." *The Journal of Appellate Practice and Process* 1:1-6.

example of what lawyers call a "hot bench." That is, the justices usually come to oral argument with a good understanding of the case, having had access to briefs and to bench memos from clerks summarizing the cases and precedents and offering some analysis. Most of the justices are not inclined to play a passive role.

When the Woodall case was argued, the first question, from Justice Kagan, came less than a minute into the presentation of Kentucky's lawyer, Susan Lenz. Ms. Lenz began with the claim that there was no clearly established law on the adverse inference instruction. Justice Kagan immediately interrupted—the justices don't raise their hands when they have something to say; they just start speaking and the lawyer stops to listen—referring to the crucial precedents and asking, "So when you put those together, *Carter* with *Estelle, Mitchell*, how—why do you think that there's a gap?" Ms. Lenz's answer was quickly challenged by Justice Sotomayor. For the next twenty minutes or so, Ms. Lenz was peppered with questions from Justices Alito, Breyer, Ginsburg, Kagan, Kennedy, and Scalia, until, in a pause, she asked the chief justice to reserve the final five minutes of her time for rebuttal. (In the standard Supreme Court case, each side gets thirty minutes to speak; the petitioner can reserve some of that time for a rebuttal to the respondent's argument.)

Laurence Komp, an attorney appointed by the Court to represent Woodall, was treated the same way. He, too, did not get a minute into his opening before being interrupted with a question, and he spent the remainder of his time fielding and parrying questions as best he could.

The first thing, then, to understand about oral argument at the Supreme Court is that it is an immensely challenging and daunting experience for lawyers, requiring them to respond respectfully to numerous questions—some surprising, some unclear or even illogical, all coming from different directions—while effectively communicating the key points favoring their clients. Even counsel with considerable experience before the Court can be reduced to stammering. The attorney's perspective is captured wonderfully in a 1995 exchange between Justice Breyer and Thomas Christ, an attorney challenging a public school's random drug testing policy for student athletes.[16] By the point at which this exchange occurred, Mr. Christ had spent nearly twenty minutes trying to answer different justices' questions about what right was infringed by the drug testing requirement. The discussion continued:

---

16   The case was *Vernonia School District v. Acton*, 515 U.S. 646 (1995).

JUSTICE BREYER: Medical exams all involve urinalyses.

MR. CHRIST: That's—

JUSTICE BREYER: I've probably had hundreds of them in my life, and so have you, and you know, what's the special thing here?

MR. CHRIST: The medical exam you're talking about is being conducted in private by the student's doctor. It is not being conducted—

JUSTICE BREYER: Well, people urinate, you know, in men's rooms all over the country. It's not necessarily . . . and I don't mean to be . . . trivialize it, but it isn't really a tremendously private thing, is it?

MR. CHRIST: I think it is private when it is being compelled by the Government, and the Government is there watching and observing and collecting specimens.

JUSTICE BREYER: All right. What I'm trying to get you to do is to pinpoint precisely what it is that's the intrusion of the privacy interest. That's what I'm trying—

MR. CHRIST: It's not—

JUSTICE BREYER: —That's what I'm aiming at.

MR. CHRIST: —It's not the mere act. We all urinate. That's . . . has to be conceded.

[Laughter]

In fact, I might do so here, if—

[Laughter][17]

---

17   You can listen to this and other oral arguments at a wonderful website, www.oyez.org. The dry transcript doesn't do justice to the moment. The volume of the laughter is closer to what you would expect at a comedy club than in a courtroom and probably reflects the audience's own tension and sympathy for Mr. Christ.

For lawyers, oral argument is about trying to hold their own, perhaps scoring a few points but mostly avoiding doing anything to hurt their cases. For the justices, oral argument has a number of purposes. Undoubtedly, many justices enjoy the give and take of oral argument, and we would not rule out enjoyment as a factor in the persistence of oral argument in the electronic age. But judges also tell us that oral argument aids them in their work.

For the Court as a whole, there is the bolstering of legitimacy that may come from opening a portion of the proceedings to public view. The Supreme Court has been strangely reluctant to expand public access to oral arguments beyond those who attend in person. Although it has made audio recordings for decades, it only recently began releasing the audio to the public the day of the oral argument. And it does not allow cameras at oral argument and does not look likely to do so any time soon. (The United Kingdom's new Supreme Court, in contrast, has a YouTube page.[18])

For individual justices, oral argument will be most helpful when the justice is on the fence. Questions to the lawyers can help fill in missing facts or bring more order to confusing ones, can illuminate the consequences of accepting or rejecting a particular position, and can provide a test of each side's reasoning to see which holds up under pressure. Judging from tone of Justice Kagan's questions and her eventual vote, it seems likely that she had not made up her mind by the time of Woodall's oral argument and was genuinely interested in testing the strength of the arguments.

Far more often, though, the main function of oral argument is to allow the justices to enter the fray, communicating their own ideas to each other through questions or statements ostensibly directed at the attorneys. This may seem surprising, as the justices work in the same building and can talk whenever they want and will have a chance to discuss the case in conference within a few days of the oral argument. However, the norms of the Court have developed in such a way that in-person conversations about cases are rare and conference discussions are generally kept quite brief. Oral argument gives the justices an important additional chance to air their views and hear what their colleagues are thinking.

Two exchanges in the Woodall oral argument illustrate this practice especially well. The first occurs early in the argument. Justice Sotomayor asks a series of questions challenging Ms. Lenz, Kentucky's lawyer. Justice Scalia, apparently feeling that Ms. Lenz's answers are inadequate, jumps in and the exchange continues:

---

18   Which you can visit at https://www.youtube.com/user/UKSupremeCourt.

JUSTICE SCALIA: Under Federal law, you don't think the judge could say, ladies and gentlemen of the jury, this defendant has already pleaded guilty to a horrible crime. This is a punishment hearing. He has chosen not to—not to testify in this—in this hearing. You—you are—if you wish, you may take his failure to testify as an indication that he does not have remorse, that he is not sorry. He could have come before you said and said I am terribly sorry, I wish I had never done it, I will never do it again. He has chosen not to testify. You may, if you wish, take that into account in determining whether—whether there is remorse. You can't say that?

MS. LENZ: Oh, absolutely. Absolutely.

JUSTICE SCALIA: Well, then your answer should have been otherwise.

MS. LENZ: Well, I guess I interpreted Justice Sotomayor's question a little bit different because she wasn't referring to facts in evidence or—or to some type of evidence. But your question asks the—the question about whether silence bears on the determination of a lack of remorse.

JUSTICE SCALIA: Of course.

Here we see Justice Scalia becoming, in effect, an advocate for Kentucky. The same thing happens in the second half of the oral arguments, but here it is Justice Sotomayor intervening to help a struggling lawyer.

JUSTICE ALITO: Let me—let me give you this example. Let me pretend to be a juror in a—in a Kentucky capital case. And the—and let's assume in this case the prosecution puts on evidence to show eligibility and some evidence of aggravating factors. The defense puts on no evidence of mitigation. Now, the judge tells me you shall consider such mitigating or extenuating facts and circumstances as have been presented to you in the evidence, and you believe to be true. Okay? . . .

And then the judge gives the instruction that you requested: A defendant is not compelled to testify, and the fact that the defendant did not testify should not prejudice him in any way.

So now I'm back in the jury room, and I say, well, now I have to consider mitigating evidence. And, you know, there are a lot of things that could be mitigating in a capital case. I'd like to know about the defendant's childhood. I'd like to know whether the defendant was—was abused. I'd like to know whether the defendant was remorseful.

And I haven't heard anything about this. And I don't know what to do because the judge told me I should consider the mitigating evidence that's been presented to me. On the other hand, the judge told me that the failure—the fact that the defendant didn't put on any mitigating evidence can't prejudice him in any way. So what am I supposed to do?

MR. KOMP: Well, in that case, again, if—if there's no mitigating evidence presented, you don't know if it's what Instruction 4 will look—look like. But taking your hypothetical and you're in that jury room, if you're given the Carter instruction—again, it wasn't given in this case. So if you're given that Carter instruction, all that prohibits is—is raising a negative inference against the defendant for the failure to exercise his right to testify.

JUSTICE ALITO: No, it doesn't really. It says the fact that he didn't testify, and he could have testified about child—about his childhood or about remorse or any of these other things, that shouldn't prejudice him in any way.

MR. KOMP: And that's right—that's the—

JUSTICE ALITO: Well, just tell me what I'm supposed to do as a juror. The judge says consider the evidence that's put before you, but the fact that the defendant didn't put this evidence before you in the form of his testimony shouldn't prejudice him in any way. I'm—I'm pulled in two different directions. I don't know what to do.

MR. KOMP: Well, but he can't—again, I think in your hypothetical that he's presented nothing. And so he can't be penalized again for presenting nothing. And you can't allow—

JUSTICE SOTOMAYOR: Nothing—zero equals zero.

MR. KOMP: Correct. And so—

JUSTICE SOTOMAYOR: And the zero just can't be added onto or taken away from. Zero is zero, not a positive, not a negative.

MR. KOMP: Right. And—

JUSTICE SOTOMAYOR: So you can't take away from the zero, create evidence from his silence, just as you can't from his silence outweigh the aggravating circumstances; correct?

MR. KOMP: Correct.

No one observing or reading these exchanges could have had much trouble predicting how the three justices involved in them would vote in the end; they gave every indication of having made up their minds before the argument began. Not only does this illustrate an important fact about the functions of oral argument, but it points us in the direction of a truth about the Supreme Court—one so fundamental that you cannot hope to understand the institution without recognizing and keeping this truth in mind.

Let us explain by way of an analysis of voting data. The nine justices who sat on Woodall's case in the 2013 term have been together on the Court since the 2010 term. In the three terms beginning with 2010, they heard fifty-five cases involving issues of criminal procedure. Using The Supreme Court Database, we can find out how often each justice voted on the defendant's side or the prosecution's side in those cases.[19] (Not every justice participated in every case.)

It turns out that Justice Alito was the most pro-prosecution, voting for the prosecution in 85% of the cases. Justice Ginsburg was the most pro-defendant, voting for the prosecution only 29% of the time. The other justices lined up as follows:

- Thomas—73% prosecution

- Roberts—73%

- Scalia—62%

- Kennedy—56%

- Breyer—49%

---

19   This database was created by Professor Harold Spaeth and is now maintained by a group of scholars. You can visit it yourself by going to http://supremecourtdatabase.org.

- Kagan—34%

- Sotomayor—33%

Now suppose you knew all this before you had learned anything about the Woodall case and we told you that the vote in the Woodall case was 6-3 in favor of the prosecution. Would you be able to make a reasonable guess as to who voted on which side? Presumably, you would say to yourself something like this: "Well, in the three years prior to this case, Justice Alito showed a very strong tendency to vote with the prosecution. If six justices supported the prosecution here, it seems extremely likely that he was one of them. On the other side, Justice Ginsburg votes for the prosecution less than a third of the time. I'd be willing to bet she voted for Woodall." Continuing with this line of reasoning, you might guess that the three justices with the strongest pro-defendant voting records were the dissenters, with the other six justices in the majority.

This guess would not be entirely correct, for in reality Justice Kagan voted with the majority and Justice Breyer dissented. But it would come awfully close, much closer than one could expect to get just choosing six justices' names at random. That is, you could make an excellent prediction about the justices' decisions based on their decisions in prior cases.

How might you account for your predictive success? Well, although criminal procedure is a fairly broad category, the same few constitutional provisions and precedents show up in many cases. A certain understanding of those provisions and precedents might lead some justices toward frequent support of prosecutors, while a different understanding could lead justices to support defendants fairly consistently.

This is a plausible hypothesis. To test it, let us examine the justices' decision making on other legal issues. Among the other categories available in the Database are Civil Rights (involving issues like voting, affirmative action, gender discrimination, immigrant rights, an poverty) and First Amendment (primarily freedom of speech and religion). To analyze votes across these various issues, we must adopt the convention of identifying some positions as liberal and others as conservative: for instance, votes in favor of immigrants, litigants claiming discrimination, and free speech claims are generally considered liberal. This approach is not free of problems, but it accords with widely held understandings of contemporary policy positions and is sound enough to provide useful data.

Here are the percentages of conservative votes in Civil Rights and First Amendment cases for each of the justices in the 2010-2012 terms.

- Thomas—77%

- Alito—73%

- Scalia—67%

- Roberts—60%

- Kennedy—51%

- Breyer—42%

- Ginsburg—33%

- Sotomayor—31%

- Kagan—27%

The pattern is not precisely the same as that we observed with criminal procedure, but there are marked similarities. Note that Justice Kennedy is in the middle again, and the blocs of four justices to his right and left are the same as in criminal procedure. Yet there is a completely different set of constitutional provisions, statutes, and precedents at play in these cases. Perhaps with some creative thinking we could find a way to salvage our hypothesis. But there is a much more plausible explanation for these patterns: the justices, like many other Americans, especially well-educated ones with an interest in politics, have deeply held values and beliefs that shape their attitudes toward policies in somewhat consistent and predictable ways. When they confront cases that raise those policy issues, their personal attitudes exert a considerable influence on their decisions.

Let us ask you to think back to your reaction to the legal argument made by Woodall's attorneys: under the Fifth Amendment, the jury in Woodall's case should have been instructed not to draw any negative inferences from his refusal to testify at his sentencing hearing. Were you inclined to agree or disagree with that argument? Now ask yourself if, as a general matter, you tend to worry more about police misconduct and excessive incarceration or about the threat to public safety posed by criminals who are released from prison. (Of course you may worry about all these things, but one set of problems probably troubles you more than the other.) You might be an exception, but we would be willing to bet a lot that most readers who worry more about public safety were less inclined to accept Woodall's argument. It is just not easy to separate our evaluations of legal claims from our feelings about the underlying issues.

You might respond that the justices are trained to put aside their personal views and follow the law. There is some truth to this, but the special characteristics of the Court really come into play here. Most importantly, the cases chosen for review at the Supreme Court are those where the law is most ambiguous, precisely the cases where legal training is least helpful for overcoming one's personal predilections. Add to this the fact that the justices need not worry about losing their jobs or having their decisions reversed by a higher court, and you can see that law's impact on justices' decisions will necessarily be limited.

Some observers go so far as to argue that the justices' attitudes utterly dominate their decisions. In the words of two scholars closely associated with this view, "Simply put, Rehnquist vote[d] the way he [did] because he [was] extremely conservative; Marshall voted the way he did because he was extremely liberal."[20] Other scholars think the law still plays a major role in many Supreme Court decisions. But virtually no careful observer of the Court takes very seriously Chief Justice Roberts' famous claim at his confirmation hearing that "Judges are like umpires. Umpires don't make the rules; they apply them" or that their job is simply to "call balls and strikes." The description is a somewhat better fit for trial judges, but even they are sometimes called on to make law where existing law fails to provide clear answers, and they must do so as individuals with strongly held views that inevitably enter into their decisions. It is an inescapable fact: what judges do is influenced not only by what they take the law to be, but by what they think it *should* be. And it is least escapable at the Court whose decisions matter the most.

■ METHODS OF INTERPRETATION

If attorneys are to use the tools of legal argumentation successfully, judges must be persuadable. For their part, most judges are conscientious and would not like to think that they decide cases simply by what feels right to them. For both attorneys and judges, then, there are strong incentives to find methods of deciding cases that allow judges to transcend their personal views, at least to some extent, even in very difficult cases. Countless hours have been devoted to developing, defending, and attacking such methods. The grandest debates have involved methods of interpreting texts, especially constitutions and statutes—that is, ways of deciding what vague or ambiguous

---

20   Jeffrey A. Segal and Harold J. Spaeth. 2002. *The Supreme Court and the Attitudinal Model Revisited.* Cambridge University Press, p. 86.

language in a statute ("requisite to protect the public health") or constitution ("a witness against [one]self") means.

Millions of lines have been written on this topic, and it would take another full book to give you a thorough grounding in even the most commonly debated methods of interpretation. However, we can offer a simplifying framework based on two questions whose answers often differentiate the different interpretive approaches: (1) From what temporal perspective should we view the text? (2) How much should we emphasize the precise language of the text?

For illustrative purposes, let us consider the question whether the Equal Protection Clause of the 14th Amendment ("No state shall . . . deny to any person within its jurisdiction the equal protection of the laws.") requires states to recognize marriages between same-sex couples. We can start by asking from whose perspective we should try to understand the clause and any application it might have to same-sex marriage. One natural response would be that we should view the question from the perspective of Americans living today. There is much to be said for this position, of course, but there are also arguments against. For instance, one might worry that the law will be too volatile and unpredictable to guide people's actions if it changes easily with society's views. And reliance on contemporary views might too easily allow judges to fall back on their personal opinions. People who make arguments of this sort often advocate approaching a text from the perspective of the people who were around at the time it was written. (This approach, sometimes called "originalism," is closely associated with Justices Scalia and Thomas on the U.S. Supreme Court.) An intermediate approach asks how a text or issue has been viewed over the course of U.S. history. Given the dramatic shifts in American attitudes toward sexuality in the last century and a half, taking a contemporary perspective on the question is much more likely to yield a decision in favor of same-sex marriage than would an originalist or even a historical perspective.

The other question is whether we should take a text literally or look beyond its words to its purpose or to broader principles that the text might be meant to invoke. A strictly literal approach to the clause would seem to favor advocates of same-sex marriage: a law offering the many benefits—financial and otherwise—of marriage only to heterosexual couples would certainly appear to deny some people the equal protection of the laws. Going beyond the text to consider the clause's purpose muddies the waters some. For instance, we might consider the fact that the Fourteenth Amendment, passed in the aftermath of the Civil War, was most obviously aimed at combating discrimination against African-Americans.

There are some important things to note. First, in our examples we tried to proceed by answering one question at a time. But a coherent approach to interpretation requires answering both questions together. If you are inclined to approach a text from an originalist perspective, will you ask how people who lived at the time it was written would have understood and used the language or what people at that time would have seen as the purpose of the text? If you think it best to ask about the general principles underlying a text, do you want to know about the general principles recognized by people at the time, by people living now, or by people living sometime in between? In practice, judges rarely answer both of these questions clearly.

Second, a given method of interpretation does not always yield a single answer. Reasonable people will often disagree about what evidence should be considered and how it should be interpreted. Different dictionaries will provide different definitions of key words in a text. Historical sources like newspapers and diaries will often contain conflicting accounts and positions. Surveys differ in the way their questions are worded and in their results. At the time the Supreme Court was deciding *Brown v. Board of Education*, historians were unable to reach any consensus about whether even the main writers and supporters of the Fourteenth Amendment meant it to bar segregation. If you were to try to determine whether contemporary Americans favor constitutional protection of same-sex marriage, where would you look? How would you deal with the problem that the answer to the question looks very different in northeastern or west-coast states than in southern or mid-western states?

Finally, there is nothing approaching a consensus in the legal community about the best method of interpreting texts, and the choice of methods is rarely neutral. That is not to say that a given method always produces similar results. Strict textualism is often thought of as a "conservative" approach that works against rights claims, but as we pointed out, a literal reading of the text of the Equal Protection Clause is likely to favor rights claimants, as is a literal reading of the First Amendment's stricture that "Congress shall make no law . . . abridging the freedom of speech." Nevertheless, it will often be apparent in advance which side would be favored by the adoption of a certain approach, and it is hard to escape the suspicion that judges are drawn to the approaches most likely to generate results they favor.

This suspicion is heightened by the fact that few, if any, judges are perfectly consistent across cases in the methods they use, that they often appeal to multiple approaches in the course of a single opinion, and that they rarely describe their method clearly. You might find it an interesting exercise to read the justices opinions in *Obergefell v. Hodges* (135 S. Ct. 2584 [2015]) and see if you can figure out how each decided what the Equal Protection Clause (and, even more, the Due Process Clause) means for same-sex marriage. ■

CHAPTER 8

Complexities and Complications

The cases we have followed—Commonwealth of Kentucky vs. Robert Woodall and Promotion in Motion vs. Beech-Nut—were complex, but in many respects these cases were simple compared to others that American courts handle. Each of our cases involved only one defendant against whom a small number of claims or crimes had been alleged, and each case involved only a few legal and factual issues to be resolved.

In many civil cases, several plaintiffs, perhaps even thousands, sue one or several defendants on multiple claims that implicate many transactions over a very long period and require resolution of numerous technical and involved factual and legal issues. Many criminal cases also involve multiple defendants charged with multiple crimes, though the most complicated criminal cases tend to be more limited in scope than the most complicated civil cases.

Although some have argued that lay juries cannot competently resolve highly complex cases, so far the U.S. Supreme Court has not accepted a complexity limitation on the right to trial by jury. Thus, whether a case involves only two parties fighting over one claim, or hundreds of parties fighting over hundreds of claims, the basic process we described applies to both cases. There is not a separate track within American legal systems for highly complex cases, although more judicial involvement and management may be necessary in such cases. (And recall from Chapter 2 that small-stakes civil cases and criminal cases involving misdemeanors and traffic violations may be resolved quickly in special courts devoted to those particular kinds of cases.)

The complexity found in many cases nowadays is the product of innovations in court procedure that permit multiple parties and multiple claims or crimes to be joined and resolved in a single lawsuit. Courts will sometimes limit the parties if it would be unfair to some of the parties to include them in a single, large case. Perhaps a subcontractor who had only a small role in the construction of a building that collapsed in an ordinary thunderstorm has been sued along with the general contractor and architect who are primarily responsible for the defects in the construction. This minor player could be subjected to large legal bills and be tarnished by association with the more culpable defendants if all of the claims are tried together in a single lawsuit. In a case such as this, the court has discretion to separate the less important defendant from the main case and have claims against that defendant tried separately. The same is true in criminal cases involving multiple defendants accused of overlapping crimes. If the judge is convinced that evidence that will be admitted against one of the defendants is likely to improperly prejudice the jury against another of the defendants, then this other defendant may be given a separate trial. Still, the general rule today is that claims and crimes arising from a common set of facts can and, if reasonable to do so, should be tried together.

Three primary reasons motivate this modern preference for joining multiple claims/crimes and for joining all of the parties implicated by those claims/crimes. First, trying all of the parties together before a single decision-maker who hears the collective evidence one time promotes efficiency: as we have seen, civil and criminal cases can be long and expensive; to the extent multiple disputes can be resolved in one case, costs are reduced. Second, a single forum for collective resolution promotes consistency in outcomes. If one defendant is tried without the other defendant, the defendant on trial is likely to point to the missing defendant—who is not there to protest—as the more culpable actor. So we may see one jury excusing the first defendant on the belief that the second, missing defendant was the responsible party and a second jury excusing the second defendant on the belief that the now missing first defendant was responsible. Or we may see a plaintiff who sues defendants sequentially rather than together, altering its theory in each case to shift more blame to each new defendant, with the potential for inconsistent verdicts and windfalls to the plaintiff. Finally, finality in dispute resolution is promoted by the modern approach to joining claims and parties. Parties can achieve full and final resolution of all facets of a dispute, without fear of multiple bites at the litigation apple, by bringing all disputants and claims together in one proceeding. The appeal process may draw out a single case for many years, but thanks to modern joinder rules, at least there will only be one case that gets drawn out, not multiple cases.

The preference for joinder of all civil claims arising from the same set of facts is so strong that American courts, both at the state and federal law, have developed what is called the "claim preclusion doctrine," which prohibits plaintiffs from withholding claims from the initial case in order to save them for another case in the event the first case is lost. For instance, Promotion in Motion filed three legally separate but factually related claims against Beech-Nut in its lawsuit, and all of those claims were dismissed before trial. If Promotion in Motion had saved one of those claims for a later case against Beech-Nut, Beech-Nut could have invoked the claim preclusion doctrine to have that claim in the second case dismissed on grounds that it was related to the claims decided in the first case. A parallel doctrine, the compulsory counterclaim rule, requires defendants to assert any counterclaims they may have that arise from the set of facts giving rise to the plaintiff's claims. Because of the compulsory counterclaim rule, Beech-Nut had to file its breach of contract counterclaims against Promotion in Motion in the lawsuit begun by Promotion in Motion, since those counterclaims arose from the same transactions on which Promotion sued. If Beech-Nut had pursued those breach of contract claims in a later case, after winning dismissal of Promotion's claims through summary judgment, those claims would have been subject to dismissal under the compulsory counterclaim rule. Together the claim preclusion doctrine and compulsory counterclaim rule motivate plaintiffs and defendants to join all factually-related claims they may have against each other in a single lawsuit.

Class Actions

Some would say that the pinnacle of efficient resolution of multiple civil claims is found in a type of civil lawsuit known as the class action, which is available in both state and federal courts. In a class action lawsuit, one or a few plaintiffs files claims on behalf of a class of persons who allegedly suffered a common injury caused by one or more defendants. Imagine that a child who was fed Fruit Nibbles suffered a serious injury from choking on the Nibbles. The mother of this child might have filed a class action complaint against Beech-Nut on behalf of all purchasers of Fruit Nibbles, alleging that Beech-Nut marketed a dangerous product.[1] This mother would be the lead plaintiff in the product liability lawsuit. If she prevailed on her claim, then each person in the class would also prevail and would be entitled to some amount of money to compensate them for harms caused them by the Fruit Nibbles. Given that several thousand packages of Fruit

---

1   Alternatively, if many individual plaintiffs filed lawsuits against Beech-Nut in federal court, those lawsuits might have been combined under a federal statute (28 U.S.C. Section 1407) that permits the consolidation of cases from multiple federal districts in one district to enable more efficient discovery and resolution of pretrial matters in those related lawsuits.

Nibbles were initially put out on the market, this class action could involve a class of several thousand seeking relief against Beech-Nut.

A plaintiff cannot simply file a class action complaint and automatically represent an entire class of plaintiffs. Special procedures apply to class actions to ensure that the named plaintiff is a proper representative of the class of plaintiffs and to ensure that the case is otherwise proper for the collective resolution of claims against the defendant or defendants. Under both state and federal law, a plaintiff who files a class action complaint must file a motion with the court to certify the case as a class action.[2] In order to get that certification, the plaintiff must convince the court that there are numerous claimants, that the named plaintiff's claims are typical of the claims of all class members, that the claims of class members present common questions of law and/or fact, and that the plaintiff and the counsel chosen by the plaintiff are adequate representatives of the class.

If the judge believes that all of these prerequisites have been met, then she must decide whether the case can be certified as a "damages class action" or as an "injunctive relief class action." In a damages class action, the class members are all seeking monetary relief. In order to certify the case as a damages class action, on top of the four basic prerequisites the judge must also find that common questions of law or fact predominate over non-common questions (i.e., questions that are unique to each individual claimant) and that a class action is superior to other forms of adjudication. If the case is certified as a damages class action, then persons in the class are given notice that the named plaintiff has sued on their behalf and are given the chance to opt out of the class action and pursue their own claims individually.

In order to certify an injunctive relief class action, the judge must conclude that it is possible to remedy the wrongs suffered by the class by ordering the defendant to do something or cease doing something. For instance, prisoners sometimes file class action complaints on behalf of all inmates of a prison that is overcrowded, arguing that their rights are being violated by exceeding the limit on inmates per cell. If the case is certified as an injunctive relief class action and the plaintiff prevails, the court may order the prison administrators to limit the number of inmates housed in each cell. With an injunctive relief class action, members of the class have

---

2   We provide here a general overview of class action rules that can in application be quite complicated. For a more detailed discussions of the history and law of class actions, as well as of controversies surrounding their use, *see* Deborah Hensler & Erik K. Molller, *Class Action Dilemmas: Pursuing Public Goals for Private Gain* (2000); Jay Tidmarsh, *Class Actions: Five Principles To Promote Fairness and Efficiency* (2013).

no right to opt out of the case because they will benefit from any injunctive relief that may be imposed.

These special requirements for proceeding as a class action exist for two primary reasons. First, if the case proceeds as a class action, then it resolves the claims of all persons who are in the class as defined by the court and who did not opt out of the class if they had a chance to do so. That is, once the case is resolved on the merits, persons who are in the class will not be able to file their own complaints and pursue their own claims. So we want to be sure that the class of plaintiffs will be well-represented. Second, if the case is certified, the defendant will be under tremendous pressure to settle the case because of the increased exposure—in terms of publicity, the substantial cost of continued litigation, and the amount of money at risk—that comes with defending against a whole class of claims instead of the claims of a few individual plaintiffs. The worry is that plaintiffs might obtain unfair leverage over a defendant if the use of the class action device is not reserved for cases where there is a large class of claimants who all probably did suffer an economic or physical injury caused by the defendant's behavior directed at the group as a whole. If the claims of each individual class member present unique questions or law or fact, then the case should not proceed as a class action.

Class actions have many supporters and many detractors. The supporters emphasize that class actions provide a vehicle to overcome a collective action problem: when many individuals have low-value claims, as may be the case for purchasers of defective consumer products, no single individual has much incentive to sue, but if these individuals can join together and share costs, then the collective may have sufficient incentive to sue. If we do not have a means of aggregating low-value claims, such as the class action complaint, then defendants who have caused a good deal of harm but have dispersed that harm over a large group of people will never be held accountable for their misconduct. Critics of class actions assert that class actions rarely result in justice for all because counsel for plaintiffs and defendants often collude to reach a settlement that gives the plaintiff's law firm a big payday but gives the individual members of the class little or no relief. It is true that most cases certified as class actions do settle, and some of these settlements do provide little relief to class members (e.g., in some settlements, class members have received only coupons to purchase goods in the future from the defendant who supposedly had wronged them), but it is difficult to gauge the extent to which class actions result in net gains for class members and deter defendants from engaging in dangerous or exploitive behaviors.

An attentive trial judge is the key to protecting against class action abuses. As noted above, before a case can proceed as a class action, the judge of the trial court has to be convinced that the case meets all of the requirements for a class action. Furthermore, because the final outcome in a class action will be binding on all members of the class, most of whom have never participated in the court proceedings or settlement negotiations, the trial judge must also approve any settlement agreement that will put an end to the class action. (Settlement agreements will provide that the case be dismissed with prejudice, meaning that members of the class will not be able to purse their own claims after dismissal.) By ensuring that the settlement is fair to all members of the class, the trial judge can avoid the worst abuses of the class action.

Collecting Judgments

When we introduced settlement agreements, we emphasized how attractive they can be to resolve uncertain cases. The plaintiff and defendant control their own fates by entering into a settlement agreement rather than by submitting their case to a judge or jury at the end of trial. There is an additional source of certainty that renders settlement agreements very attractive: settlement agreements require parties to dismiss the claims pending in court as a condition of the settlement, but the dismissal of those claims is itself usually contingent on settlement funds being placed into an attorney's escrow account for distribution following the dismissal. In other words, a plaintiff who enters into a settlement agreement can be sure that it will be paid in exchange for dismissing its claims. A plaintiff who wins a case at trial receives only a judgment in its favor, not an immediate payment. After winning at trial, the plaintiff must survive any appeal the defendant takes and then must convert the judgment into money. Judgments awarding damages on a civil claim are like promissory notes: they can be used to obtain money from the losing party, or the "judgment debtor," but the judgment is not itself money.

Collecting a judgment can be easy when the losing party has plenty of liquid assets or a steady stream of income and has not taken steps to hide or shelter those assets from collection. In those cases, the losing party's wages or bank funds can be garnished through laws each state has for converting judgments into money. Apparently, Promotion in Motion had ample liquid assets, because Beech-Nut's judgment against Promotion in Motion was quickly converted to cash following the conclusion of Promotion appeal. We know this because

Beech-Nut filed notice with the court that Promotion had satisfied the judgment held by Beech-Nut against it.[3]

But when the losing party has few liquid assets or has taken steps to hide its assets, converting a judgment to cash can be very difficult.[4] In cases such as this, a whole new round of litigation may occur in which claims are filed for fraudulent transfer of assets, discovery becomes focused on finding the judgment debtor's assets, and additional parties to whom the losing party transferred assets in an effort to thwart collection of the judgment are sued to compel them to return those assets.

Alternative Dispute Resolution

The complexities and uncertainties of civil lawsuits have driven many businesses to avoid American courts altogether. They do this by including in contracts they sign a provision that any disputes arising from the contract will submitted, not to the courts, but to some alternative form of dispute resolution, most commonly arbitration. (We presented an example of such a clause at the end of Chapter 1.) Arbitration is conducted by a single arbitrator or a panel of three arbitrators who either have been chosen by the parties or have been appointed by an arbitration organization with the consent of the parties. The arbitrators can decide all legal and factual questions presented by the dispute before them—including whether the contract properly provided for arbitration of that dispute. When a contract includes an arbitration clause in it, there is a strong presumption that any disputes between the parties to the contract will be resolved through arbitration rather than the courts. To overcome this presumption, the party that wants to take the case to court rather than arbitration will have to convince the arbitrator or a court that the arbitration clause either was not properly agreed to (perhaps one party deceived the other about the meaning of the clause) or that the clause is against the public policy of the jurisdiction whose laws govern the contract. Otherwise, arbitrators and courts will enforce the arbitration clause and not allow the case to be heard in court.

---

3   It is likely that Promotion in Motion promptly paid the judgment after appeal because, as a condition of taking an appeal, it had to post what is called a "supersedeas bond" for $2,550,000 million with the trial court to secure payment of the judgment. That is, after it lost on appeal, the bonding company would have had to pay the judgment due to Beech-Nut if Promotion in Motion did not pay from its own funds.

4   Unless the party has appealed and had to post a bond securing payment of the judgment as a condition of appeal. Losing parties who cannot obtain a bond can ask the trial court or appellate court to waive the bond requirement as a condition of filing the appeal.

In arbitration, the parties have access to some of the discovery tools discussed in Chapter 3 to obtain information about the case from the other side, but discovery tends to be much more circumscribed than in court. Arbitrators can hold evidentiary hearings that resemble bench trials, but these hearings usually only loosely follow the rules of evidence that would apply in courts, and they are usually shorter than trials and come earlier in the case than they would were the case in court. After hearing the evidence and considering any briefs submitted by the parties, the arbitrator or panel of arbitrators will issue a decision that resolves the civil dispute and awards damages if the party with a claim for relief prevails. An arbitration award can be enforced in a court just like a court's judgment—that is, if the losing party refuses to pay what is due under the arbitration award, then collection proceedings in court can be initiated by the prevailing party.

A party unhappy with the outcome in arbitration can appeal the arbitration award to a court, but it is very difficult to convince a court to overturn an arbitration award. The disgruntled party has to prove some kind of misconduct on the part of the arbitrator or prove that the arbitrator acted outside of her authority under the contract that contained the arbitration clause. Errors of fact or errors in the application of law are not sufficient to overturn an arbitration award.

This finality of arbitration awards and arbitration's generally quicker and lower-cost route to dispute resolution have made arbitration an attractive alternative to courts for many businesses. There is also a belief among many business people that arbitrators tend to be business friendly, though it is difficult to test this belief and there is little empirical evidence on whether arbitrators generally favor businesses over consumers. Another attraction of arbitration clauses is that they can be used to avoid class action lawsuits. This is because the Supreme Court has ruled that a plaintiff who signed an agreement to arbitrate any claims against a defendant company can be compelled to arbitrate those claims individually rather than collectively through a class action filed in court, at least for contracts involving interstate commerce that are subject to federal law.[5]

As the popularity of arbitration clauses has grown, more and more companies have added arbitration clauses to their standard contracts, even adding them after consumers have begun a relationship with a business. For instance, many banks have updated the contract terms that apply to credit cards they issue to provide that disputes over credit card payments must be submitted to

---

5   *AT&T Mobility v. Concepcion*, 563 U.S. 321 (2011).

arbitration. Even if these updated terms of service were issued after you signed a credit card application that did not contain an arbitration clause, the new arbitration clause will probably be binding on you under state and federal law so long as the bank gave reasonable advance notice that this arbitration clause was being added to the contract. The idea is that by continuing to use the credit card issued by the bank after receiving this notice, you are agreeing to this new term in the contract. If a dispute arises between you and any big business, you should look closely at the full contract terms that apply to your transactions. Some of those contracts will probably require that you submit any claims you have to arbitration, and the contract will probably specify where you need to do this and what procedures you must follow to activate the arbitration.

Of course, if you had no pre-existing contractual relationship with the person or business against whom you have a claim—perhaps someone negligently drove his car into your car and now you have a tort claim against that person—then your claim can be submitted to a court rather than to arbitrators. However, you and the party you are suing could agree to submit the dispute to an arbitrator rather than to a court, and you might want to do that, especially if the amount of the claim is not great and you do not need to conduct a lot of discovery to develop your case. But in order for arbitration to be binding on the parties, the parties must first agree to submit their dispute to arbitration. Unlike the courts, which can compel defendants to appear and respond to complaints filed against the defendant, arbitrators only have power over parties who have agreed to submit a dispute to arbitration.

Another form of alternative dispute resolution is often used in conjunction with litigation in court: parties who are already engaged in litigation agree to meet with a mediator who will attempt to facilitate a settlement agreement between the parties. Successful mediation really involves two forms of alternative dispute resolution: the mediation itself and the resulting voluntary settlement of the dispute by the parties, both alternatives to resolving claims in courts.

In a mediation session, the mediator, who is supposed to be a neutral third party, meets with the parties and helps them evaluate the strengths and weaknesses of each side's case. If the mediator is perceived as being biased in favor of one side, then the success of the mediation will be compromised. The goal is to create a zone of possible agreement by having both sides come to a realistic assessment of the likely outcomes in the case and the likely costs of continued litigation in court. Experienced attorneys often serve as mediators because they will understand the legal issues presented by a case as well as the uncertainties and expense of continued litigation. Mediation is so helpful in getting civil cases resolved that many courts now require parties to submit their cases to mediation with a court-appointed mediator before the case can be scheduled for a trial.

Party-driven settlement, mediated settlement, and arbitration are the most popular forms of alternative dispute resolution, but many other forms exist. For instance, parties sometimes conduct a "mini-trial" before a group of persons recruited from the community to be jurors, with the trial being very abbreviated and the parties agreeing to be bound by the decision of the jury if it falls within a certain range. Likewise, parties sometimes use "third-party case evaluations," in which one or more retired judges reads a case file and provides an assessment on liability and damages, with the parties agreeing in advance to be bound by the evaluations if they fall within a specified range (e.g., the parties may agree that if the evaluations favor the plaintiff and set damages below $50,000, then they will agree to settle for the average of the amounts set by the judges). Parties can agree to any mechanism they want for resolving the dispute, so long as it is not against the law (duels are no longer legal in the United States[6]). Within these legal bounds, parties are only limited by their creativity in devising a method for resolving a dispute without the aid of a court.

Final Thoughts

You should now have the basic information you need to understand how criminal and civil cases make their way into American courts and how American courts handle both kinds of cases. As with any introductory treatment of a complex topic, we have glossed over some of the complexities that may arise in litigating any particular criminal or civil case, whether it be in a state court located in Kentucky or a federal court located in New Jersey. But we have tried to give you a realistic portrait of the many decisions that parties must make as they navigate American courts and have tried to give you a flavor of just how complicated and drawn-out even seemingly simple cases can become.

Our focus has been on the law of procedure: how cases get filed in court and how they progress through the state and federal courts. In Chapter 2, we gave a broad overview of the substantive laws that can give rise to civil claims and criminal charges, but we only scratched the surface. Entire books are devoted to particular areas of substantive law, and some lawyers devote their

---

6   For an interesting history of the law on duels, *see* C. A. Harwell Wells, (2001), "The End of the Affair? Anti-dueling Laws and Social Norms in Antebellum America," VANDERBILT LAW REVIEW, 54, 1805-1847.

whole practice to a narrow area of substantive law, such as federal law on the taxation of employee pension plans (this type of legal practice is more interesting than it may sound). Much of law school, perhaps two-thirds, is devoted to giving law students a good grounding in different areas of substantive law, such as the law on property ownership, contracts, and white collar crimes. The remainder of law school is devoted to the law of criminal procedure and civil procedure that we have covered in this book. There is much more to learn about American legal systems, both its substance and procedure, as you will realize if you become a party in a case or if you participate eventually as a lawyer, judge, or juror.

Whatever you may think of the legal systems that we have described, you should not doubt that American courts are powerful forces within our federalist system of government. If people cannot resolve a civil dispute on their own, they can turn to taxpayer-funded courts for a compulsory resolution. And before the federal government or any state government can imprison a person or put a person to death as a penalty for a crime, prosecutors representing the government must follow rules designed to protect against unjustified penalties based on undisclosed evidence, including the requirement that the prosecutor convince a judge or a jury that the defendant committed the crimes beyond any reasonable doubt at a public trial. The multi-layered system of courts means that every criminal defendant and every civil litigant can have his or her case examined by at least two courts (though there is no guarantee that either or both courts will take their arguments very seriously). And the rulings of courts higher in the system will shape the law not just for lower courts and potential litigants but for governmental officials including elected legislators, governors, and presidents.

This complex, expensive, time-consuming system for administering justice can be maddening and is sometimes unfair, and we hope you are already thinking about ways that it might be improved. At the same time, it is a system that citizens living in many other countries of the world would choose over their own. We hope you leave this book with an understanding and appreciation of the sometimes frustrating, but usually explicable, intricacies of American courts. ■

Appendix A

The Constitution of the United States

PREAMBLE

We the People of the United States, in Order to form a more perfect Union, establish Justice, insure domestic Tranquility, provide for the common defence, promote the general Welfare, and secure the Blessings of Liberty to ourselves and our Posterity, do ordain and establish this Constitution for the United States of America.

ARTICLE I

SECTION 1. All legislative Powers herein granted shall be vested in a Congress of the United States, which shall consist of a Senate and House of Representatives.

SECTION 2. The House of Representatives shall be composed of Members chosen every second Year by the People of the several States, and the Electors in each State shall have the Qualifications requisite for Electors of the most numerous Branch of the State Legislature.

No Person shall be a Representative who shall not have attained to the Age of twenty five Years, and been seven Years a Citizen of the United States, and who shall not, when elected, be an Inhabitant of that State in which he shall be chosen.

Representatives and direct Taxes shall be apportioned among the several States which may be included within this Union, according to their respective Numbers, which shall be determined by adding to the whole Number of free Persons, including those bound to Service for a Term of Years, and excluding Indians not taxed, three fifths of all other Persons. The actual Enumeration shall be made within three Years after the first Meeting of the Congress of the United States, and within every subsequent Term of ten Years, in such Manner as they shall by Law direct. The number of Representatives shall not exceed one for every thirty Thousand, but each State shall have at Least one Representative; and until such enumeration shall be made, the State of New Hampshire shall be entitled to choose three, Massachoosetts cight, Rhode-Island and Providence

Plantations one, Connecticut five, New-York six, New Jersey four, Pennsylvania eight, Delaware one, Maryland six, Virginia ten, North Carolina five, South Carolina five, and Georgia three.

When vacancies happen in the Representation from any State, the Executive Authority thereof shall issue Writs of Election to fill such Vacancies.

The House of Representatives shall choose their Speaker and other Officers;and shall have the sole Power of Impeachment.

SECTION 3. The Senate of the United States shall be composed of two Senators from each State, chosen by the Legislature thereof, for six Years; and each Senator shall have one Vote.

Immediately after they shall be assembled in Consequence of the first Election, they shall be divided as equally as may be into three Classes. The Seats of the Senators of the first Class shall be vacated at the Expiration of the second Year, of the second Class at the Expiration of the fourth Year, and of the third Class at the Expiration of the sixth Year, so that one third may be chosen every second Year;and if Vacancies happen by Resignation, or otherwise, during the Recess of the Legislature of any State, the Executive thereof may make temporary Appointments until the next Meeting of the Legislature, which shall then fill such Vacancies.

No Person shall be a Senator who shall not have attained to the Age of thirty Years, and been nine Years a Citizen of the United States, and who shall not, when elected, be an Inhabitant of that State for which he shall be chosen.

The Vice President of the United States shall be President of the Senate, but shall have no Vote, unless they be equally divided.

The Senate shall choose their other Officers, and also a President pro tempore, in the Absence of the Vice President, or when he shall exercise the Office of President of the United States.

The Senate shall have the sole Power to try all Impeachments. When sitting for that Purpose, they shall be on Oath or Affirmation. When the President of the United States is tried, the Chief Justice shall preside: And no Person shall be convicted without the Concurrence of two thirds of the Members present.

Judgment in Cases of Impeachment shall not extend further than to removal from Office, and disqualification to hold and enjoy any Office of honor, Trust or Profit under the United States: but the Party convicted shall nevertheless be liable and subject to Indictment, Trial, Judgment and Punishment, according to Law.

SECTION 4. The Times, Places and Manner of holding Elections for Senators and Representatives, shall be prescribed in each State by the Legislature thereof; but the Congress may at any time by Law make or alter such Regulations, except as to the Places of choosing Senators.

The Congress shall assemble at least once in every Year, and such Meeting shall be on the first Monday in December, unless they shall by Law appoint a different Day.

SECTION 5. Each House shall be the Judge of the Elections, Returns and Qualifications of its own Members,and a Majority of each shall constitute a Quorum to do Business; but a smaller Number may adjourn from day to day, and may be authorized to compel the Attendance of absent Members, in such Manner, and under such Penalties as each House may provide.

Each House may determine the Rules of its Proceedings, punish its Members for disorderly Behaviour, and, with the Concurrence of two thirds, expel a Member.

Each House shall keep a Journal of its Proceedings, and from time to time publish the same, excepting such Parts as may in their Judgment require Secrecy; and the Yeas and Nays of the Members of either House on any question shall, at the Desire of one fifth of those Present, be entered on the Journal.

Neither House, during the Session of Congress, shall, without the Consent of the other, adjourn for more than three days, nor to any other Place than that in which the two Houses shall be sitting.

SECTION 6. The Senators and Representatives shall receive a Compensation for their Services, to be ascertained by Law, and paid out of the Treasury of the United States. They shall in all Cases, except Treason, Felony and Breach of the Peace, be privileged from Arrest during their Attendance at the Session of their respective Houses, and in going to and returning from the same; and for any Speech or Debate in either House, they shall not be questioned in any other Place.

No Senator or Representative shall, during the Time for which he was elected, be appointed to any civil Office under the Authority of the United States, which shall have been created, or the Emoluments whereof shall have been increased during such time; and no Person holding any Office under the United States, shall be a Member of either House during his Continuance in Office.

SECTION 7. All Bills for raising Revenue shall originate in the House of Representatives; but the Senate may propose or concur with Amendments as on other Bills.

Every Bill which shall have passed the House of Representatives and the Senate, shall, before it become a Law, be presented to the President of the United States; If he approve he shall sign it, but if not he shall return it, with his Objections to that House in which it shall have originated, who shall enter the Objections at large on their Journal, and proceed to reconsider it. If after such Reconsideration two thirds of that House shall agree to pass the Bill, it shall be sent, together with the Objections, to the other House, by which it shall likewise be reconsidered, and if approved by two thirds of that House, it shall become a Law. But in all such Cases the Votes of both Houses shall be determined by Yeas and Nays, and the Names of the Persons voting for and against the Bill shall be entered on the Journal of each House respectively. If any Bill shall not be returned by the President within ten Days (Sundays excepted) after it shall have been presented to him, the Same shall be a Law, in like Manner as if he had signed it, unless the Congress by their Adjournment prevent its Return, in which Case it shall not be a Law.

Every Order, Resolution, or Vote to which the Concurrence of the Senate and House of Representatives may be necessary (except on a question of Adjournment) shall be presented to the President of the United States; and before the Same shall take Effect, shall be approved by him, or being disapproved by him, shall be repassed by two thirds of the Senate and House of Representatives, according to the Rules and Limitations prescribed in the Case of a Bill.

SECTION 8. The Congress shall have Power To lay and collect Taxes, Duties, Imposts and Excises, to pay the Debts and provide for the common Defence and general Welfare of the United States; but all Duties, Imposts and Excises shall be uniform throughout the United States;

To borrow Money on the credit of the United States;

To regulate Commerce with foreign Nations, and among the several States, and with the Indian Tribes;

To establish an uniform Rule of Naturalization, and uniform Laws on the subject of Bankruptcies throughout the United States;

To coin Money, regulate the Value thereof, and of foreign Coin, and fix the Standard of Weights and Measures;

To provide for the Punishment of counterfeiting the Securities and current Coin of the United States;

To establish Post Offices and post Roads;

To promote the Progress of Science and useful Arts, by securing for limited Times to Authors and Inventors the exclusive Right to their respective Writings and Discoveries;

To constitute Tribunals inferior to the supreme Court;

To define and punish Piracies and Felonies committed on the high Seas, and Offenses against the Law of Nations;

To declare War, grant Letters of Marque and Reprisal, and make Rules concerning Captures on Land and Water;

To raise and support Armies, but no Appropriation of Money to that Use shall be for a longer Term than two Years;

To provide and maintain a Navy; To make Rules for the Government and Regulation of the land and naval Forces;

To provide for calling forth the Militia to execute the Laws of the Union, suppress Insurrections and repel Invasions;

To provide for organizing, arming, and disciplining, the Militia, and for governing such Part of them as may be employed in the Service of the United States, reserving to the States respectively, the Appointment of the Officers, and the Authority of training the Militia according to the discipline prescribed by Congress;

To exercise exclusive Legislation in all Cases whatsoever, over such District (not exceeding ten Miles square) as may, by Cession of particular States, and the Acceptance of Congress, become the Seat of the Government of the United States, and to exercise like Authority over all Places purchased by the Consent of the Legislature of the State in which the Same shall be, for the Erection of Forts, Magazines, Arsenals, dock-Yards and other needful Buildings;-And

To make all Laws which shall be necessary and proper for carrying into Execution the foregoing Powers, and all other Powers vested by this Constitution in the Government of the United States, or in any Department or Officer thereof.

SECTION 9. The Migration or Importation of such Persons as any of the States now existing shall think proper to admit, shall not be prohibited by the Congress prior to the Year one thousand eight hundred and eight, but a Tax or duty may be imposed on such Importation, not exceeding ten dollars for each Person.

The Privilege of the Writ of Habeas Corpus shall not be suspended, unless when in Cases of Rebellion or Invasion the public Safety may require it.

No Bill of Attainder or ex post facto Law shall be passed.

No Capitation, or other direct, Tax shall be laid, unless in Proportion to the Census or Enumeration herein before directed to be taken.

No Tax or Duty shall be laid on Articles exported from any State.

No Preference shall be given by any Regulation of Commerce or Revenue to the Ports of one State over those of another: nor shall Vessels bound to, or from, one State, be obliged to enter, clear, or pay Duties in another.

No Money shall be drawn from the Treasury, but in Consequence of Appropriations made by Law; and a regular Statement and Account of the Receipts and Expenditures of all public Money shall be published from time to time.

No Title of Nobility shall be granted by the United States: And no Person holding any Office of Profit or Trust under them, shall, without the Consent of the Congress, accept of any present, Emolument, Office, or Title, of any kind whatever, from any King, Prince, or foreign State.

SECTION 10. No State shall enter into any Treaty, Alliance, or Confederation; grant Letters of Marque and Reprisal; coin Money; emit Bills of Credit; make any Thing but gold and silver Coin a Tender in Payment of Debts; pass any Bill of Attainder, ex post facto Law, or Law impairing the Obligation of Contracts, or grant any Title of Nobility.

No State shall, without the Consent of the Congress, lay any Imposts or Duties on Imports or Exports, except what may be absolutely necessary for executing it's inspection Laws: and the net Produce of all Duties and Imposts, laid by any State on Imports or Exports, shall be for the Use of the Treasury of the United States; and all such Laws shall be subject to the Revision and Controul of the Congress.

No State shall, without the Consent of Congress, lay any Duty of Tonnage, keep Troops, or Ships of War in time of Peace, enter into any Agreement or Compact with another State, or with a foreign Power, or engage in War, unless actually invaded, or in such imminent Danger as will not admit of delay.

ARTICLE II

SECTION 1. The executive Power shall be vested in a President of the United States of America. He shall hold his Office during the Term of four Years, and, together with the Vice President, chosen for the same Term, be elected, as follows:

Each State shall appoint, in such Manner as the Legislature thereof may direct, a Number of Electors, equal to the whole Number of Senators and Representatives to which the State may be entitled in the Congress: but no Senator or Representative, or Person holding an Office of Trust or Profit under the United States, shall be appointed an Elector.

The Electors shall meet in their respective States, and vote by Ballot for two Persons, of whom one at least shall not be an Inhabitant of the same State with themselves. And they shall make a List of all the Persons voted for, and of the Number of Votes for each; which List they shall sign and certify, and transmit sealed to the Seat of the Government of the United States, directed to the President of the Senate. The President of the Senate shall, in the Presence of the Senate and House of Representatives, open all the Certificates, and the Votes shall then be counted. The Person having the greatest Number of Votes shall be the President, if such Number be a Majority of the whole Number of Electors appointed; and if there be more than one who have such Majority, and have an equal Number of Votes, then the House of Representatives shall immediately choose by Ballot one of them for President; and if no Person have a Majority, then from the five highest on the List the said House shall in like Manner choose the President. But in choosing the President, the Votes shall be taken by States, the Representation from each State having one Vote; A quorum for this Purpose shall consist of a Member or Members from two thirds of the States, and a Majority of all the States shall be necessary to a Choice. In every Case, after the Choice of the President, the Person having the greatest Number of Votes of the Electors shall be the Vice President. But if there should remain two or more who have equal Votes, the Senate shall choose from them by Ballot the Vice President.

The Congress may determine the Time of choosing the Electors, and the Day on which they shall give their Votes; which Day shall be the same throughout the United States.

No Person except a natural born Citizen, or a Citizen of the United States, at the time of the Adoption of this Constitution, shall be eligible to the Office of President; neither shall any person be eligible to that Office who shall not have attained to the Age of thirty five Years, and been fourteen Years a Resident within the United States.

In Case of the Removal of the President from Office, or of his Death, Resignation, or Inability to discharge the Powers and Duties of the said Office, the Same shall devolve on the Vice President, and the Congress may by Law provide for the Case of Removal, Death, Resignation or Inability, both of the President and Vice President, declaring what Officer shall then act as President, and such Officer shall act accordingly, until the Disability be removed, or a President shall be elected.

The President shall, at stated Times, receive for his Services, a Compensation, which shall neither be increased nor diminished during the Period for which he shall have been elected, and he shall not receive within that Period any other Emolument from the United States, or any of them.

Before he enter on the Execution of his Office, he shall take the following Oath or Affirmation:—"I do solemnly swear (or affirm) that I will faithfully execute the Office of President of the United States, and will to the best of my Ability, preserve, protect and defend the Constitution of the United States."

SECTION 2. The President shall be Commander in Chief of the Army and Navy of the United States, and of the Militia of the several States, when called into the actual Service of the United States; he may require the Opinion, in writing, of the principal Officer in each of the executive Departments, upon any Subject relating to the Duties of their respective Offices, and he shall have Power to grant Reprieves and Pardons for Offenses against the United States, except in Cases of Impeachment.

He shall have Power, by and with the Advice and Consent of the Senate, to make Treaties, provided two thirds of the Senators present concur; and he shall nominate, and by and with the Advice and Consent of the Senate, shall appoint Ambassadors, other public Ministers and Consuls, Judges of the supreme Court, and all other Officers of the United States, whose Appointments are not herein otherwise provided for, and which shall be established by Law: but the Congress may by Law vest the Appointment of such inferior Officers, as they think proper, in the President alone, in the Courts of Law, or in the Heads of Departments.

The President shall have Power to fill up all Vacancies that may happen during the Recess of the Senate, by granting Commissions which shall expire at the End of their next Session.

SECTION 3. He shall from time to time give to the Congress Information of the State of the Union, and recommend to their Consideration such Measures as he shall judge necessary and expedient; he may, on extraordinary Occasions, convene both Houses, or either of them, and in Case of Disagreement between them, with Respect to the Time of Adjournment, he may adjourn them to such Time as he shall think proper; he shall receive Ambassadors and other public Ministers; he shall take Care that the Laws be faithfully executed, and shall Commission all the Officers of the United States.

SECTION 4. The President, Vice President and all civil Officers of the United States, shall be removed from Office on Impeachment for, and Conviction of, Treason, Bribery, or other high Crimes and Misdemeanors.

ARTICLE III

SECTION 1. The judicial Power of the United States, shall be vested in one supreme Court, and in such inferior Courts as the Congress may from time to time ordain and establish. The Judges, both of the supreme and inferior Courts, shall hold their Offices during good Behaviour, and shall, at stated Times, receive for their Services, a Compensation, which shall not be diminished during their Continuance in Office.

SECTION 2. The judicial Power shall extend to all Cases, in Law and Equity, arising under this Constitution, the Laws of the United States, and Treaties made, or which shall be made, under their Authority;—to all Cases affecting Ambassadors, other public Ministers and Consuls;—to all Cases of admiralty and maritime Jurisdiction;—to Controversies to which the United States shall be a Party;—to Controversies between two or more States;—between a State and Citizens of another State;—between Citizens of different States;—between Citizens of the same State claiming Lands under Grants of different States, and between a State, or the Citizens thereof, and foreign States, Citizens or Subjects.

In all Cases affecting Ambassadors, other public Ministers and Consuls, and those in which a State shall be Party, the supreme Court shall have original Jurisdiction. In all the other Cases before mentioned, the supreme Court shall have appellate Jurisdiction, both as to Law and Fact, with such Exceptions, and under such Regulations as the Congress shall make.

The Trial of all Crimes, except in Cases of Impeachment; shall be by Jury; and such Trial shall be held in the State where the said Crimes shall have been committed; but when not committed within any State, the Trial shall be at such Place or Places as the Congress may by Law have directed.

SECTION 3. Treason against the United States, shall consist only in levying War against them, or in adhering to their Enemies, giving them Aid and Comfort. No Person shall be convicted of Treason unless on the Testimony of two Witnesses to the same overt Act, or on Confession in open Court.

The Congress shall have Power to declare the Punishment of Treason, but no Attainder of Treason shall work Corruption of Blood, or Forfeiture except during the Life of the Person attainted.

ARTICLE IV

SECTION 1. Full Faith and Credit shall be given in each State to the public Acts, Records, and judicial Proceedings of every other State. And the Congress may by general Laws prescribe the Manner in which such Acts, Records and Proceedings shall be proved, and the Effect thereof.

SECTION 2. The Citizens of each State shall be entitled to all Privileges and Immunities of Citizens in the several States.

A Person charged in any State with Treason, Felony, or other Crime, who shall flee from Justice, and be found in another State, shall on Demand of the executive

Authority of the State from which he fled, be delivered up, to be removed to the State having Jurisdiction of the Crime.

No Person held to Service or Labour in one State, under the Laws thereof, escaping into another, shall, in Consequence of any Law or Regulation therein, be discharged from such Service or Labour, but shall be delivered up on Claim of the Party to whom such Service or Labour may be due.

SECTION 3. New States may be admitted by the Congress into this Union; but no new State shall be formed or erected within the Jurisdiction of any other State; nor any State be formed by the Junction of two or more States, or Parts of States, without the Consent of the Legislatures of the States concerned as well as of the Congress.

The Congress shall have Power to dispose of and make all needful Rules and Regulations respecting the Territory or other Property belonging to the United States; and nothing in this Constitution shall be so construed as to Prejudice any Claims of the United States, or of any particular State.

SECTION 4. The United States shall guarantee to every State in this Union a Republican Form of Government, and shall protect each of them against Invasion; and on Application of the Legislature, or of the Executive (when the Legislature cannot be convened) against domestic Violence.

ARTICLE V

The Congress, whenever two thirds of both Houses shall deem it necessary, shall propose Amendments to this Constitution, or, on the Application of the Legislatures of two thirds of the several States, shall call a Convention for proposing Amendments, which, in either Case, shall be valid to all Intents and Purposes, as Part of this Constitution, when ratified by the Legislatures of three fourths of the several States, or by Conventions in three fourths thereof, as the one or the other Mode of Ratification may be proposed by the Congress; Provided that no Amendment which may be made prior to the Year One thousand eight hundred and eight shall in any Manner affect the first and fourth Clauses in the Ninth Section of the first Article; and that no State, without its Consent, shall be deprived of its equal Suffrage in the Senate.

ARTICLE VI

All Debts contracted and Engagements entered into, before the Adoption of this Constitution, shall be as valid against the United States under this Constitution, as under the Confederation.

This Constitution, and the Laws of the United States which shall be made in Pursuance thereof; and all Treaties made, or which shall be made, under the Authority of the United States, shall be the supreme Law of the Land; and the Judges in every State shall be bound thereby, any Thing in the Constitution or Laws of any State to the Contrary notwithstanding.

The Senators and Representatives before mentioned, and the Members of the several State Legislatures, and all executive and judicial Officers, both of the United States and of the several States, shall be bound by Oath or Affirmation, to support this Constitution; but no religious Test shall ever be required as a Qualification to any Office or public Trust under the United States.

ARTICLE VII

The Ratification of the Conventions of nine States, shall be sufficient for the Establishment of this Constitution between the States so ratifying the Same.

AMENDMENT I

Congress shall make no law respecting an establishment of religion, or prohibiting the free exercise thereof; or abridging the freedom of speech, or of the press; or the right of the people peaceably to assemble, and to petition the Government for a redress of grievances.

AMENDMENT II

A well regulated Militia, being necessary to the security of a free State, the right of the people to keep and bear Arms, shall not be infringed.

AMENDMENT III

No Soldier shall, in time of peace be quartered in any house, without the consent of the Owner, nor in time of war, but in a manner to be prescribed by law.

AMENDMENT IV

The right of the people to be secure in their persons, houses, papers, and effects, against unreasonable searches and seizures, shall not be violated, and no Warrants shall issue, but upon probable cause, supported by Oath or affirmation, and particularly describing the place to be searched, and the persons or things to be seized.

AMENDMENT V

No person shall be held to answer for a capital, or otherwise infamous crime, unless on a presentment or indictment of a Grand Jury, except in cases arising in the land or naval forces, or in the Militia, when in actual service in time of War or public danger; nor shall any person be subject for the same offence to be twice put in jeopardy of life or limb; nor shall be compelled in any criminal case to be a witness against himself, nor be deprived of life, liberty, or property, without due process of law; nor shall private property be taken for public use, without just compensation.

AMENDMENT VI

In all criminal prosecutions, the accused shall enjoy the right to a speedy and public trial, by an impartial jury of the State and district wherein the crime shall have been committed, which district shall have been previously ascertained by law, and to be informed of the nature and cause of the accusation; to be confronted with the witnesses against him; to have compulsory process for obtaining witnesses in his favor, and to have the Assistance of Counsel for his defence.

AMENDMENT VII

In suits at common law, where the value in controversy shall exceed twenty dollars, the right of trial by jury shall be preserved, and no fact tried by a jury, shall be otherwise reexamined in any Court of the United States, than according to the rules of the common law.

AMENDMENT VIII

Excessive bail shall not be required, nor excessive fines imposed, nor cruel and unusual punishments inflicted.

AMENDMENT IX

The enumeration in the Constitution, of certain rights, shall not be construed to deny or disparage others retained by the people.

AMENDMENT X

The powers not delegated to the United States by the Constitution, nor prohibited by it to the States, are reserved to the States respectively, or to the people.

AMENDMENT XI

The Judicial power of the United States shall not be construed to extend to any suit in law or equity, commenced or prosecuted against one of the United States by Citizens of another State, or by Citizens or Subjects of any Foreign State.

AMENDMENT XII

The Electors shall meet in their respective states and vote by ballot for President and Vice-President, one of whom, at least, shall not be an inhabitant of the same state with themselves; they shall name in their ballots the person voted for as President, and in distinct ballots the person voted for as Vice-President, and they shall make distinct lists of all persons voted for as President, and of all persons voted for as Vice-President, and of the number of votes for each, which lists they shall sign and certify, and transmit sealed to the seat of the government of the United States, directed to the President of the Senate; — The President of the Senate shall, in the presence of the Senate and House of Representatives, open all the certificates and the votes shall then be counted; — The person having the greatest number of votes for President, shall be the President, if such number be a majority of the whole number of Electors appointed; and if no person have such majority, then from the persons having the highest numbers not exceeding three on the list of those voted for as President, the House of Representatives shall choose immediately, by ballot, the President. But in choosing the President, the votes shall be taken by states, the representation from each state having one vote; a quorum for this purpose shall consist of a member or members from two-thirds of the states, and a majority of all the states shall be necessary to a choice. And if the House of Representatives shall not choose a President whenever the right of choice shall devolve upon them, before the fourth day of March next following, then the Vice-President shall act as President, as in case of the death or other constitutional disability of the President.— The person having the greatest number of votes as Vice-President, shall be the Vice-President, if such number be a majority of the whole number of Electors appointed, and if no person have a majority, then from the two highest numbers on the list, the Senate shall choose the Vice-President; a quorum for the purpose shall consist of two-thirds of the whole number of Senators, and a majority of the whole number shall be necessary to a choice. But no person constitutionally ineligible to the office of President shall be eligible to that of Vice-President of the United States.

AMENDMENT XIII

SECTION 1. Neither slavery nor involuntary servitude, except as a punishment for crime whereof the party shall have been duly convicted, shall exist within the United States, or any place subject to their jurisdiction.

SECTION 2. Congress shall have power to enforce this article by appropriate legislation.

AMENDMENT XIV

SECTION 1. All persons born or naturalized in the United States, and subject to the jurisdiction thereof, are citizens of the United States and of the State wherein they reside. No State shall make or enforce any law which shall abridge the privileges or immunities of citizens of the United States; nor shall any State deprive any person of life, liberty, or property, without due process of law; nor deny to any person within its jurisdiction the equal protection of the laws.

SECTION 2. Representatives shall be apportioned among the several States according to their respective numbers, counting the whole number of persons in each State, excluding Indians not taxed. But when the right to vote at any election for the choice of electors for President and Vice-President of the United States, Representatives in Congress, the Executive and Judicial officers of a State, or the members of the Legislature thereof, is denied to any of the male inhabitants of such State, being twenty-one years of age, and citizens of the United States, or in any way abridged, except for participation in rebellion, or other crime, the basis of representation therein shall be reduced in the proportion which the number of such male citizens shall bear to the whole number of male citizens twenty-one years of age in such State.

SECTION 3. No person shall be a Senator or Representative in Congress, or elector of President and Vice-President, or hold any office, civil or military, under the United States, or under any State, who, having previously taken an oath, as a member of Congress, or as an officer of the United States, or as a member of any State legislature, or as an executive or judicial officer of any State, to support the Constitution of the United States, shall have engaged in insurrection or rebellion against the same, or given aid or comfort to the enemies thereof. But Congress may by a vote of two-thirds of each House, remove such disability.

SECTION 4. The validity of the public debt of the United States, authorized by law, including debts incurred for payment of pensions and bounties for services in suppressing insurrection or rebellion, shall not be questioned. But neither the United States nor any State shall assume or pay any debt or obligation incurred in aid of insurrection or rebellion against the United States, or any claim for the loss or emancipation of any slave; but all such debts, obligations and claims shall be held illegal and void.

SECTION 5. The Congress shall have the power to enforce, by appropriate legislation, the provisions of this article.

AMENDMENT XV

SECTION 1. The right of citizens of the United States to vote shall not be denied or abridged by the United States or by any State on account of race, color, or previous condition of servitude.

SECTION 2. The Congress shall have the power to enforce this article by appropriate legislation.

AMENDMENT XVI

The Congress shall have power to lay and collect taxes on incomes, from whatever source derived, without apportionment among the several States, and without regard to any census or enumeration.

AMENDMENT XVII

The Senate of the United States shall be composed of two Senators from each State, elected by the people thereof, for six years; and each Senator shall have one vote. The electors in each State shall have the qualifications requisite for electors of the most numerous branch of the State legislatures.

When vacancies happen in the representation of any State in the Senate, the executive authority of such State shall issue writs of election to fill such vacancies: Provided, That the legislature of any State may empower the executive thereof to make temporary appointments until the people fill the vacancies by election as the legislature may direct.

This amendment shall not be so construed as to affect the election or term of any Senator chosen before it becomes valid as part of the Constitution.

AMENDMENT XVIII

SECTION 1. After one year from the ratification of this article the manufacture, sale, or transportation of intoxicating liquors within, the importation thereof into, or the exportation thereof from the United States and all territory subject to the jurisdiction thereof for beverage purposes is hereby prohibited.

SECTION 2. The Congress and the several States shall have concurrent power to enforce this article by appropriate legislation.

SECTION 3. This article shall be inoperative unless it shall have been ratified as an amendment to the Constitution by the legislatures of the several States, as provided in the Constitution, within seven years from the date of the submission hereof to the States by the Congress.

AMENDMENT XIX

The right of citizens of the United States to vote shall not be denied or abridged by the United States or by any State on account of sex. Congress shall have power to enforce this article by appropriate legislation.

AMENDMENT XX

SECTION 1. The terms of the President and the Vice President shall end at noon on the 20th day of January, and the terms of Senators and Representatives at noon on the 3d day of January, of the years in which such terms would have ended if this article had not been ratified; and the terms of their successors shall then begin.

SECTION 2. The Congress shall assemble at least once in every year, and such meeting shall begin at noon on the 3d day of January, unless they shall by law appoint a different day.

SECTION 3. If, at the time fixed for the beginning of the term of the President, the President elect shall have died, the Vice President elect shall become President. If a President shall not have been chosen before the time fixed for the beginning of his term, or if the President elect shall have failed to qualify, then the Vice President elect shall act as President until a President shall have qualified; and the Congress may by law provide for the case wherein neither a President elect nor a Vice President shall have qualified, declaring who shall then act as President, or the manner in which one who is to act shall be selected, and such person shall act accordingly until a President or Vice President shall have qualified.

SECTION 4. The Congress may by law provide for the case of the death of any of the persons from whom the House of Representatives may choose a President whenever the right of choice shall have devolved upon them, and for the case of the death of any of the persons from whom the Senate may choose a Vice President whenever the right of choice shall have devolved upon them.

SECTION 5. Sections 1 and 2 shall take effect on the 15th day of October following the ratification of this article.

SECTION 6. This article shall be inoperative unless it shall have been ratified as an amendment to the Constitution by the legislatures of three-fourths of the several States within seven years from the date of its submission.

AMENDMENT XXI

SECTION 1. The eighteenth article of amendment to the Constitution of the United States is hereby repealed.

SECTION 2. The transportation or importation into any State, Territory, or Possession of the United States for delivery or use therein of intoxicating liquors, in violation of the laws thereof, is hereby prohibited.

SECTION 3. This article shall be inoperative unless it shall have been ratified as an amendment to the Constitution by conventions in the several States, as provided in the Constitution, within seven years from the date of the submission hereof to the States by the Congress.

AMENDMENT XXII

SECTION 1. No person shall be elected to the office of the President more than twice, and no person who has held the office of President, or acted as President, for more than two years of a term to which some other person was elected President shall be elected to the office of President more than once. But this Article shall not apply to any person holding the office of President when this Article was proposed by Congress, and shall not prevent any person who may be holding the office of President, or acting as President, during the term within which this Article becomes operative from holding the office of President or acting as President during the remainder of such term.

SECTION 2. This article shall be inoperative unless it shall have been ratified as an amendment to the Constitution by the legislatures of three-fourths of the several States within seven years from the date of its submission to the States by the Congress.

AMENDMENT XXIII

SECTION 1. The District constituting the seat of Government of the United States shall appoint in such manner as Congress may direct: A number of electors of President and Vice President equal to the whole number of Senators and Representatives in Congress to which the District would be entitled if it were a State, but in no event more than the least populous State; they shall be in addition to those appointed by the States, but they shall be considered, for the purposes of the election of President and Vice President, to be electors appointed by a State; and they shall meet in the District and perform such duties as provided by the twelfth article of amendment.

SECTION 2. The Congress shall have power to enforce this article by appropriate legislation.

AMENDMENT XXIV

SECTION 1. The right of citizens of the United States to vote in any primary or other election for President or Vice President, for electors for President or Vice President, or for Senator or Representative in Congress, shall not be denied or abridged by the United States or any State by reason of failure to pay poll tax or other tax.

SECTION 2. The Congress shall have power to enforce this article by appropriate legislation.

AMENDMENT XXV

SECTION 1. In case of the removal of the President from office or of his death or resignation, the Vice President shall become President.

SECTION 2. Whenever there is a vacancy in the office of the Vice President, the President shall nominate a Vice President who shall take office upon confirmation by a majority vote of both Houses of Congress.

SECTION 3. Whenever the President transmits to the President pro tempore of the Senate and the Speaker of the House of Representatives his written declaration that he is unable to discharge the powers and duties of his office, and until he transmits to them a written declaration to the contrary, such powers and duties shall be discharged by the Vice President as Acting President.

SECTION 4. Whenever the Vice President and a majority of either the principal officers of the executive departments or of such other body as Congress may by law provide, transmit to the President pro tempore of the Senate and the Speaker of the House of Representatives their written declaration that the President is unable to discharge the powers and duties of his office, the Vice President shall immediately assume the powers and duties of the office as Acting President. Thereafter, when the President transmits to the President pro tempore of the Senate and the Speaker of the House of Representatives his written declaration that no inability exists, he shall resume the powers and duties of his office unless the Vice President and a majority of either the principal officers of the executive department or of such other body as Congress may by law provide, transmit within four days to the President pro tempore of the Senate and the Speaker of the House of Representatives their written declaration that the President is unable to discharge the powers and duties of his office. Thereupon Congress shall decide the issue, assembling within forty-eight hours for that purpose if not in session. If the Congress, within twenty-one days after receipt of the latter written declaration, or, if Congress is not in session, within twenty-one days after Congress is required to assemble, determines by two-thirds vote of both Houses that the President is unable to discharge the powers and duties of his office, the Vice President shall continue to discharge the same as Acting President; otherwise, the President shall resume the powers and duties of his office.

AMENDMENT XXVI

SECTION 1. The right of citizens of the United States, who are eighteen years of age or older, to vote shall not be denied or abridged by the United States or by any State on account of age.

SECTION 2. The Congress shall have power to enforce this article by appropriate legislation.

AMENDMENT XXVII

No law, varying the compensation for the services of the Senators and Representatives, shall take effect, until an election of representatives shall have intervened.

Appendix B

The Structure of Kentucky State Courts[1]

Kentucky

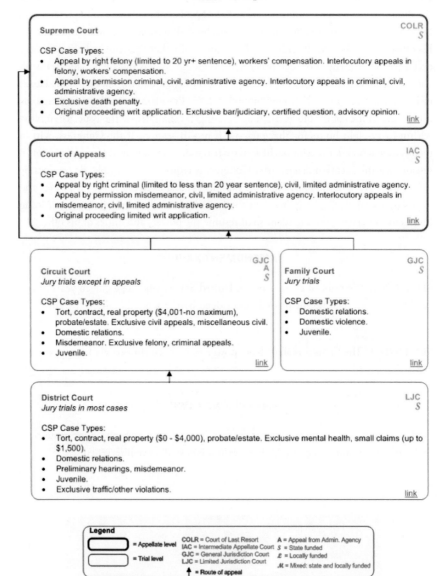

Supreme Court   COLR
                                                                                      S

CSP Case Types:
- Appeal by right felony (limited to 20 yr+ sentence), workers' compensation. Interlocutory appeals in felony, workers' compensation.
- Appeal by permission criminal, civil, administrative agency. Interlocutory appeals in criminal, civil, administrative agency.
- Exclusive death penalty.
- Original proceeding writ application. Exclusive bar/judiciary, certified question, advisory opinion.
                                                                                      link

Court of Appeals   IAC
                                                                                      S

CSP Case Types:
- Appeal by right criminal (limited to less than 20 year sentence), civil, limited administrative agency.
- Appeal by permission misdemeanor, civil, limited administrative agency. Interlocutory appeals in misdemeanor, civil, limited administrative agency.
- Original proceeding limited writ application.
                                                                                      link

Circuit Court   GJC   **Family Court**   GJC
Jury trials except in appeals   A   *Jury trials*   *S*
                                                             S
CSP Case Types: CSP Case Types:
- Tort, contract, real property ($4,001-no maximum),   - Domestic relations.
  probate/estate. Exclusive civil appeals, miscellaneous civil.   - Domestic violence.
- Domestic relations.   - Juvenile.
- Misdemeanor. Exclusive felony, criminal appeals.
- Juvenile.
                                                 link   link

District Court   LJC
Jury trials in most cases   *S*

CSP Case Types:
- Tort, contract, real property ($0 - $4,000), probate/estate. Exclusive mental health, small claims (up to $1,500).
- Domestic relations.
- Preliminary hearings, misdemeanor.
- Juvenile.
- Exclusive traffic/other violations.
                                                                                      link

Legend

☐ = Appellate level   COLR = Court of Last Resort   A = Appeal from Admin. Agency
                       IAC = Intermediate Appellate Court *S* = State funded
☐ = Trial level   GJC = General Jurisdiction Court *£* = Locally funded
                       LJC = Limited Jurisdiction Court *M* = Mixed: state and locally funded
↑ = Route of appeal

---

1   Reproduced from http://www.courtstatistics.org/Other-Pages/State_Court_Structure_Charts/Kentucky.aspx

Appendix C

The Structure of New Jersey State Courts[2]

New Jersey

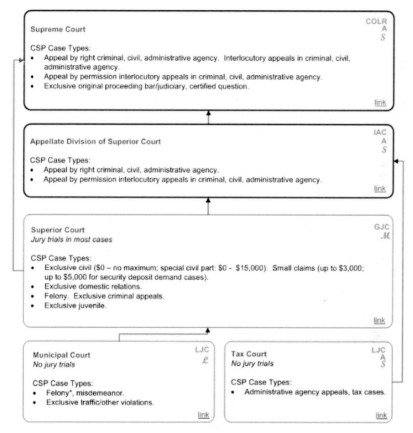

*Felony cases are handled on first appearance in the Municipal Courts and then are transferred through the county Prosecutor's office to the Superior Court.

2   Reproduced from http://www.courtstatistics.org/Other-Pages/State_Court_Structure_Charts/New-Jersey.aspx

Appendix D

The Structure of New York State Courts[3]

New York

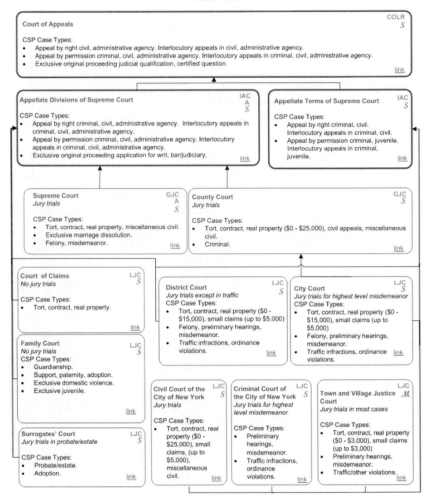

Appendix E

Additional Sources of Information on American Courts

Current information on the composition of the federal judiciary can be found at the website maintained by the Administrative Office of the U.S. Courts: http://www. uscourts.gov/Home.aspx.

The National Center for State Courts maintains a website that contains a wealth of information about all of the state courts within the U.S.: http://www.ncsc.org/.

The U.S. Congress created the National Constitution Center to "disseminate information about the United States Constitution on a non-partisan basis in order to increase the awareness and understanding of the Constitution among the American people." You can find many useful resources on the American Constitution at the Center's website: http://constitutioncenter.org/.

The Federal Judicial Center, which is a center for research and education within the federal judicial branch, published a short and useful guide to the federal courts in 2006. This publication, *Federal Courts & What They Do*, is available online: http:// www.fjc.gov/public/pdf.nsf/lookup/fctswh06.pdf/$file/fctswh06.pdf. You can find many other interesting resources on the federal courts at the Federal Judicial Center website: http://www.fjc.gov/.

A good history of the common law can be found in Arthur R. Hogue, *The Origins of the Common Law* (Liberty Press, 1966). Karl N. Llewellyn's *The Case Law System in America* (University of Chicago Press, 1989) provides an influential account of America's common law system, and Benjamin N. Cardozo's *The Nature of the Judicial Process* (Yale University Press, 1921) provides a classic account of the role of courts in the creation, interpretation, and application of law.

More detailed information on appellate courts can be found in the following books: Ruggero J. Aldisert, *The Judicial Process*, 2d ed. (West Publishing Co., 1996); Paul D. Carrington, Daniel J. Meador, & Maurice Rosenberg, *Justice on Appeal* (West Publishing Co., 1976); David G. Knibb, *Federal Court of Appeals Manual*, 5th ed. (West Publishing Co., 2007); Daniel J. Meador, Thomas E. Baker & Joan E. Steinman, *Appellate Courts: Structures, Functions, Processes, and Personnel*, 2d ed. (Lexis Nexis Publishing, 2006); Daniel J. Meador & Jordana S. Bernstein, *Appellate Courts in the United States* (West Publishing Co., 1994).

Jonathan Harr's *A Civil Action* (Vintage Books, 1995) provides a detailed and suspense-filled account of a civil lawsuit in which residents of a neighborhood in Woburn, Massachusetts claimed that they had been harmed by drinking water contaminated by chemical wastes from plant operated by W.R. Grace & Co. Many of the documents from the case that is the centerpiece of the book have been collected in Lewis A. Grossman

& Robert G. Vaughn, *A Documentary Companion to A Civil Action* (Foundation Press, 2008, 4th ed.).

Another interesting and detailed discussion of a civil case, as told by the plaintiff's lawyer, is Gerald M. Stern's *The Buffalo Creek Disaster* (Vintage books, 1976).

Anthony Lewis's book, *Gideon's Trumpet* (Vintage Books, 1964), chronicles the case of *Gideon v. Wainwright*, which resulted in the Supreme Court ruling that criminal defendants facing serious criminal charges have the constitutional right to an attorney whether they can afford to pay for an attorney or not.

Also be sure to consult the book's website, www.amcourtsbook.com, for additional resources.

This glossary provides basic definitions of many of the legal terms you will encounter in this book. A number of our entries are modifications to the definitions found in the glossary provided by the federal judiciary (which is available online at http://www.uscourts.gov/Common/Glossary.aspx). For more detail on any of the terms, please consult *Black's Law Dictionary* or another legal reference book.

Abuse of Discretion: A standard of review applied by a court reviewing the decision of a lower court. Under the "abuse of discretion" standard of review, an appellate court should not reverse the decision under review unless there is no evidence or law that reasonably supports the decision. This scope of review is narrow and deferential to the judgment of the lower court (i.e., if reasonable judges could disagree on the issue at the heart of the decision, then the lower court's decision should be upheld). This standard of review is very similar to, and often treated as synonymous with, the "arbitrary and capricious" standard of review.

Administrative Law: Regulations promulgated by government agencies and the laws that govern the making of such regulations.

Adversarial System: A type of judicial system in which the burden is on the parties (and their attorneys) to identify the legal and factual issues in dispute and to develop and present evidence to a judge or jury to resolve those issues. The American federal and state judicial systems are all adversarial systems of litigation. (Compare to Inquisitorial System.)

Affidavit: A declaration about facts relevant to a case. Affidavits are commonly used in conjunction with motions for summary judgment. The declaration must be made under oath or affirmation that the statements are true. Submission of a false affidavit may subject the person making the declaration to a prosecution for perjury.

Affirmance: Outcome in a court of appeals in which the appellate court upholds, or "affirms," the decision of the lower court that is the subject of the appeal. The decision under review, if it involves multiple issues, may be affirmed in whole or in part.

Affirmative Defense: A defense that does more than deny the allegations made against the defendant. An affirmative defense adds a new basis for defending against a claim in a civil case or a crime in a criminal case. If a defendant fails to raise an affirmative defense before trial, the judge may not allow the defendant to rely on the affirmative defense at trial.

Amicus Curiae: Latin for "friend of the court." An amicus curie brief is submitted by a person or entity interested in, but not a party, to the case pending before the court Amicus briefs are much more common in courts of appeals than in trial courts.

Answer: A type of pleading in civil litigation. In the answer, the defendant responds to the allegations in the complaint and asserts affirmative defenses to the allegations in the complaint.

Appellant: The party who appeals a trial court's decision, usually seeking reversal of that decision.

Appellate Judge: A judge who sits on a court of appeals.

Appellee: The party who won in the trial court and who opposes an appellant's request for reversal of the trial court's decision.

Arbitrary and Capricious: A standard of review applied by a court reviewing the decision of a lower court. Under the "arbitrary and capricious" standard of review, an appellate court should not reverse the decision under review unless the decision was illogical, unsupported by substantial evidence, or clearly erroneous under the governing law. This scope of review is narrow and deferential to judgment of the lower court (i.e., if reasonable judges could disagree on the issue at the heart of the decision, then the lower court's decision should be upheld).

Arbitration: A form of dispute resolution in which a single arbitrator or a panel of arbitrators considers the evidence and legal arguments put forth by the disputants and issues a decision that resolves the dispute. Arbitrators are supposed to be persons with no interest in the outcome who have some expertise in law and/or in the subject matter of the dispute. A decision by an arbitrator or arbitration panel can be enforced in a court of law just as a judgment by a court can be. Decisions by arbitrators can be appealed to trial courts, but courts have very limited power to overturn an arbitration decision.

Arraignment: A proceeding in which a criminal defendant is brought into court, told of the charges in an indictment or information, and asked to plead guilty or not guilty.

Attorney: A person with legal training who has been admitted to practice law in a particular state, usually by passing an examination. Attorneys may be admitted temporarily to practice in courts outside that state on an as-needed basis by submitting an application to appear in the court "pro hac vice" (which means "for this turn" in Latin).

Bankruptcy Court: The federal court devoted to hearing and resolving cases in which the party filing the case is seeking legal relief from its creditors. Federal courts have exclusive jurisdiction over bankruptcy cases.

Bench Trial: A trial conducted without a jury, with the verdict rendered by the judge.

Beyond a Reasonable Doubt: A standard of proof that must be met in order to convict an individual of a criminal charge. It does not require that the proof be so clear that no possibility of error exists, but it does mean that the evidence should be so clear that a reasonable person could not doubt that the defendant committed the charged crime.

Binding Precedent: A decision by a prior court that a subsequent court is bound to abide by. Decisions of the U.S. Supreme Court on federal questions are binding precedent on all other courts in the U.S.

Brief: Papers submitted to a trial or appellate court explaining one side's legal and factual arguments.

Burden of Production: The responsibility of a party to produce evidence to support a position being advocated in the case. For instance, in a civil case, a plaintiff has the burden to produce evidence sufficient to support all elements of the civil claim for which a remedy is sought in order to avoid dismissal of the case on grounds of insufficient evidence. The judge will decide whether the burden of production has been met, whereas the jury will typically decide whether the burden of proof has been met.

Burden of Proof: The duty to prove disputed facts by a specified degree of likelihood. In civil cases, a plaintiff usually has the burden of proving his or her case by a preponderance of the evidence (i.e., the plaintiff must prove that the facts needed to support each element of a civil claim is more likely than not true). In criminal cases, the government has the burden of proving the defendant's guilt beyond a reasonable doubt.

Case: The individual-level unit of analysis for matters being handled by American courts. When a prosecutor or plaintiff files the required documents with a clerk of a court to initiate proceedings against a defendant, the matter as a whole is referred to as a case. Case is synonymous with lawsuit, though the term lawsuit is often used to refer to civil cases alone rather than criminal and civil cases.

Cause of Action: The basis on which a party seeks relief in a civil case. The term is often used interchangeably with right of action or claim.

Certification: When a court asks another court to give a special opinion on a given case. For example, if a state is making a determination regarding another state's laws, it may certify the question for a court in the other state to give its opinion on the question. Not to be confused with class certification, which involves a court's determination that a case can proceed as a class action.

Certiorari: A writ of certiorari is issued by a superior court to get the records of a case from an inferior court. This term is generally used in referring to the Supreme Court of the United States, when that court determines whether it will hear an appeal of a case from a lower court. Where there is no right to appeal a decision from an inferior court, the dissatisfied party may petition the higher court for a writ of certiorari. The higher court grants the petition if it agrees to decide the case.

Challenge for Cause: A request by an attorney to dismiss a prospective juror on the grounds that the juror cannot be trusted to decide the case fairly. There is no limit on the number of challenges for cause, but they must be approved by the judge.

Circuit Court: In some state court systems, the circuit court is a trial court. In the federal court system, circuit court are the first court of appeals above the district court. The United States is divided into several judicial circuits, with one court of appeals handling all appeals from the district courts within each circuit. Originally, judges would ride from court to court within each circuit to handle cases. Nowadays circuit courts hold sessions in a few courthouses located within the circuit on arranged dates, with one courthouse serving as the court's primary location.

Civil Law: The body of law relating to private rights rather than criminal rights.

Civil Law System: A legal system based in codes that can be traced back to the Roman Empire. Precedent is generally understood to play a smaller role in civil law systems than in common law systems.

Claim: The legal basis on which relief can be sought in civil court. Each claim specifies the facts that must be proved to obtain relief.

Class Action: A lawsuit in which one or more members of a large group, or class, of individuals sue on behalf of the entire class. A number of special requirements apply to civil cases that seek to proceed as class actions.

Clear and Convincing Evidence: A burden of proof requiring that the evidence supporting a party's claim be clear and convincing in order to issue a verdict for that party. This standard of proof requires a higher degree of certain than the usual burden of proof in civil cases, the preponderance standard.

Clerk: A judge's personal legal assistant. Typical duties include legal research and drafting of opinions. Clerks are usually young attorneys who serve an individual judge for one or two years. Not to be confused with a Clerk of the Court, who is the top administrative official for a court.

Clerk of the Court: The court officer who oversees administrative matters for a court, including the filing of new cases and the preparation of a docket that records events in filed cases.

Code: A compilation of laws or legal principles that is arranged by subject. Statutes passed by the U.S. legislature and signed by the President are compiled in the U.S. Code, and each state maintains a code containing laws passed within each state.

Common Law System: The legal system that originated in England and is now in use in the United States. This system relies on the articulation of legal principles through a historical succession of judicial decisions that build on one another. Common law principles can be overridden or changed by legislation.

Compensatory Damages: Damages that are set in an amount that should compensate a party for injuries suffered as a result of a violation of the party's civil law rights.

Complaint: A type of pleading in civil litigation. This document is filed by a plaintiff to initiate a civil case. It contains a statement of civil law claims against a defendant, including a statement of the facts allegedly showing how the defendant violated one or more civil laws, and it specifies the relief sought for the alleged violation of those civil laws.

Concurrence: An option for an appellate judge who agrees with the outcome favored by the majority of appellate judges considering a decision on appeal but who disagrees with all or part of the reasoning by the majority to support that outcome. For instance, a majority of judges may agree that a lower court's decision may be affirmed, but these judges may disagree on why the lower court's decision should be affirmed. Any judge who disagrees with the reasoning by the majority's opinion may issue a concurring opinion offering an alternative rationale for the affirmance.

Constitution: The basic principles and laws of a nation, state, or group, often recording in a single document that may be amended, that determine the power and duties of the governing power.

Contract: An agreement between two or more people or entities that creates an obligation to do or not to do something.

Counterclaim: A type of pleading in civil litigation that is analogous to a complaint but which is submitted by a defendant rather than a plaintiff. In the counterclaim, which is usually submitted in conjunction with the answer, a defendant alleges facts showing that the plaintiff violated one or more civil laws and that these violations somehow harmed the defendant. The counterclaim also specifies the relief sought for the harms caused by the alleged violations of civil law.

Criminal Law: The body of law codifying acts that constitute crimes and specifying the facts that must be proven to prosecution someone for committing a particular crime.

Cross-Examination: The questioning of a witness who was called to the witness stand by another party and who has already answered questions from that party or its counsel during direct examination.

Damages: A monetary amount sought by a civil party to remedy a violation of that party's civil law rights.

De Novo: A standard of review applied by a court reviewing the decision of a lower court. Under the "de novo" standard of review, an appellate court considers the issues decided by the lower court on its own, without any deference to the lower court's reasoning or decision. The de novo standard of review typically applies only to questions that can be decided solely by analyzing the applicable law and does not require judgments about facts in dispute in the case. (Compare to the "abuse of discretion" and "arbitrary and capricious" standards of review.)

Declaratory Judgment: A judge's statement declaring the rights of the parties under a law or contract.

Defendant: In a civil case, the person or entity against whom the plaintiff filed a lawsuit; in a criminal case, the person accused of a crime who is being prosecuted.

Deposition: An oral statement made under oath before an officer authorized by law to administer oaths (usually a stenographer or court reporter). Deposition testimony may be used as part of discovery in a case and may be used court hearings and trials.

Dictum: A view expressed by a judge that is not essential or necessary to the ultimate holding in the opinion. Dicta are not binding precedent but may have persuasive value.

Direct Examination: The first questioning of a witness by the party calling that witness to the give testimony at trial or a court hearing.

Directed Verdict: An order from a judge in a jury trial that disposes of a claim against a civil party or a criminal charge against a criminal defendant; the judge must conclude that no reasonable jury could find in favor of the defendant party before directing the verdict. Now synonymous with judgment as a matter of law.

Discovery: Legally authorized procedures used to obtain disclosure of information and evidence from parties and non-parties for use in a case. Information gathered through discovery often promotes settlement of cases, and evidence gathered during discovery is often used at trial if a case does not settle.

Dissent: An option for an appellate judge who disagrees with the outcome favored by the majority of appellate judges considering a decision on appeal. A judge who dissents from the majority opinion may do so without explanation or may issue a dissenting opinion explaining why this judge disagrees with the outcome favored by the majority of judges.

District Attorney: See Prosecuting Attorney.

District Court: Trial level court in the federal court system and in some state court systems.

Diversity Jurisdiction: The jurisdiction federal courts have over civil claims involving parties with diverse citizenship where the matter in controversy exceeds a statutorily required amount (presently $75,000).

Docket: The official record of cases begun in a particular court and of the actions and events taken by the parties and court with respect to each case. Most courts today maintain electronic dockets.

En Banc: Latin for "the bench" or "entire bench," this phrase refers to all members of a court coming together to hear and decide a case.

Equitable Remedy: An order from a judge that someone must do something or cease doing something or declaring the relative rights of the parties. In English legal history, the courts of "law" and "equity" were separate courts. In American courts, trial courts have both legal and equitable power, but the distinction is still an important one. For example, judges typically consider civil claims seeking equitable remedies.

Evidence: Information presented in testimony or in physical form that is used to persuade the fact finder (judge or jury) to decide factual questions in favor of one side or the other.

Expert Witness: A witness with a special skill, knowledge, or training who testifies in order to aid the fact finder in matters going beyond the scope of the common knowledge of laypersons. For example, a doctor may testify about what is visible in an X-ray to help the judge or jury understand the nature of a plaintiff's injury from a car wreck.

Federal Circuit: A federal court of appeals that has nationwide jurisdiction over appeals of cases involving claims against the United States or claims for violation of federal trademark and patent law.

Federal District: Each state within the U.S. and its territories are divided into one or more judicial districts with one federal district court having jurisdiction over federal cases filed within that district. Federal districts are located within federal circuits.

Federal Question Jurisdiction: Jurisdiction given to federal courts in cases involving the interpretation and application of the federal laws.

Federalism: Distribution of power between a central authority and constituent units. In the United States, this distribution of power is between the federal government and the state governments.

Grand Jury: A body of citizens who listen to evidence of criminal allegations presented by prosecutors and determine whether there is probable cause to believe an individual committed an offense. If so, the grand jury issues an indictment of the person.

Habeas Corpus (and Writ of Habeas Corpus): Latin, meaning "you have the body." A writ of habeas corpus is a judicial order forcing law enforcement authorities to produce a prisoner they are holding and to justify the prisoner's continued confinement. Prisoners held in state prisons may petition federal district judges for a writ of habeas corpus on grounds that the imprisonment somehow violates the prisoner's rights under federal law.

In Forma Pauperis: Latin, meaning "in the manner of a pauper." A person who does not have sufficient funds to pay a court's filing fees with respect to a complaint or appeal may ask the permission of the court to proceed "in forma pauperis." If permission is granted, then the filing fees will be waived. Also, a criminal defendant who has the right to defense counsel may proceed "in forma pauperis" if he or she has insufficient funds to pay an attorney; if the application is accepted by the court, then the court will appoint and pay for an attorney for the criminal defendant.

Indictment: The formal charge issued by a grand jury stating that there is sufficient evidence the defendant committed a crime to justify having a trial. Indictments are used primarily for felony crimes.

Information: An alternative means of beginning a criminal case in which a prosecutor alleges facts sufficient to show that a defendant committed a crime. Analogous to a Complaint in a civil case.

Injunction: An order from a trial judge that the named party and persons under the control of the party are to stop doing something or are to take the specified actions. A preliminary injunction is sometimes issued on a temporary basis to preserve the status quo while the case proceeds to a final determination.

Inquisitorial System: A type of judicial system in which a judge (or group of judges) determines the issues for resolution, is actively involved in developing the evidence needed to resolve the case, and then decides the case. Parties (and their attorneys) are responsible for initiating cases and are involved in evidence gathering and legal argumentation, but the judge serves as the inquisitor who controls many facets of the case. Many European countries have inquisitorial systems of litigation. (Compare to Adversarial System.)

Intentional Tort: Civil laws that provide a basis for claims against persons or entities who have taken some intentional or knowing action that harmed another person or entity. Civil law claims for fraud and battery are examples of intentional torts.

Interlocutory Appeal: An appeal of a trial judge's ruling that occurs before a verdict has been reached. Interlocutory appeals are exceptions to the general rule that appeals must wait until the trial is completed.

Intermediate Appellate Court: A court beneath the court of last resort in a jurisdiction but above the trial court. In state courts, intermediate appellate courts have different names. In federal courts, these courts are Courts of Appeals, which are also known as Circuit Courts.

Interrogatory: A form of discovery consisting of written questions submitted by one party to another party which are to be answered in writing within a legally prescribed amount of time.

Judgment: An order from the trial court judge that ends one or more claims at issue in a civil case. A judgment may dismiss an invalid or procedurally defective claim without granting any relief or may authorize relief on the basis of a valid claim. Jury verdicts are reduced to a judgment unless the trial judge disagrees with the verdict and sets it aside.

Judgment Notwithstanding the Verdict: If a judge sets aside a verdict on grounds that no reasonable jury could have found as the jury did, then the judge enters a judgment in favor of the party who lost in the jury's verdict. Thus, the judge enters judgment notwithstanding the verdict. This judicial action is also called entry of judgment as a matter of law. See also Directed Verdict.

Judicial Clerk: See Clerk.

Judicial Election: The process whereby a judge is elected to office by popular vote.

Judicial Review: The act of declaring a statute null and void on the ground that it violates a constitution.

Judicial Selection: The process by which a judge is chosen for a seat on the bench. In federal courts the president selects judges with the approval of the Senate. State courts use a wide variety of selection methods, including direct election.

Jurisdiction: The legal authority given to a court to hear and decide a certain type of case (subject matter jurisdiction) or to assert power over a defendant in the case (personal jurisdiction).

Jury and Jurors: The jury is the group of persons selected to hear the evidence in a trial and to render a verdict (not to be confused with Grand Jury). Individual members of the jury are called jurors.

Lawsuit: See Case.

Legal Remedy: A remedy involving an order to pay a sum of money. In English legal history, the courts of "law" and "equity" were separate courts.

Litigant: A party of a case, but the term is often reserved for civil cases. The usual litigants in civil cases are the plaintiff and defendant, and in criminal cases are the prosecuting attorney and defendant.

Magistrate Judge: A judge who assists the trial judge in the handling of cases. Magistrate judges have limited authority to issue judgments and binding decisions in cases. In most courts, the parties may consent to the magistrate judge issuing binding decisions in the case.

Missouri Plan (for Judicial Selection): A type of judicial selection that started in Missouri in 1940 which has been adopted by several other states since that time. Under the plan, a committee creates a list of candidates for a judicial vacancy based on merit rather than partisanship, and then sends that list to the governor to choose from. After their initial appointment, judges must periodically face voters in a retention election.

Motion: A request by a party to a judge for a decision on an issue of some importance in the case.

Motion in Limine: A pretrial motion requesting the court to prohibit the other side from presenting, or even referring to, evidence on matters said to be so highly prejudicial that no steps taken by the judge can prevent the jury from being unduly influenced. Alternatively, a party planning to submit evidence to which an objection is expected can file a motion in limine asking the court to declare before trial that the evidence is admissible. Motions in limine are often denied without prejudice to raising the same questions or objections during the trial.

Motion to Dismiss: A request to dismiss one or more claims in a civil case or one or more charges in a criminal case. Typically a motion to dismiss is based on an opposing party's failure to observe some legal requirement.

Negligence: Failure to exercise the degree of care that a reasonable person in similar circumstances would be expected to exercise. Negligence is a type of unintentional tort.

Notice of Appeal: A document submitted by party who lost a decision in a trial court that gives notice that the losing party seeks review of the decision by a court of appeals. A notice of appeal initiates the appeal process and must be filed within a prescribed time period after issuance of the decision to be appealed in order to pursue an appeal. Usually only decisions that dispose of the case at the trial level can be appealed, but a court of appeals will occasionally allow parties to appeal intermediate decisions that are crucial to how a case proceeds (see Interlocutory Appeal).

Objection: A statement of opposition to evidence or an argument presented by another party in a case, usually during trial.

Oral Argument: An opportunity for parties or their lawyers to summarize their positions in a case and to answer the judge or judges' questions.

Order: A ruling or command by the judge to the parties. Orders dispose of motions made by the parties. Orders can take many different forms, including, but not limited to, cease-and-desist orders, restraining orders, and final orders (or final judgments) that disposes of a case (at least with respect to proceedings in that court).

Overrule: To declare a prior decision or opinion incorrect and no longer binding precedent. A court can choose to overrule only a portion of a prior opinion, in which case the opinion is considered "overruled in part."

Panel: A subset of a court's membership (usually of an appellate court) that comes together to hear and decide a case.

Party: A person or entity who is officially named in a legal document instituting legal proceedings by or against that person or entity. A party will often be represented in a case by an attorney.

Peremptory Challenge: A demand by an attorney to dismiss a prospective juror. Peremptory challenges need not be justified and do not have to be approved by the judge unless there is an objection that the challenge was based on a characteristic of the potential juror that is an improper basis for exclusion, such as the juror's race or gender.

Personal jurisdiction: The jurisdiction granted a court over the parties in the case that allows the court to issue judgments in the case that will dispose of the claims or criminal charges pending in the case. Most commonly, personal jurisdiction is established through consent or through a party's contacts with the jurisdiction.

Petitioner: An individual who presents a formal, written request to the court, requesting action in a particular manner. The party who files a writ of certiorari with the U.S. Supreme Court is referred to as the petitioner.

Plaintiff: A person or entity initiating a civil lawsuit by filing of a Complaint with the court.

Pleading: A document filed with the court, such as the plaintiff's Complaint, setting out the party's legal and factual assertions about the case.

Precedent: A court decision in an earlier case with facts and legal issues similar to a dispute currently before a court.

Preponderance of the Evidence: A standard of proof requiring that the fact finder conclude that any facts that have to be proven by the party with the burden of proof must be more likely than not true before the fact finder can decide those facts in favor of the party with the burden of proof. If the evidence is too ambiguous to decide what facts really occurred, then the fact finder should conclude that the party with the burden of proof failed to prove necessary facts by a preponderance of the evidence.

Pretrial Order: An order by the trial judge establishing procedures to be used during trial and the issues to be decided at trial.

Prosecutor: See Prosecuting Attorney

Prosecuting Attorney: An individual (normally a government attorney) who institutes a criminal case and who presents evidence that the criminal defendant committed any charged crimes. Each federal district has a federal prosecuting attorneys who has been appointed by the President and who are referred to as U.S. Attorneys. In most states, each county will have its own popularly elected prosecuting attorney.

Punitive Damages: A sum of money awarded in an amount that is mean to punish past misconduct and deter future misconduct.

Record on Appeal: The materials from the lower court that are compiled and provided to the court of appeals when an appeal has been taken from a decision of the lower court. The record on appeal from a trial court typically includes a transcript of the trial (as recorded by a court reporter) and the documents that the parties introduced into evidence or sought to introduce into evidence at the trial. Other physical evidence offered at trial, such as the weapon allegedly used in a crime, will not usually be contained in the record on appeal, but it is retained by the trial court in the event the court of appeals wishes to see other physical evidence.

Recusal: A judge's decision not to participate in a case that was assigned to him or her, because of a perceived or actual conflict of interest.

Remedy: Relief that can be ordered by a court to prevent or rectify a wrong. Remedies can be either legal (such as punitive or compensatory damages) or equitable (such as an injunction).

Request for Admission: Written assertions submitted by one party to another party asking the other party to admit or deny, in writing within a legally prescribed time period, that the assertions are true.

Request for Production: A written request submitted by one party to another party that the other party make available for inspection the specified documents or other things within a legally prescribed time period.

Remand: Outcome in a court of appeals in which the appellate court sends a case back to the lower court for further proceedings or consideration in light of the opinion and directions issued by the court of appeals. Remand occurs when the court of appeals reverses the decision of the lower court or believes that additional actions are necessary in the lower court before the case can be finally adjudicated.

Respondent: A party who answers or responds to a petition.

Retention Election: A form of judicial selection used for state court judgeships. In a retention election, the public votes on whether a judge may keep his or her position. Retention elections are held after a judge appointed by the governor of a state has served a probationary period. Voters' only options in a retention election are yes or no. If a sufficient percentage (usually over 50%) of the electorate votes in favor of retention, the judge stays in the position for the full term; otherwise the judge loses the position, and the governor must choose a new judge who will also be subject to a retention election. Judges who survive the initial retention election must face another retention election at the end of the several-year term if they want to remain in the position.

Reversal: Outcome in a court of appeals when the appellate court determines that the lower court made an error in its decision. Following reversal of the lower court's decision, the court of appeals may issue a final binding decision on the issue or issues that were the subject of the appeal or may remand the case to lower court for further proceedings in accordance with the opinion and directions issued by the court of appeals. For instance, the appellate court may remand the case for a new trial, with directions not to permit certain evidence at the trial.

Senatorial Courtesy: The practice of allowing a senator to veto the President's nominee for a district court judgeship in the senator's state.

Settlement Agreement: An agreement by one party in a civil case to dismiss a civil claim against another party in the case in return for money or something else of value. Persons sometimes settle claims before they have been officially filed with a court, in which case one party agrees not to file the claims in return for money or something of value.

Specific Performance: An equitable remedy directing the performance of a contract according to, or substantially in accordance with, the terms of the contract. For instance, a homeowner who entered into a purchase agreement might be directed to give custody of the property to the buyer who paid in full for the house.

Standard of Review: The standard used by a higher court reviewing the decision of a lower court. The Abuse of Discretion and Arbitrary and Capricious standards are deferential to the judgment of the lower court, whereas the De Novo standard gives no deference to the judgment of the lower court.

Standing: A right to make a legal claim, or a right to seek enforcement of a protected right.

Stare Decisis: Latin for "to stand by things decided." It is essentially a way of referring to the doctrine of precedent.

Statute: A law passed by a legislature.

Subject Matter Jurisdiction: The authority of a court to hear cases of a particular type. Many state courts have general jurisdiction, allowing them to hear a case of any subject matter. Federal courts are courts of limited subject matter jurisdiction, with their jurisdiction set by federal statutes.

Subpoena: A command, issued under a court's authority, for a witness to appear and give testimony.

Subpoena Duces Tecum: A command, issued under a court's authority, for a witness to appear and produce documents or other things as specified in the subpoena document. "Duces tecum" is Latin for "bring with you."

Summary Judgment: A decision to enter judgment on one or more civil claims that is made on the basis of statements and evidence presented to the judge in the form of documentary evidence instead of through witnesses testifying at trial. A judge is not supposed to grant a motion for summary judgment unless there is no reasonable dispute on any facts that are material to the outcome of the case (i.e., facts that must be decided to determine whether a law has been violated). The party who pursues a motion for summary judgment has the burden of convincing the judgment that summary judgment is warranted, and the judge in deciding a motion for summary judgment is supposed to resolve factual ambiguities in favor of the non-moving party. Summary judgment is proper when, in light of the undisputed facts in the record, the moving party is entitled to judgment as a matter of law.

Summons: A written notification that a person or entity has been named as a defendant in a Complaint filed in the court issuing the summons and notifying the defendant that a response to the Complaint must be submitted within a legally prescribed time period or the defendant may lose the case by default.

Supremacy Clause: The second clause in Article VI of the U.S. Constitution that declares the constitution and laws of the federal government to be the supreme law of the land.

Tort: A civil, not criminal, wrong. A negligent or intentional injury against a person or property. Torts are distinct from civil wrongs based on a breach of contract.

Venue: The geographic area within a state or federal district that has personal jurisdiction over the parties to a case and that is a proper location for filing suit under the rules that govern venue. A change or transfer of venue is a move from one court to another court within the same court system.

Voire Dire: The process of questioning prospective jurors to ascertain their qualifications and beliefs to determine whether there is a basis for excluding the person from serving as a juror at the trial. Also, the preliminary questioning of a witness to establish the witness should be allowed to testify (most commonly used with respect to persons offered as expert witnesses).

With Prejudice or Without Prejudice: When a complaint or part of a complaint is dismissed by a court, the dismissal is either with prejudice or without prejudice. A dismissal with prejudice means that the claims that have been dismissed should not be pursued in court again or, if they are, they are subject to prompt dismissal. A dismissal without prejudice means that the claims that were dismissed may be pursued in court again. A dismissal without prejudice occurs when a plaintiff has filed in the wrong court or has failed to give proper notice of the filing of the complaint to the defendant. Any other dismissal will be considered a dismissal with prejudice unless the order of dismissal specifies otherwise.

Witness: A person called upon by either side in a lawsuit to give testimony at a hearing or trial.

Index

References are to pages.